Please return or renew by
latest date below

LOANS MAY BE RENEWED BY PHONE
657-7310

OCT. 14.1982 OK

D0205338

Economic Democracy

The Challenge of the 1980s

Economic Democracy

The Challenge of the 1980s

MARTIN CARNOY and DEREK SHEARER

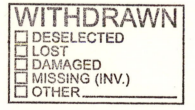

M. E. Sharpe INC.
WHITE PLAINS, NEW YORK

Copyright © 1980 by M. E. Sharpe, Inc.
901 North Broadway, White Plains, New York 10603

All rights reserved. No part of this book may be reproduced in any form without written permission from the publisher.

Design: Laurence Lustig

Library of Congress Catalog Card Number: 79-55934

Publisher's International Standard Book Number (cloth): 0-87332-162-6
Publisher's International Standard Book Number (paper): 0-87332-163-4

Distributor's International Standard Book Number (cloth): 0-394-51107-7
Distributor's International Standard Book Number (paper): 0-394-73889-6

Distributed by Pantheon Books, a division of Random House, Inc.

Printed in the United States of America

For our parents, who gave us democratic values.

Contents

Acknowledgements

The research for this book was supported largely by a grant from the Ford Foundation to the Center for Economic Studies in Palo Alto, California. The aim of the research effort was to analyze structural economic reforms in advanced industrial societies such as Western Europe and Canada and to consider the applicability of these reforms to the American economy.

The authors wish to thank Bill Behn, Maria Leal, and Marc Weiss, who worked as research associates on the project. We owe a particular debt to Marc Weiss for his work on Chapter 3, "Democratic Control of Investments," and to Bill Behn for his work in gathering source material and checking our source citations. Joyce Crain of the Center staff administered the grant and made certain that all bureaucratic details were taken care of.

Steve Babson, Peter Barnes, Richard Flacks, Bill Domhoff, and Ben Harrison all read parts of the manuscript and offered helpful suggestions. Neither these individuals nor the Ford Foundation, however, bear any responsibility for the final content of the book. While we have benefited from the comments and work of others, the critical perspective and conclusions of this work are the authors'.

MARTIN CARNOY
DEREK SHEARER
September, 1979

"We must realize that the democratic form of government is bound to penetrate our industrial life as well. It cannot be confined merely to our political institutions."

—SIDNEY HILLMAN, President,
   Amalgamated Clothing Workers Union,
   1924

Economic Democracy

The Challenge of the 1980s

Introduction:
A Strategy for a New Economy

This book is a discussion of and an argument for
alternatives to the present structure of production in
the United States; alternatives that would change the
control of capital and how it is used. The U.S.
economy is faced with a set of economic problems that
appear to be *unsolvable* by corporate capitalist development. If changes are to be made, then the way
the economy is governed and the way things are
produced will have to be changed as well. The essence
of such transformation is economic democracy—the
transfer of economic decision making from the few to
the many. The very same arguments that for two
centuries supported the ceding of political choice to
the mass of people rather than its retention by a single
individual or a small group, also provide the rationale
for production and investment decision making by
workers and consumers, not by individual capital
owners or their managers. For all of its imperfections,
a democratic choice, when it is allowed expression,
best reflects people's needs and desires. Democratic
capitalist countries have evolved into more equitable
societies than nondemocratic capitalist countries. But
this process has its limitations in an economy such as
the United States, where investment and production

decisions are not made democratically. Democratic, worker-controlled production would extend democratic choice to work, employment, income, and technology.

Is this an ideal impossible to achieve?

We don't think so. Like any serious political change, this one requires a strategy, a strategy that is consistent with the context in which it is applied and reflects an understanding of the economic and political consequences of each of its aspects. For us, the two essential elements of any strategy of fundamental reform in the United States today are: (1) the shift of investment control from corporate domination to the public; and (2) the reconstruction of economic decision making through democratic, worker- and worker/consumer-controlled production.

Investment decisions in the United States are made almost entirely by private companies. These are not the small, independent, entrepreneur-run firms of "free enterprise" mythology (although many of them still exist), but corporate giants. Many are in industries where one or sometimes two or three corporations completely dominate the market for their products. They employ thousands of workers, and decisions about how many people will work and what and how much they will produce are made in offices usually distant from the plant. These corporations are impersonal and powerful; in their relations with another set of large corporations—the banks—they govern the capital accumulation process and, with it, employment technology, income distribution, work organization, consumption patterns, and, in large part, our relations with other nations.

Any alternative economic and social strategy must start by dismantling, or at least restricting, the power of these corporations. They are the antithesis of democracy. But we are not proposing a return to a competitive capitalism of the past. America is no longer a nation of farmers and artisans. Today, we are a nation of employees; that is our reality. Nòr do we think that the best way to work is necessarily to compete individually one against another for bread and status. Employees can produce cooperatively; their wages can be largely the direct fruit of their labor, and they themselves can decide the best way to produce and how much to produce in a democratically planned economy.

A strategy of reform must transfer capital from the corporations to the public, so that the people who work and consume can collectively and democratically decide what to do with it. The logical vehicle for that process should be the government—our democratically elected legislature and executive. Yet the government is heavily influenced (if not controlled) by these very same corporations. This is one of the many dilemmas we face: how to move the government to restrict corporate power instead of aiding and abetting it.

It is essential, over the next two decades, to build a mass political movement on the basis of a program such as ours and to win a majority of local, state, and national governing bodies. That should be part of an overall strategy. Even though economic democracy is not one of the virtues of American society, political democracy is, at least for the present. But other, nonelectoral work is also important for limiting corporate options. We discuss such work in the last section of the book: democratizing unions and broadening their goals; sponsoring legislation and getting it passed under pressure from organized public groups; and working with local, decentralized organizations to build segments of the movement around specific issues. All of these efforts assume that there is enough political space in American society to make change, to restrict control of capital by large private firms, and to shift that control to the public sector and to workers in individual plants and industries—or at least to move in that direction.

But how, specifically, should we do this? What policies should we use to transform the economy? To find answers, we have researched experiences in industrial, politically democratic countries, primarily in Western Europe (but also in the United States itself) and analyzed whether and how these experiences could be applied to a reform strategy for the United States. It is to this investigation that we now turn.

PART ONE
The American Setting

CHAPTER ONE

The American Economy: Is This All There Is?

In 1800 the United States was a rural and village society. Its biggest cities—New York, Boston, and Philadelphia—were provincial by European standards. Its industry was limited to a few textile and flour mills, and workshops manufacturing simple iron products, shoes, and other light consumer goods. Over 90 percent of the population was self-employed. One hundred and seventy-five years later—an extremely short time in human history—steel, automobiles, electrical products, railroads, petroleum synthetic textiles, as well as agricultural products and metals all are being produced in greater quantity in the United States than anywhere else in the world. Consumption per capita has also become the highest ever. The mass of Americans live in cities. Rather than working on farms or as shop owners, they are increasingly employed in large corporations. Their rate of work has become controlled by the speed of machines; the way they live outside the factory is governed by the pace and demands of urban existence. Ninety percent of the working population are now employees.

How did all this happen? Why, after centuries of almost no change in human life-styles, did the United States and other societies become transformed so rapidly and so irrevocably? Many reasons have been given: technological innovation, the availability of raw materials from the New World, rising grain prices in Europe, and religious revolutions. But all of these can be subsumed under the emergence in Western Europe, during the seventeenth century, of a new economic system: capitalism. That development was marked by rising prices for staples, previously unheard of amounts of capital accumulation by merchants, the beginning of manufacturing, religious wars, and the rise of a philosophy that put individual liberty and the right of individuals to run their own economic lives above the power of the Crown.

This was a profound revolution. It gave to individuals much more power to amass capital and use it in the way each one saw fit. During the eighteenth century, the remnants of feudalism gradually crumbled in England, Holland, France, and other countries of northwest Europe. In France, the overthrow of these remnants was violent. But in the United States, there was no feudalism to overthrow. The colonies were settled as part of European economic expansion, and the institutions that grew up here were part and parcel of that development. One of the distinguishing features of American society is that it grew up free of feudal fetters. It is natural that this child of European capitalism should in this century become the symbol of its success.

Capitalist development made possible incredible changes in how people lived and what they thought possible. People's feelings about change itself were altered. In the United States, which had no feudal past, the flight from tradition to "progress" became a way of life. This process has had its costs. Working hundreds and then thousands of people in a factory for long hours at low wages sacrificed the health and welfare of many generations of workers to today's high levels of consumption. Rapid growth under capitalism required workers to move quickly to locations where wages were highest and jobs were available. Urban areas provided a highly concentrated source of labor for industry, and workers migrated to growing urban areas to find jobs. These new cities had little in common with the old European towns, which were more a collection of neighborhoods than an industrial labor market. The new cities did have some sense of community and even communities within them, but for most they were places to live to find work rather than places to live a life. The security of the towns and villages—as well as their more stifling aspects—were rapidly destroyed under capitalism.

The greatest threat to security, however, was the new phenomenon of the business cycle, accompanied by the unemployment, hunger, and instability that represent the worst aspects of capitalist development. In the United States, the first major capitalist recession lasted from 1837 to 1850. Much of the decade of the 1870s (following the panic of 1873) was a serious downturn; 1893, then 1907, 1919, and the great crisis of 1929 all marked the beginnings of depressions. The working class suffered greatly during such downturns, marked by widespread hunger, anxiety, and despair.

Attainment of a long-term growth rate—an eventual increase in material consumption—meant a series of booms and busts. While feudal times were marked by droughts and disease, man-made distresses such as unemployment and hunger in the midst of plenty were relatively absent. Capitalism by its very nature was good for some, yet very costly for others.

The new philosophy also had difficulty delivering on its ideals. The concept of the individual making rational free choices and, through this rationality and freedom, bringing society to some optimum performance and general welfare was contradicted by the separation of workers from their means of work. Once that separation occurred, the workers lost control over the things that were produced. The ideology of capitalism shifted significantly in the nineteenth century to accommodate the fact that rapidly increasing numbers of workers were employed in factories and had nothing to say about the conditions of their work. By the end of the century, the idea that all (white) men are created equal had given way in the United States to the concept of equality *within social classes.* Democracy was limited to suffrage and consumer choice. The work place was governed by the laws of private property, not the Bill of Rights. The struggle of unions for worker protection and bargaining rights theoretically was unnecessary in the free enterprise system; yet it became a regular part of capitalist life. The growth of monopolies was an unforeseen product of unbridled competition; they, too, became a dominant factor in capitalist development.

As the United States emerged from the Great Depression and World War II to be the leader of the capitalist world, the possibilities for progress seemed boundless. But within a generation, the country was racked by social strife during a period of rapid growth. The typical middle-class American family had two cars, a house, and children taking post-secondary education, but happiness was frequently beyond its grasp. Divorces increased, political participation decreased, use of drugs became commonplace, and crime became an integral part of the urban scene. Continued economic growth did not reduce poverty, unemployment, inadequate health care, or old-age insecurity. Taxes went up, but services were no better. Foreign wars took 100,000 American lives in Korea and Vietnam. Unemployment increased after Vietnam—as after every war—but this time it scarcely went down after the recession was over; worse, along with unemployment came inflation—steady, long-run inflation that put homes out of the reach of many families, decreased real wages, raised taxes rapidly, and caused pensioners to suffer. Pollution, energy shortages, and corporate corruption added to these problems.

Capitalism has certainly brought us somewhere. The new question is, where? We have run a long way and we have run very hard. But is this it?

Economists cannot seem to solve these problems. The technicians, with their mathematical models and computer simulations, cannot eliminate poverty, reduce unemployment significantly, lower inflation, predict the oil crisis, make working more fun, lower taxes, or give Americans the security they seek. Affluence has not stopped the anxiety, the crises, the dissatisfaction. Is this simply a human characteristic of never being satisfied? Perhaps, but on the other hand people see around them enormous wealth to which they seem to have no access. Young couples have high incomes compared to those of a generation ago, but cannot afford to buy a house; old people are lonely; young people have more education than their parents could have ever imagined and can find only routine work or are unemployed; the statistics on real income show increases in the last ten years, but significant portions of the population are actually worse off than a decade ago.

So the problems are real. Traditional economists still view them in terms of increasing real output: if the economy can just be made to grow more quickly with low increases in prices, unemployment will be reduced and consumption will rise. Undoubtedly, raising real output and consumption will solve some problems such as poverty and unemployment, provided the expansion is general and spread throughout the potential labor force and increases the demand for unskilled and young workers, in particular. Economists assume that this is what will happen if real growth can be sustained. Their assumptions about the labor market, however, may not be correct. Why is it so difficult for growth to occur now without inflation, and why does unemployment decline so little with higher growth?

More important, is the orthodox economists' answer to America's problems—increased growth with stable prices—really a solution to these difficulties? This is not just a question of assumptions about the way labor markets work, or the relationship between inflation and employment. The issue concerns the nature of society and the structure of the economy. Orthodox economists treat pollution and the energy crises as soluble by means of the marketplace. Are these really pricing problems? Is it even possible to think about a free market in today's corporate economy? What about work satisfaction? the control of wealth and power? the relationship of the United States to other countries? the use of resources for military ends rather than other purposes? Are these pricing problems, or even political voting model problems?

We believe that economists and other governmental policymakers cannot improve the situation primarily because they choose to look at economic and social problems in the way they do. And they choose to look at them this way because, consciously or unconsciously, they accept a set of ideological assumptions about the "naturalness" and "perfectability" of capitalism as an economic order. Most economists would find our statement "radical," since it challenges their scientific objectivity. Yet, we think that it is crucial to political-economic discussion to accept openly the fact that assumptions about ownership and power are part and parcel of the economic problem.

The Council of Economic Advisors does not discuss the relationship between economic problems and economic power. This might be understandable in the context of a governmental bureaucracy in which economists are supposed to give technical advice to executives and legislators who deal with the power issue. But these same economists conspicuously fail to question that relationship even when they return to their universities. The discussion of America's economy among "mainstream" economists waxes hot but only rarely inquires into issues that combine politics and economics. Nor does it question whether capitalism in its present or previous forms is the most appropriate production organization to deal with today's needs. And it rarely focuses on what the nature of capitalist society is and how the assumptions of orthodox economics relate to today's institutions. United States economic policy discussions are unique in that they include almost no debate of alternatives to corporate capitalist production.

We believe that the debate by economists and policymakers is largely misplaced. Rather than discussing the best methods for "fine tuning" the economy, we want to shift the debate to strategies for changing the structure of the economy so that it better serves the interests and needs of all Americans. Such a shift implies questioning the assumptions of neoclassical economics and moving the discussion to issues raised by "radical" political economists concerning economic policy in a corporate capitalist society, including a discussion of the nature of that society. This is the ground on which economics is debated in most of the rest of the capitalist world, particularly in Western Europe.

Neoclassical economics represents a point of view, a political position, a set of assumptions about the way the world should be and about human behavior. We will present an alternative view based on an alternative set of assumptions. We will also analyze American economic problems from this point of view and deal with possible solutions to these problems. Although we start from the assumption that certain problems cannot be resolved until the structure of production is altered, much of our analysis will examine this assumption itself: do changes in the structure help solve our problems? Will changes in income distribution result from changes in production organization? Will workers relate to each other differently when ownership of firms is transfered from the private to the public sector, or from absentee stockholders to workers? or are the relations in production fixed in whole or part by technology rather than by ownership? What is the role of technology in the production process? What is the relation between the macroeconomy (ownership, political power) and the microeconomy (the work socialization process, worker productivity, worker alienation)? What is the effect of ownership and technology on individual freedom inside and outside the production process?

These are very broad questions, but they are crucial to any plan designed to solve societal difficulties through alternative economic structures. Solving difficulties also requires defining a view of the political economy. In our case, this view is shaped by the American reality: What are the political conditions in the United States that give it its special character? How do these political conditions affect the criteria by which we evaluate the appropriateness of various policy alternatives in the American scene? Any change in the organization of production must take this reality into account.

We realize that the questions we are asking are not fashionable at the moment. While the media plays up the alleged trend to the right, purveyors of conservative economic snake oil are in vogue. For example, a book by Nixon's secretary of the treasury, William Simon—A Time for Truth—hit the bestseller charts in 1978. Nobel laureate Milton Friedman contributed a glowing introduction to the book, which blames all our society's problems on government regulation and warns that America is well on its way to becoming a totalitarian state because free enterprise is increasingly hampered and shackled by government. Simon's book is a kind of temper fit by a member of America's power elite who is angry and confused by the unruliness and spunk that appear occasionally in a society with democratic political institutions. Simon wants corporations to be totally free to do whatever they wish without interference from Congress, whose members he labels "self-appointed economic planners" (at least congressmen, unlike corporate managers, are elected by someone), or from civil servants in agencies such as the Occupational Health and Safety Administration (OHSA), whose mission is to protect the lives and health of working men and women.

Simon appears sincerely to believe that liberal, antibusiness individuals have been in charge of the country since the New Deal and that they have saddled business with petty regulations and productive citizens with burdensome taxes, all in order to redistribute income to the poor. Not only is this conspiratorial explanation of recent history at odds with the facts—a quick look at the preponderance of corporate executives in every presidential cabinet since the Depression (including all of Roosevelt's administrations) suggests otherwise—even if it were true, if Robin Hood liberals had been in charge of the federal government, their efforts would have to be judged weak and ineffective. As numerous academic and government studies have demonstrated, the distribution of wealth and income in the United States has changed little in the direction of greater equality since the turn of the century, and hardly at all since World War II.

In our view, most government programs have come into being either at the request of or with the support of specific business interests; and others have been introduced to save the capitalist system from itself— when there are no jobs for some people, a welfare system is created to prevent them from riot or starvation.

The public declarations of men like Simon are part

of a general conservative attack on the few modest government programs that do benefit the poor and working Americans with moderate to middle incomes.

What is ironic is that conservatives like Simon do not even understand how the American economy really works, although it serves their interests more than they realize. Their proposals for "reform" are intellectually spurious and, if enacted, would cause more trouble in the long run for their cherished free enterprise system than they will ever know.

It is not our purpose here to defend the few social programs under our current economic arrangements that actually help the poor or the middle class. That struggle is ongoing and will continue, and we leave it for the moment to community organizers, trade union lobbyists, and public interest activists. Our task is more long range. We are interested in possible structural reforms in the American economy that will make short-run, defensive fights against cutbacks in welfare and employment programs unnecessary by substantially reducing the economic distress which creates the need for such assistance programs.

Earlier in this century, the discussion of reforms under capitalism inevitably led to heated debates over "reform vs. revolution." We will not repeat this debate. Suffice it to say that we believe that, under certain political circumstances, it is possible in a politically democratic country like the United States to win significant structural changes in capitalist society— what French sociologist André Gorz calls nonreformist reforms—changes that substantially add to the democratic rights and power of "average" citizens in their daily lives as workers and consumers. An example of what we mean is the right to organize unions, embodied in law by the Wagner Act of 1935, but won by the sit-down strikes and mass organizing efforts of the CIO.

What is important and key is that these nonreformist reforms lead in the direction of a more democratic and more equal society, and that they help to build a popular movement whose long-range goal is the construction of such a society.

To make our discussion of *desirable* reforms meaningful, we must keep in mind what is *possible* by considering the nature of American society and the sociopolitical context in which economic reforms might be carried out.

American Issues and Their Implications for Economic Alternatives

Americans are heavily committed to democratic ideals. Individual freedom and individual rights are an integral part of the American culture. Any proposed reform that ignores this crucial ideological element could not gain support from many citizens. The issue of democracy is central to a new vision of American society. In America, democracy is identified with capitalism. This is not just an ideological mystique; there is a great deal of individual freedom in the United States compared with previous epochs and with other societies today. Not everyone has the same amount of freedom, and freedom is more limited than it might be, as we shall argue throughout this book; but the fact is that the American capitalist economy has reached a high level of economic development in which citizens are allowed *some* (albeit limited) voice in the way society is run. It is that "some" that most Americans want to preserve.

The existing alternatives to a capitalist economic system—particularly the Soviet Union and her East European satellites—seem to Americans to have eliminated democracy without replacing it by something better. So despite the frequent contradictions between the democratic ideal and the actual operation of our capitalist system, any "socialist" alternative conjurs up images of tyranny in the political as well as economic aspects of daily life. Ironically, Marxist economic and social philosophy, which—as the basis for a political movement—was and is an attempt to *humanize* economic and social life, is associated with dehumanization. In part this is a false image: American visitors to China and Cuba, for example, will attest to the austerity of life in those countries; yet, they also comment on the spirit of cooperativeness and well-being that pervades Chinese and Cuban life. On the other hand, we know that the oldest socialist society, the Soviet Union, actively crushes any dissent and is a model of anti-individualism at every level. The high degree of bureaucratization and centralized decision making in socialist societies does tend to dehumanize both economic and political life. Such realities of socialist development raise real problems for those who offer centralized socialism as the model for an American alternative to corporate capitalism.

At least, reason most Americans, under capitalism they get to vote if they wish (even if the choice is limited) and to consume a multitude of products if they have the income. And there is always that small chance of realizing the American dream—a high income, a beautiful home in a fashionable suburb, a flashy car. Advocates of structural reforms have to convince people that as a result of reform they will live in a more, not less, humanistic society, that democracy will be extended, and that their material well-being will not be reduced.

Americans are idealists about democracy, but economic power is not distributed very democratically. Distribution *is* an issue, in part because a significant fraction of Americans have difficulty sharing in consumption increases and in part because of the clear relationship of material wealth to political power. Who gets what and why they get it has always been reduced to a minor issue in capitalist ideology, assumed away by an idealized view of equal opportunity and meritocracy. The Horatio Alger myth told the poor that the rich had more wealth and power because they worked harder, had greater intelligence, and were more frugal. This mythology continues to underlie much of the American meritocratic ideology today; but along with it is the inescapable cynicism that comes with almost daily revelations on TV or in the press of huge corporate bribes to foreign government, political payoffs, bank manipulations, and tax avoidance by oil companies showing huge profits. Numerous polls show that the majority of Americans view the corporations as too powerful—irresponsibly powerful. This reaction fits well with the American view of democracy and the contradiction that corporate concentration poses to that view.

As Yale political scientist Charles E. Lindblom concluded in his study, *Politics and Markets,* "The large private corporation fits oddly into democratic theory and vision. Indeed, it does not fit."[1]

Lindblom's judgment merits attention. For many years, Lindblom has been regarded as one of the country's leading mainstream political scientists. When one of the authors was a student at Yale in the 1960s, Lindblom was a leading proponent of the pluralist view of American society—that is, the view that no one group had inordinate power. Now, after careful reexamination of the evidence in *Politics and Markets,* Lindblom has moved to a "radical" analysis: namely, that business, particularly the corporate sector, converts economic power into political power and uses that power to block legislation and administrative reforms inimicable to corporate interests. America is a business society. Its dominant ideology is a business one, and the dominant group in America is business. The form of this business domination is important for any reform strategy.

Is American power in the hands of dispensable and constantly changing managers—the new technocratic elite—or do rich financiers (Wall Street) exercise most of the control? The answer to this question is important for the issue of distribution: if it is a set of individuals—the rich financiers—that is especially important, then finding means to divest their personal capital would open the way toward a redistribution of wealth. But if it is the corporations and their managers who are important, as we believe to be the case, then a much more complex problem arises. Corporate wealth and its distribution become the issue, and it is the control of corporations, not of personal capital, that carries implications for employment, growth, income distribution, and the structure of the economy.

Distribution has another facet: who is to bear the costs of pollution, run-down cities, traffic jams, and the social problems of advanced capitalism? In traditional capitalist thinking, these are pricing problems—choices to be made by individuals faced by particular circumstances. If an individual does not like pollution, he or she can move to an area where there is none. This will lower housing rents in polluted areas, so that those who remain will be compensated for the bad air they breathe. But should not citizens in an affluent society have the living conveniences of urban areas without pollution? And should not corporations bear a significant part of the cost of cleaning up? Will this mean a reduction of jobs? Perhaps for high-polluting kinds of production it will. Yet, there are other goods and services that can be produced with much less pollution and perhaps with greater labor intensity.

Americans are concerned about pollution and social problems such as crime, drugs, and mental health because these directly affect the quality of their lives. What good is more income if the enjoyment of what that income buys is offset by increased personal difficulties? This raises another question: how much of the desire for increased economic growth and higher individual income is motivated by the need to escape oppressive social conditions? The history of post–World War II America is characterized by a flight from cities to suburbs. How much of that costly move was prompted by a "pure" preference for suburban living (no matter how peaceful and pleasant the cities were) and how much by the increased unpleasantness of urban life—unpleasantness caused by the absence of any public policy that dealt seriously with poverty, employment, and pollution?

The government is the institution responsible for distribution policy. Although a sizeable percentage of economists would disagree that government should play this role, believing instead that the competitive marketplace is the most efficient income allocator, postwar economic policy has definitely given government, particularly the federal government, increasing distributional powers. Under the present configuration of economic power in corporate capitalist society, it makes sense to recognize distribution as a *political* issue. If everyone worked on small farms and in small shops, if women had the same economic rights as men, if there had been no slaves or racism, then a free market might be the best way to allocate wages and income. But this is not the case.

Giving increased power to the government to allocate incomes appears to contradict the American democratic ideal: if the government has more economic power, won't the individual lose a measure of freedom? In many ways, the fear that governmental bureaucracy will limit individual rights seems a bigger factor in American minds than the benefits provided by government. Social Security, health benefits, unemployment insurance, welfare, and expenditures on jobs in the public sector (including education) or in government contract sectors—of which Lockheed and General Dynamics are a part—

represent about one-third of the U.S. national product. But it is the individual taxpayer who bears a large fraction of the cost of those benefits, and apparently he feels that he is not getting his money's worth. At least, that appears to be the message of recent "tax revolts." The main problem may be that the government does not use its distributional power in ways that really satisfy most citizens' needs. Individuals feel, in turn, that they are giving up individual rights (through taxes) to the government without receiving adequate benefits in return. They see the failure of the government to solve obvious social problems despite accessibility to a large portion of the national product. Their frustration turns against those public institutions closest to them: the schools, the welfare system, and the public bureaucracy itself.

From the standpoint of ideology as well as the reality of performance, Americans mistrust government. Is government inherently corrupt, inefficient, and self-centered? Or is the configuration of economic power in the United States responsible for much of the government's performance? One thing is clear: government at all levels favors corporate interests and helps preserve corporate capitalism, but at the same time a large and growing public sector has served as a means for the poor in America to make *some* gains at the expense of the rich. Without free schooling, working-class mobility might be less than it is now. Without public employment (and equal employment opportunity laws), particularly in schools and local government services, blacks and women would have much less access to professional jobs than they have. State, local, and federal governments employ more than 50 percent of all professional blacks and women working in the United States, at higher salaries than they would earn in private sector jobs. The poor and working class may mistrust government, but these groups—particularly minority groups and women—are also aware of where the better employment opportunities lie, and how to gain access to those opportunities. The affluent society has shortchanged the poor; whatever they have achieved has been gained through the struggle over government power. Since the organization and control of government is and will continue to be one very important arena of political conflict, it seems crucial that proposed alternatives to the present production system deal with government as an element in the economic system as well as its role in the distribution of wealth, income, and employment.

One of the most important aspects of American life and values is the continuing improvement in the material standard of personal life. We have already suggested that Americans count on these material increases to offset or at least soften the personal costs of capitalist development, such as pollution, poor working conditions, stress, and disintegrating family life. Many rely on increases in output to raise their standard of living higher than that of their parents. It has come to be expected that children do "better" than the generation before them. Many also rely on periods of growth just to have a job. Recessions mean unemployment; growth means jobs.

Though there has been talk of "limits to growth," the reality of the idea has not gone much further than discussions among environmentalists and intellectuals. Yet, there may really be limits to growth in the next generation. Capitalism, which is predicated on growth and expansion, will have great difficulties in coping with such limits.

As economist Robert Heilbroner notes in *Boom and Crash,* his recent book on the American economy,

the constraints of the environment, which are the great determining element in the era into which we are moving, suggest that we will have perhaps twenty-five years of "safe," although increasingly difficult growth, followed by curtailments that promise to be more and more drastic [and which] . . . would pose a truly historic challenge to capitalism.[2]

Distribution of jobs at the existing level of output will become increasingly important, not only within the United States, but among countries.

At the moment, workers' organizations are pitted against environmentalists over choices about growth patterns. Many unions see any limit on growth as a direct threat to employment and wages. Environmentalists view unbridled expansion as a direct threat to the environment. Both concerns are valid; they are not dealt with adequately under the present production system, however, which stresses the expansion of output, but not necessarily the creation of more jobs in proportion to output increases.

Ostensibly less important—because it is much harder to measure—is the issue of worker satisfaction and worker participation. There are indications that workers are dissatisfied with their work; nevertheless, some polls also show that workers are generally satisfied, especially in recessions when almost any job is better than unemployment. The issue of participation is even more obscure: workers in capitalist societies are socialized to limit their democratic ideals to the political (voting) sphere and to freedom of choice in consumption. They do not expect to participate in production decisions. Any outright worker demand for control over production transcends that socialization and the whole concept of private property. It also conflicts with the goals of worker organizations: unions are chartered to perform particular functions—collective wage bargaining and grievance mediation. Any worker activity outside of that charter creates conflicts between the rank and file and union officers.

Yet, there are many indications that working in capitalist hierarchies is alienating. Absenteeism, high rates of drug use and alcoholism among workers, and wildcat strikes are manifestations of this alienation. Is capitalist hierarchy to blame, or is industrial production alienating no matter what the system of organization? The only way to answer this question is to examine similar types of production under capitalist and alternative democratic organizations. Consistency with democratic ideals should make work place participation an important reform issue. Whether it is or not depends on the willingness and ability of political organizations to make the mass of American workers aware of its possibilities. Unlike unemployment, inflation, pollution, and distribution, however, worker alienation and its solution through participation and control of production are vague issues. If alienation in work is an accepted fact of life and workers do not connect that alienation with poor interpersonal relations outside the work place, a tremendous effort will be required to make them aware of alternative arrangements. This effort will have to be even greater because of the opposition to increased worker awareness by employers and many unions themselves.

American Political Reality and Economic Change

Americans have one of the highest levels of consumption achieved by any society in history. While this affords opportunities for moving beyond the limited goal of satisfying basic material needs, there are also important limitations on the structural changes that can be made in an affluent and well-organized society. Institutions have been developed that not only increase production and distribute it in a particular way but also defend the system from any significant change. Consciousness is shaped by these institutions—for example, commercial television and advertising. Not only must external conditions change for people in a way that makes them willing to develop new institutions, but they must reject their own relationship with existing structures and actively strive to change these structures.

In spite of the many problems and insecurities associated with capitalist development, most Americans are not compelled by hunger and economic desperation to make drastic changes in the system that governs their lives. As French sociologist André Gorz has pointed out, in the economically advanced countries, the imperative to overthrow existing institutions has lost its natural base of misery. Destitute peasants and workers rise up against the existing order because for them it is blatantly oppressive and they have little to lose. But to corporate employees who have attained higher living standards, it is not so clear that the present situation represents a great evil; most Americans are cautious about risking what they have for vague and unclear alternatives.

Not only are Americans generally well off financially, they are consumption, not production, oriented. Since democratic ideals cannot be implemented in the capitalist work place, people are socialized to believe in a democracy that is limited to the non-production aspects of life. It is through consumption that they allegedly can influence the types and amounts of goods produced and can express their creativity. Even though they are only employees, they can own their own homes, furniture, cars, stereos, and so on. The emphasis on consumption has made Americans much more aware of and interested in inflation, environment, truth in packaging, monopoly pricing, and television programming issues than in job health and safety, job relations and hierarchies, and even unemployment. Ralph Nader understood this in the 1960s. He also understood that any effort to organize the basis of production issues had been successfully delegitimized in American minds as "socialist." This delegitimization has changed somewhat—socialism is not as bad a word as it was ten years ago—but the focus on consumption remains. So there is a temptation for activists to organize largely on these issues.

In addition, no institutional base exists around which to organize for changes in the structure of production. Corporations have grown larger and the corporate sector has gained tremendous power in the American political scene. There is no countervailing force to that power. In other capitalist societies, labor organizations have traditionally been the source of opposition to the concentration of wealth and power in the hands of capital owners. But unlike other industrialized countries, the United States does not have a political organization (party) tied directly into the labor movement, although in some respects the Democratic Party does fill this role.

The American labor movement has been successful in winning legislation that aids workers and has been an important force in pushing for welfare, social insurance, and civil rights; but the unions have never moved out from their production base to develop an overall labor political program. Labor union membership as a share of the total labor force has declined since 1950. The American labor movement enrolls one of the smallest percentages of the labor force among industrialized countries (22 percent). In addition to labor's political limitations, there are other problems in mobilizing around the existing trade union movement to achieve structural change. An important gap exists between trade union leadership and the rank and file. Sociologist Stanley Aronowitz, in his study of the American trade union movement, found that while blue and white collar workers regard their unions as their only weapons against the deterioration of working conditions and the inflation responsible for recent downward pressure on real wages, the labor movement's leadership has failed to extend workers' rights or decentralize and democratize union organizations. Instead, the unions have evolved into a force for integrating workers into the corporate capitalist system.[3]

The modern labor contract serves as a means of insuring some benefits to workers and, in return, providing a stable, disciplined labor force to the employer. The growth of union bureaucracy and the decline of rank-and-file initiatives is built into the theory and practice of collective bargaining. As unions grow and collective bargaining becomes increasingly complex, union officials, like their counterparts in business and government, become bureaucrats whose first obligation is to preserve and protect the institution they serve—in this case, the trade union. As a result, labor leaders have become more concerned with maintaining their own powers and privileges than with organizing the unorganized, contributing to innovative trends in unionism, or promoting a general program of labor reform. So trade unions serve contradictory functions under capitalism. On the one hand, they exist to improve the conditions of work for their members (collective bargaining was, after all, the result of union struggles on behalf of the working class); but, on the other, they compromise themselves to deliver disciplined labor to capital owners and their managers. For the unions to serve as a political base for structural reform, the organization and goals of the unions themselves would have to be changed. As we shall discuss later, there are signs that, to some extent, such a change has begun to occur in the 1970s.

The U.S. political situation is therefore very different from that in Europe, where labor unions are intimately involved with major political organizations, and labor governments are generally committed to promoting working class legislation. Of course, the meaning of a labor program differs from country to country and from decade to decade, but the labor program is discussed in a political context, not just in the context of collective bargaining.

To a much greater extent than in Europe, the government in the United States is bound to a corporate ideology and corporate goals. Rather than a struggle between these corporate interests and the interests of an active labor movement extending workers' rights, the struggle in the United States has been waged by minorities and women seeking greater equality and, in the sixties, by youth and its allies against the Vietnam war, although consumer groups and environmentalists have directly challenged corporate power. While women and minorities are organized around the issue of workers' rights, they are struggling for the rights of particular workers, even if it means lowering the employment possibilities for white males. The women's, minorities', consumer, and environmental movements are an important reality in the American political scene and certainly have their own validity. In the absence of forces to unite these movements into a coherent whole, however, they also tend to fractionalize a broader movement for structural change.

One additional factor deserves mention—the structure of the American political system. This is a basic fact that, until recently, has been overlooked or underemphasized by groups seeking social and political change in the United States in this century. Unlike Europe, the United States does not have a parliamentary form of government. We have a system with a strong president and a Congress elected from single-member, winner-take-all districts. Such an arrangement produces a two-party system and makes the development of third or fourth parties almost impossible. A vote for a third party, in the American context, is understood by most voters as a vote for the other major party. Consequently, most working and middle class voters have never deserted the Democratic Party in large numbers, understanding that to vote for a third party—a labor or a socialist party—would aid Republicans—the party of big business.

The nonparliamentary structure of American government, along with the other factors already mentioned, has doomed efforts by reform groups to build third-party challenges to corporate policies. The fate of the Progressive Party in 1948, which received less votes than the racist Dixiecrats, is a good example of the futility of such efforts.

Significant gains have come where reformers and radicals have chosen to operate within the two-party framework: for example, in California in 1934, when Socialist author Upton Sinclair won the Democratic primary and was almost elected governor on his EPIC (End Poverty in California) platform; in Minnesota in the 1930s, when the Farmer-Labor Party merged with the weaker Democratic Party to become the reform-oriented Democratic Farmer-Labor Party; and in North Dakota in 1919, when populists and socialists formed the Non-Partisan League, captured the Republican Party nominations for state office in the primaries, and swept into the statehouse for two terms, enacting a number of structural reforms such as a state-owned bank that still serves the people of that state today.

The American emphasis on democracy and consumption, the absence of a labor program and party, the hierarchical and compromised labor unions, American aversion to bureaucracy, and the strong two-party political system, all shape American political reality. Any structural reforms proposed for the United States must be framed by the context of this reality, or they will have little chance of serving as the basis of a movement for change.

PART TWO

Corporations and Capital

CHAPTER TWO

Public Ownership

Most reform or revolutionary movements in capitalist economies have viewed public ownership—usually the nationalization of entire industries—as an essential goal that, if realized, would lead to a more equitable society. When public ownership has actually been adopted, however, it has not proved to be the panacea its proponents had hoped.

One of the most important lessons to be learned from the experience of Soviet-style economies is that ownership of the means of production is not a simple issue. The transfer of ownership to the government does not automatically guarantee the establishment of an egalitarian, democratic society. As has been noted by E. F. Schumacher, an economist with the British Coal Board: "Ownership, whether public or private, is merely an element of framework. It does not by itself settle the kind of objectives to be pursued within the framework. . . ."

Schumacher did point out that private ownership severely limits the firm's freedom of objectives. "While private ownership is an instrument that by itself largely determines the ends for which it can be employed," wrote Schumacher, "public ownership is an instrument the ends of which are undetermined and need to be consciously chosen."[1]

What is important in economics is *control* as well as ownership. To the extent that public ownership is now advocated in Western economies, it is often presented as social ownership—that is, the owner is not always the state, but can be the workers themselves, the community, the city or region, or a combination of public and private owners. In this view, a variety of ownership patterns in states and cities would be balanced by public control and guidance at the national level. Accountability and participation would be built into the system for all enterprises no matter what their form of ownership, and certain permissible standards of economic behavior would be set. Both plan and market would function.

British political writer C. A. R. Crosland summed up this pluralistic theory of ownership as follows:

The ideal (or at least my ideal) is a society in which ownership is thoroughly mixed-up—a society with a diverse, diffused, pluralist, and heterogeneous pattern of ownership, with the State, the nationalised industries, the Co-operatives, the Unions, Government financial institutions, pensions funds, foundations, and millions of private families all participating.[2]

Of course, this pluralistic ideal raises many serious and complicated questions.

The best way to consider them is by examining the experience of pluralistic economies—Western mixed economies with public enterprise—and discovering what lessons might be drawn.

The political impetus for public enterprise in Western Europe derives primarily from the socialist tradition, though many public enterprises have been created out of economic necessity by conservative governments. In Europe, particularly in France, there is an "etatist" tradition whereby the government engages in certain economic activities in the interests of overall national development. This is, of course, very different from the Left's case for public owner-ship, which has come primarily in the form of a political economic brief for nationalization. The tra-ditional left-wing arguments for nationalization in-clude the following.

Public utility. Where a natural monopoly exists, duplication of economic facilities makes little sense. Falling into this category are such industries as elec-tric power, railroads, gas and coal, municipal transit. In this area, the "etatist" and socialist traditions merge.

Monopoly. In cases where large firms might be justified on grounds of economic efficiency, there is no reason for the public to suffer from the monopolistic control of an industry. Instead, the public, through public ownership, should run the monopoly in the public interest.

Basic industry. There are certain commodities such as steel which are so basic to the economy and on which so many other firms rely, that only public ownership can insure that their level of output and prices are set in the overall interests of the public.

Planning. The profit motive and public interest are in conflict; thus, only long-range public planning of vital investment in key industries can insure long-term stability and economic growth.

Taken together, these economic arguments con-stitute the "commanding heights" rationale for nationalization that until recently held sway with most Western European socialist parties. The public must take political control over the commanding heights of the economy and guide it in a way that benefits work-ing people, rather than a handful of capitalists. Em-bedded in this outlook is the conclusion that large-scale, monopolistic industry is inevitable and that, as G. D. H. Cole wrote earlier in the century, "the choice to-day is no longer between competition and monopoly, but between monopoly-capitalism and socialism."[3]

There are also noneconomic arguments for public ownership. These have had great ideological force in Western Europe and remain influential around the world (and particularly among the American Left). Such arguments include:

—the belief that the profit motive is ethically bad and will be eliminated by nationalization;

—the belief that industrial democracy will be instituted under public ownership;

—the belief that all egalitarian society can come about only by abolishing private incomes from property.

"We nationalize," wrote one British political economist, "in order to extinguish the great unearned incomes which are to-day derived, not from anything that those who draw them do, but from what they own. . . . The real purpose of socialization is to secure the proper distribution of the net national product among those who create."[4]

Many of the high hopes of the European Left for nationalization have not been realized in practice. Before we examine the actual record of public enterprise, however, it is important to point out that public enterprise in Western Europe has been used in ways not originally envisioned by its proponents, and that many public enterprises came into being by force of circumstance, which has served to confuse the rationale for their existence and impede their smooth operation, as well as to cloud any sort of consensus on what their societal purposes should be.

In the decades since World War II, Western European governments have consciously employed public enterprise for a number of purposes: to aid in regional development; to promote industrial restructuring through government shareholding and control of companies rather than simply through loans and occasional shareholding; to meet the challenge to key companies posed by multinational corporations; to promote import substitution and export as a supplementary policy for maintaining the favorable trade balance necessary for sustained economic growth; to aid in maintaining domestic investment in the face of threats of a general economic recession; to promote advanced-technology industry.

A growing number of economists in Western Europe have adapted their theories to encompass these new uses of public enterprise. Public ownership in many cases was brought about by war and depression, not by conscious left-wing political action. For example, the Italian state holding company, the Industrial Reconstruction Institute (IRI), had its genesis in bank failures in the 1930s in fascist Italy. In bailing out the banks, Mussolini's government took over their enormous and varied stockholdings. After the war, these extensive holdings remained in government hands and served as the basis for the Italian state holding company. In France, the Renault factory was confiscated not for any particular economic reason, but to punish the owners for collaboration with the Nazis. And in West Germany, the government inherited a number of government-owned companies such as Volkswagen that were built as part of the Third Reich's industrial-military machine. More recently, Rolls-Royce company in England slipped into public ownership through its own market failure. In the United States, passenger railway transportation has taken a similar route. These latter cases (Rolls-Royce and U.S. railroads) are examples of what public interest lawyer Mark Green calls "lemon socialism"—the nationalization of industries or firms necessary to the national economy but unprofitable in private hands.

The most complete theory of the need for public enterprise in a capitalist economy has been put forward by Professor Pasquale Saraceno, chief economist of Italy's IRI. Saraceno argues that, as capitalist development progresses, competition is retarded by monopolistic tendencies and growth itself is restricted by structural deficiencies which the market mechanism alone cannot rectify. These structural problems cannot be resolved by Keynesian demand management and will manifest themselves in (1) structural unemployment; (2) regional unemployment and underemployment; and (3) sectoral underinvestment.

In all three of these conditions, the time period of profit on investment is too long or the return too low to attract private investment. According to Saraceno, the government must take the initiative through direct intervention and economic planning. Stuart Holland has summarized Saraceno's views as follows:

> In effect, the state should itself become an entrepreneur. It must do this not simply to help private enterprise to help itself, but to enable the economy and society as a whole to enjoy the benefits which are feasible within a democratic political framework from fuller utilisation of the growth potential of the economy. To maximise this potential within socially desirable limits, macro-economic planning and micro-economic intervention in key firms and sectors should permit a wider degree of political freedom than possible in the wholly state-planned economies of Eastern Europe, while avoiding the degree of underconsumption and stagnation which could result from implementation of pure market principles.[5]

Not surprisingly, there are difficulties in Saraceno's theory as it has been carried out in practice by the IRI.

The importance of Saraceno's contribution is that it joins a critique of capitalist development with a policy option—the government as entrepreneur and indicative planner—that does not suffer from many of the problems of more fully state-owned and planned economies.

Andrew Shonfield, in his classic work *Modern Capitalism,* argued along similar lines. According to Shonfield, one of the key factors in the sustained growth of Western mixed economies in the post–

World War II period has been "the vastly increased influence of the public authorities in the management of the economic system." In Western Europe and the United States, government economic management has included a wide array of public enterprises.

A closer look at that experience can provide some insights regarding the uses and limitations of public enterprise as part of a reform strategy for the United States.

France

The public sector has been the cutting edge of the French economy since World War II. Immediately after the war all major banks and insurance companies, as well as coal, electricity, and gas, were nationalized. These nationalizations were complemented by prewar government ownership of the railroads, the telephone system, and oil and gas exploration firms. Sud Aviation, partly owned by the government since the 1930s, was taken over, and the auto giant Renault was nationalized as retribution for the family's collaboration with the Nazis. A national planning commission was established that worked out jointly determined targets with government firms. French "indicative" planning, which some observers in the 1960s—such as Bernard Nossitter in his book, *The Myth Makers*—viewed as a possible model for the United States, was successful only because of the large amount of public enterprise in the economy. As Shonfield pointed out,

what is called "indicative planning," that is a system which relies on pointing out desirable ends rather than on giving orders to achieve them, can be relied upon to work effectively only in a situation *where there is a central core of important enterprises which are more responsive to the desires of the state than ordinary private firms*. It should be noticed that these are not passive instruments of state power; that is not at all what is required for the tasks which they are designed to fulfill. They are supposed to show initiative, and they are not to be expected to be inhibited about making big profits. Of the four French firms which showed the largest net earnings in 1961, three were mixed enterprises engaged in the profitable oil business. Rather, what is required of a mixed enterprise is that the management would be equipped with a special set of antennae which will be in contact with the centres of state authority, reacting with more than usual sensitiveness to any messages from them.[6] [Emphasis added.]

The government as entrepreneur is taken seriously in France. There are talented government planners, as well as dynamic management in public and mixed enterprises. The planners have directed investment toward industries with high rates of innovation, and these have been concentrated in the public and mixed sectors.

French public enterprises, for the most part, have been competitive and profitable. For example, the Banque Nationale de Paris—the largest bank in the world outside the United States—has been responsible for a number of innovations, including ventures into Arab banking, Far East banking, student lending, sale-and-lease bank financing, tanker financing, mutual funds, and general branch banking services. The bank has provided money and management services for small companies and has sometimes taken an equity interest in them.

Along with the Société General de Paris and the Crédit Lyonnais, the nationalized banks make up 60 percent of French commercial banking. The nationalized banks, however, do not operate very differently from *dynamic* private banks.

These banks certainly do not treat their employees in an "enlightened" manner. Press reports described the French "Lordstown Syndrome" as the prime cause of a strike of clerks at the nationalized banks in

1974. These young workers complained about the depersonalization of bank work and the authoritarian manner of the banks' management. Middle-level managers—forty-seven vice-presidents of Crédit Lyonnais—signed a petition supporting the clerks' demands for reforms in personnel policy and organization of bank work.

What difference does ownership make to the nationalized French banks? There seem to be two main results: the profits do not go into private hands; and the government has close contact with the nation's top bankers. Three bankers representing almost two-thirds of the French banking industry can easily be assembled for a meeting with the finance minister and top planning officials. Such informal relationships—an "old boy" network, according to economist Stuart Holland—does help make indicative planning work.

As noted in a recent British-government-sponsored study of public enterprise:

common educational background, the evident intellectual calibre and all around ability of the top civil servants and the French tradition of respect for the role of the State as economic innovator and director, all conduce to understanding and collaboration between enterprises and Ministries.[7]

Of course, French public enterprises do not always listen to the planning commission. Renault has often ignored the planners' regional policies in locating its new plants. It has operated with as much autonomy and freedom as any similar private enterprise. On the other hand, Sud Aviation lost the competitive edge in the world market it had gained with the development of the Caravelle when it followed the government's request to produce the supersonic Concorde for reasons of national interest rather than economics.

In the area of worker participation, French public

enterprises have fared little better than private ones. In reviewing the hopes that accompanied the postwar nationalizations, a 1967 interministerial report, known as the Nora Report after its chairman, commented:

The composition, the evolution and the influence of the public sector for the last twenty years constitutes in effect a good illustration of the ruses of history ... born of a profound aspiration for the liberation of workers, [the nationalizations] have not overturned the condition of the workers; very much on the contrary, they and their unions consider themselves today legally disarmed in the face of the state as boss.[8]

In the immediate postwar period, French public enterprises were governed by boards with tripartite representation: government, workers, and consumers in equal proportions. The French Communist Party, however, used its cabinet positions to place sympathetic persons in the slots reserved for workers and consumers. This maneuver caused backlash among the public; the government stepped in and reduced the importance of the worker and consumer representatives. A new principle became operative: "It is more important to select persons representing states of mind than persons representing interests."

French managers run the public enterprises much as American managers run private firms in this country. "The technocrats in the nationalized sector are much more autocratic than those in the private sector," Andrew Shonfield commented. The bitterness expressed by striking workers at Renault and other plants in 1968 supports this conclusion.

One lesson from the French experience is that representation on the board of directors is not the central issue with regard to worker participation. Rather, it is a question of management style and the extent of worker participation and control at the plant level. As long as French managers are trained in elitist engineering schools, it is highly unlikely that they will participate willingly in the development of nonhierarchical modes of decision making for French public enterprises.

Certain cosmetic changes were made as a result of the 1968 upheaval and, more recently, the worker takeover of the Lip watch factory. The government began to offer shares in Renault free of charge to workers. As of 1973, 5.5 percent of the stock had been distributed. Certain restrictions are enforced, however: 75 percent of the stock must remain in government hands; workers must have five years' seniority to receive shares; shares are not transferable for five years; and the number of shares per person is limited. A representative of the shareholding workers is now elected to the board. When worker stock reaches 20 percent of the total, the board will include three representatives for shareholding workers, ten for the state, and six for the staff. Similar experiments are being tried in other public enterprises; such reforms, however, are minor.

Other developments in French public enterprise have included: new mergers; the decentralization of newly merged enterprises; publication in 1967 of the Nora Report, which urged clearer delineation of the relation between the government and public enterprises; and responses to the energy crisis and the challenge of American multinationals.

In 1970, Sud Aviation was merged with Nord Aviation—a joining of commercial and military production—to form Aerospatiale; in 1973, the latter firm was reorganized into four autonomous divisions, in a structure similar to that of large American aerospace companies. The reorganization was carried out to enable the company to compete better with American multinational aerospace firms. Government share control was reduced to 92.75 percent in line with the law allowing for one-third of the capital to be owned by shareholders other than the state.

An Institute of Industrial Development was established in 1970. Its role is complementary to that of the banking system, and its goals are to encourage the expansion of medium-sized firms, to aid in regional development, and to support technological innovation. The institute takes equity interest in firms. It also offers management advice and operates as a facilitator.

The major public enterprises, such as Renault, have engaged in reshuffling and restructuring aimed primarily at the rationalization and decentralization of management functions. Public enterprises have also entered into the creation of new companies and joint ventures with major private companies. For example, Renault and Peugeot established jointly owned transmission plants to be located in the north, an area with relatively high unemployment.

Decentralization of the management functions of public enterprises to regional cities away from Paris has been part of a deliberate attempt to bring economic growth to the regions. Public banks are playing a key role in developing regional industry.

The French public housing sector is expanding strongly. A national new-town law authorizes the creation of new local entities in each new town site that supersede existing suburban political bodies. Land prices are frozen within the project area until the public new-town corporation buys what it wants. The corporation builds public facilities and sells land to private developers at a profit for residential and commercial construction. This approach has some merit for its flexibility, but it allows developers and speculators too much profit at the expense of public goals. To keep some projects solvent, public companies have had to rely more and more on private developers—and what the developers do with the land they buy is what they would have done in the first place: build suburbs. This approach—using the power of government, in effect, to assist developers in overcoming local resistance to development—is similar to the American experience with urban renewal.

The French planning mechanism as it has functioned since the war has been neither authoritarian nor decentralized. Rather, it has been a consultative process with much interaction between planners and the management of public enterprise. Economist John Sheahan cited the case of the French electric company in contrasting the American regulatory approach with that of indicative planning.

Where the American regulatory boards do little more than wait for the company's plan and on some occasions delay it, the French Planning Commission asks for alternative programs, examines the criteria used, and in at least some instances recommends methods and targets that differ from the company's proposed package.

Sheahan concluded that

government intervention that takes the form of multilateral consultation through a systematic planning process is not the same kind of intervention as a specific, ad hoc, directive from a President or other political office. The systematic kind of intervention through a planning process is much more likely to be constructive in the first place, and it has the fundamental added value of permitting dialogue.[9]

In his examination of French public enterprise, Sheahan pointed out that, in the postwar period, it has *never* been the policy of the French government to attract business away from private firms. Public enterprises have expanded by starting new activities or purchasing existing ones, not by exerting independent competitive pressure to expand the public's share of the market.

"The French government has treated public enterprise essentially as a support for private profit: a means to provide essential services in fields in which profitability is difficult to ensure." French public monopolies thus have kept prices low to business users to encourage growth and development. The accumulation of capital has been given priority over income redistribution or collective consumption. This is not surprising given the relatively conservative governments that have ruled France during the postwar period.

In the fall of 1978, for example, moderate French President Giscard d'Estaing announced that, because of the troubled state of France's two privately owned major steel companies—Usinor and Sacilor, and Chiers-Chatilon—the government and government-owned banks were converting the loans owed them by these private firms into stock—in effect, forgiving the loans and giving the government majority control of the firms' capital. Other private steel firms denounced the plan as "a nationalization that dares not speak its name."

Because of the chaos and inefficiency in the steel industry and its importance to the French economy, Giscard had little choice in whether to act—but he hesitated to apply the term "nationalization" to the measure. He was acting in the overall interest of existing economic arrangements, while the left-wing parties in France—the Communist Party and the Socialist Party—have proposed extensive nationalization of leading, healthy French firms and of a number of branches of foreign multinationals operating in France as part of the Common Program of the Left to transform the French economy in a socialist direction.

The Common Program of the French Left included a list of companies (by actual name) which the Left would nationalize once in power, and other planks such as a substantive increase in the minimum wage. Giscard and his moderate coalition argued that the Left's program, if enacted, would prove both expensive and inflationary. A sense that this, in fact, would be the case did appear to influence some voters and contributed to the defeat of the Left in the 1978 national elections.

Great Britain

By 1951, coal, airlines, railroads, gas and electricity, iron and steel, and radio and television had been nationalized in Great Britain. Most of the activity took place in the immediate postwar period under a Labour government. Britain, however, nationalized the "commanding heights" of the economy as they existed in the *nineteenth* century. Relatively "sick" utility-type industries were taken over, rather than firms of a more dynamic, leading nature.

Given this limitation, nationalized industries in Britain have performed efficiently in the public interest. A massive study by economist Richard Pryke documented that the nationalized industries, in terms of efficiency and productivity, have tended on average to surpass the performance of private industry.

Pryke compared increases in output per employee-hour in each of the nationalized industries with those in numerous private manufacturing industries, and with private manufacturing as a whole. Using the best available statistics, he found that "between 1948 and 1968 the nationalized industries' productivity increased by 3.4 percent per annum as against a rise of 2.8 percent in manufacturing (and 2.5 percent in the private sector as a whole)."[10]

W. A. Robson, in his study *Nationalised Industry and Public Ownership,* also documented the successes of British public ownership.

Robson noted:

The truest answer that can be given to the question about the performance of the nationalised industries since they were taken over, is that each one of them is undoubtedly in a better condition than it would have been under private enterprise or, as was the case with gas and electricity, divided between private and municipal ownership. By this I mean that its operating efficiency is higher, its equipment more up-to-date, and its future prospect brighter than they would have been if the industry had not been nationalized.

With regard to prices and wages, Robson was equally laudatory of the nationalized sector:

It is virtually certain that if the nationalized industries had been under unregulated private ownership, prices would have risen much more steeply than they had done since 1964. . . . Wages and conditions of employment, while not uniformly satisfactory throughout the nationalized industries, are almost certainly better than they would otherwise have been.[11]

In the most recent assessment, economist William Shepherd of the University of Michigan concluded:

The broad experience of British public enterprises is that performance can be equal or better than what private enterprises would probably yield. This has involved a complex set of guidelines, good managers in the firms, and a fairly delicate balancing of external supervision with autonomy for the public firm. Such a balance has been achieved over fairly long periods of time. It has been achieved despite the high complexity of relationships among public firms, such as among coal, electricity and gas in the energy sector.[12]

The Coal Board decentralized the industry into a number of quasi-firms, thereby realizing the benefits of decentralized management. The British have applied sophisticated cost-benefit analysis in the field of transport planning. For example, planners calculated that while the expense of a new subway line through the heart of London could not be justified on the basis of expected revenues alone, it reduced other costs to the city by decreasing traffic and pollution on London streets. Nationalized industries have been ahead of private firms in offering educational opportunities to employees. Management and unions engage in joint consultation over issues such as health and safety.

The coal industry provides an example of the responsiveness of public versus private enterprise. Coal mining is the most hazardous occupation in the United States: the injury-frequency rate (number of disabling work injuries per one million employee hours worked), which reached 41.6 in 1970, is the highest of all industry groupings. The United States has consistently lagged behind other industrialized nations in improving mine safety. In 1970, the fatality rate in the United States was 1.25 deaths per million employee hours worked, compared with 0.22 in the United Kingdom and 0.43 in the European Economic Community.

While British public enterprises have scored significant accomplishments in modernizing rundown and disorganized industries, they have not brought about economic democracy. The public firms closely resemble private corporations. Prominent members of Britain's financial and industrial elite sit on the boards. Parliamentary control tends to come after the fact and deals only with the most general policies. Worker and consumer participation in decision making is minimal.

Consumer councils are attached to each nationalized industry; some of them (such as the gas boards) also have local consumer councils attached to their decentralized units. The councils have no power except to advise the responsible board and the minister. The council is also financially dependent on the board for staff, information, technical assistance, and so on, and is thus prevented from engaging in its own educational and publicity program. A number of critics have recommended that consumer councils be given an independent staff and budget so they might play a more active role as advocate of the consumer.

Little progress has been made in increasing worker participation and control in the nationalized industries, though the topic is now hotly debated in Britain. Worker representatives have been placed on the board of British Steel, and job enrichment programs have been started in the postal service and in the public auto firm, British Leyland. The British Trades Union Congress (TUC) has not been in the forefront of the workers' control movement; until the mid-1970s, declared TUC policy called for union independence from management responsibility.

In the seventies, the existing British public enterprises have continued to rationalize their operations. In 1973, for example, the two state airlines (BEA and BOAC) merged to form British Airways. From 1963 through 1971, their combined average rate of return on assets before interest and taxes had been 9.1 percent, compared with 5.1 percent for Pan Am, 4.7 percent for TWA, and 8 percent for KLM. British Steel, under the leadership of new top management, has been engaged in large-scale modernization including the construction of large, Japanese-style oxygen mills at deepwater ports that can be served by large ore carriers. British Steel ran at a profit in 1972 and 1973, then incurred heavy losses. One of its problems was that management wanted to raise prices, but the Conservative government pressured it not to as part of the government's anti-inflation strategy. The British government has used pricing policies in the nationalized industries as a means of slowing inflation.

In 1971, the Conservative government nationalized the ailing Rolls-Royce company. This move constituted a bail-out of a sick capitalist firm. As Gordon Adams concluded in his study of the case, the nationalization of Rolls-Royce was necessary because of the vital importance of that firm to the overall position of British capitalism domestically and internationally. The Rolls managers made clear to the government during January and February 1971 that private capital would no longer invest the resources necessary to ensure the survival of the firm. The research and development costs of the RB-211 contract meant that Rolls would no longer earn profits. Nationalization was therefore the only alternative.[13]

The Labour government elected in 1974 brought with it but did not implement a new program of proposed nationalization that was coupled with a call for extensive industrial democracy. The previous Labour government of 1964-70 had made almost no effort to introduce new programs of public ownership. It contented itself with direct government aid to high-cost, advanced-technology industries and with the encouragement of mergers in the private sector through an Industrial Reorganization Corporation, which served mainly to increase the concentration of private capital in the economy.

The new nationalization program was developed by a group of younger left-wing economists and had the support of a number of leading party members, particularly Anthony Wedgwood-Benn. The plan called for the nationalization of twenty-five leading firms in the most dynamic manufacturing and service sectors. Public ownership of these "leaders" is vital, argued the program. Only with a public presence in the leading sectors of each industry can the government effectively guide the economy. The program also called for a system of planning agreements under which private and public firms would be obliged to reveal to government planners data on investment, employment, prices, product development, marketing, and export and import requirements. Citing the French and Italian experience, the program's authors pointed out that such planning agreements with private firms work only when the government has public enterprises of its own with which it can compare the data provided by private firms. This is in line with Shonfield's conclusion, cited earlier, that noncoercive planning works only in an economy with a significant share of public ownership.

The new Labour program was also based in large measure on Saraceno's theory of the inadequacy of Keynesian demand management in solving the problems of capitalist development. The program envisioned that new public firms would play an entrepreneurial role—pointing out new opportunities to sluggish private firms and stimulating new growth in the British economy, as well as improving its international position.

Finally, the program strongly endorsed industrial democracy for the nationalized sector of the economy. The program, however, did distinguish between strategy and tactics in implementing worker control. In small and medium-sized firms, workers should effectively control all aspects of company behavior subject to the constraints of the market as well as regulations on pollution, unsafe products, and so on. The constituent plants of the larger firms would also be under extensive worker control. Because they are bigger, however, and their behavior influences national pricing, trade, and regional development, the government must be able to exercise influence over these strategic questions.

This does not mean to say that the central government should hand down directives to the workers in the firm concerned,

explained Stuart Holland, one of the program's drafters.

Worker-managed companies, like companies under conventional management, have a much better on-the-ground idea of markets, techniques and opportunities than central planners. The process of bargaining on such strategic issues therefore would run more as an extension of traditional bargaining procedures than as central limitation from the outset of what worker-managed firms might or might not do.

Holland concluded the case for the new program:

the strength of the proposals lies in a positive harnessing of the power of giant enterprise rather than in negatively confronting it. In the rationale for new public ownership among the economic leaders, the government can move from ineffective indirect pressures to direct intervention through new public enterprise in the public interest. In the rationale for workers' bargaining on the main features of that planned intervention, unions can move from negative confrontation on wage bargaining to positive negotiation of the wider role which companies should play in serving society as a whole.[14]

This new program for the public ownership of leading firms has not been put into practice. The Labour government did establish a state holding company, the National Enterprise Board (NEB), embodying one of the proposals made by the Left. In practice, however, the NEB has operated in the service of private enterprise. When British Leyland, England's major car firm, fell upon hard times and threatened to close, it was taken under public ownership by means of the NEB. Similarly, the Upper Clyde Shipyards in Glasgow were nationalized and placed under the NEB.

In addition to operating Leyland and the Upper Clyde works, the NEB has provided equity capital and technical advice to middle-sized high-technology firms. The goal has been to rationalize and develop Britain's technology-based industries, so that they can compete better on the international market, not to promote economic democracy.

The Conservative government elected in 1979 and

led by Margaret Thatcher began an assault on existing British public enterprises. Plans were announced in late 1979 to begin selling shares in British Aerospace, British Airways, and British Petroleum to private owners. The NEB was to remain a graveyard for unprofitable firms taken into public ownership, such as Rolls-Royce and the Clyde shipyards; but if they become profitable, these firms too will be offered for sale to private buyers.

Both the extension of public ownership in Britain and a democratization of existing public firms will have to await a new Labour government—and then only one headed by a member of the party's left wing, such as Wedgwood-Benn.

Italy

The Italian Industrial Reconstruction Institute (IRI) is Europe's largest market-oriented public enterprise operation. Together with Ente Nazionale Idrocarburi (ENI), the oil and gas conglomerate, it dominates the public sector of the Italian economy. In 1978, the IRI employed over 525,000 people, making it Europe's largest industrial employer. It is a highly diversified group. The IRI owns three of the largest national banks accounting for one-fifth of total bank deposits. It owns the national airlines, Alitalia, the main shipping companies, Italian radio and television, and most of the telephone system. It has built over half of the nation's highways. In manufacturing, it produces three-fifths of Italian steel, owns the Alfa-Romeo auto company, and has interests in other engineering firms. It is the most diversified and dynamic state holding company in the world.

The IRI was born in 1933 after the collapse of the leading Italian banks. These banks held equity positions in many companies for which they provided financing, and a number of these companies, in turn, held stock in the banks. The IRI was created to sort out the chaos and keep the companies going. Other state firms such as the General Italian Petroleum Corporation were created before the war for special purposes. After the war, the latter formed the nucleus for ENI, the state gas and oil holding company.

In reaction to Mussolini's corporate state, after the war Italy chose to run a decentralized economy with few central controls. The existing public enterprises remained in public hands, however, and were left to compete in the market with private firms. The IRI was restructured into various groups, each with its own financial intermediaries. The major groups are: Finsider for steel; Finmeccanica for engineering, including auto production; Stet for telephones; Finmare for shipping; and Fincantieri for shipbuilding.

In 1953, the government converted the General Italian Petroleum Corporation into a new energy holding company, ENI, which under the leadership of Enrico Mattei expanded across the international oil scene and across a wide spectrum of Italian industry. ENI moved into new fields such as chemicals, atomic power, and synthetic fabrics.

The same procedure was utilized in 1959 to combine holdings in electric power into another independent state holding company, Ente Nazionale per l'energia Elettrica (ENEL).

In its operations, the IRI followed Saraceno's theory as to the role of public enterprise in a capitalist economy. As Holland summarized the IRI formula:

the method adopted by IRI is to create (or recreate) enterprises that are subject to the discipline of a private business operating in a commercial market with the maximum of managerial autonomy. In some cases, the enterprises which IRI creates are only a minor part of a sector in terms of size but they make up for lack of size by becoming "pace-setters." The means which IRI relies on to run its enterprises are initial state capital supplemented by the profits of the enterprises themselves but in a number of cases there is also specific state compensation for what are called "oneri imorop" (exceptional liabilities).[15]

From 1958 to 1969, market sources accounted for nearly two-thirds of total IRI finance compared with less than a tenth from government grants; the remainder came from self-financing. The IRI has proven commercially competitive by private enterprise cash-return standards. The major difference, as Saraceno expounds in his theory, is that IRI investment differs from private investment in the time period of profitability. Public firms can have a longer time horizon on monetary return than many private firms. The IRI maintains a number of training and management institutes to educate workers, technicians, and managers. The quality of IRI personnel is considered to be outstanding at most levels.

IRI and ENI management have enjoyed a substantial degree of autonomy. In 1956 legislation created a Ministry of State Holdings to oversee public enterprises. It was given positions on the boards of the top holding companies, but has restricted itself to considerations of general policy and has avoided intervening in detailed management decisions.

The state holding company formula has served the Italian economy well. Finsider, for example, converted the backward Italian steel industry into one of the most modern and efficient in the world. In shipbuilding, however, it took over a decade for noncompetitive military-oriented facilities to be closed down or converted because of the problem of maintaining employment in local shipbuilding areas.

Both the IRI and the ENI have played key roles in the country's regional policy. Early in the postwar period, the government relied on tax and credit policies to stimulate development in the south. These incentives had little effect, however. In 1957, the IRI and the ENI were required by the government to locate 60 percent of their new industrial investment and 40 percent of their total investment in the south. Subsidies were provided in cases where extra financial costs would have put the public enterprise at a competitive disadvantage.

While following this general requirement of locating in the south, public enterprises were free to decide on the exact nature of the investment. For example, the government wanted Alfa-Romeo to locate a major new car plant at Naples, but the design, specifications, market slot, and production volume of the new vehicle were left to the company's management.

This specific policy of using public enterprise for regional development has been a qualified success. Noted Sheahan:

The experience was a demonstration that social directives, if they can ever be clearly formulated in operational terms, can in fact be implemented through public enterprise without implying the need for any authoritarian apparatus of control.[16]

Requiring investment by the IRI and the ENI in the south has not, by itself, been a totally adequate development policy. Their investment has tended to be capital intensive—large auto plants, large steel plants, relatively large food-processing plants, highways, and so on. The south also badly needs small and medium-sized firms that are labor intensive and deal with the problems of underdevelopment more directly by training workers. The lack of national planning from the central government has prevented the formulation of a comprehensive development policy for the south.

Labor relations have been somewhat better in public enterprises than in private industry, but the public enterprises certainly have not pioneered any significant worker participation or worker control experiments. Industrial democracy is a public issue in Italy and, should a more left-wing government come to power, it is likely that public enterprises might be required by the government to adopt a more democratic management approach.

In the seventies, Italian public firms began increasing their claim on public funds rather than relying on their own internal funds for growth. The problem is not with public enterprise per se; it is a manifestation of Italian political life. Public firms have been drawn more and more into providing financial support and a power base for members of the governing Christian Democratic coalition. Top management positions have gone increasingly to party politicians in need of jobs, rather than to the most competent managers trained by the IRI's institute. "The high standards of the initial postwar Italian governments wore down as the same party stayed in power too long," concluded Sheahan.

West Germany

In the postwar period, West Germany has relied essentially on government support of private economic expansion. A number of the largest West German companies, however, including Volkswagen, Veba, and Lufthansa, are wholly or partly owned by the government. Veba, involved in metals, was formed by a government-sponsored merger of several smaller companies; the federal government owns only 44 percent. Ruhr Kohle, a consortium organized to rescue the coal industry, is only 25 percent government owned.

The government has invested heavily in industry through a central development bank, the Kreditanstadt für Wiederanfban (Reconstruction Loan Corporation); most of the companies involved, however, are relatively autonomous and are managed like private firms. Top management is composed of businessmen, not civil servants. The West German government, at all levels, exercises indirect influence on private companies through government-owned banks, bank holdings, and more than 800 savings banks owned by local authorities.

"As everywhere in Germany," noted *The Economist,* "this control is exercised more by persuasion than by the tenuous powers of ownership."[17]

In addition to promoting growth, major governmental priority has been given to keeping unemployment low; consequently, public firms have been encouraged to keep open marginal operations and make up losses with state subsidies. A system of co-determination—worker representation on the board—was introduced in the iron and steel industry after the war and extended to other major firms in 1976 (co-determination will be analyzed in detail in a later chapter).

West Germany is unique in its extensive network of locally owned public financial institutions and housing authorities. Nearly all the municipalities and counties in the country own savings banks or other financial institutions such as housing finance corporations. Public savings banks are permitted a 5 percent rate of profit. There is no tax-exempt municipal bond market, and the government taxes interest on the bonds of public enterprises at the same rate as the interest on private firm bonds. Many of the local savings banks own home construction firms. In addition, there are over 300 publicly owned nonprofit housing corporations in West Germany, and hundreds of other nonprofit housing firms owned by churches and trade unions. By 1970, the nonprofit housing sector had built over 3 million rental units and had an annual construction rate of 120,000 to 150,000 new dwellings.[18]

Many regional governments own insurance firms

offering life, liability, and accident coverage as well as fire and theft insurance.

West German public enterprise has provided a basic infrastructure (iron and steel, railroads) and quasi-welfare goods (housing, medical services, insurance) within the context of a hierarchical, private-ownership economy. Its key role has been in the financing of private economic growth.

United States

Corporations established and owned by the public in order to accomplish specialized economic development have appeared throughout American economic history. In almost all cases, these enterprises have complemented and aided private enterprise, rather than replaced or competed with it. Public, nonprofit corporations have built bridges, dug canals, created ports, run airports, managed turnpikes, and performed dozens of other tasks. They have ranged in size from municipal parking services to the Port of New York Authority. Rarely has the government engaged directly in the production or distribution of economic goods. When this has happened, as in the case of the Tennessee Valley Authority, it has been as much the result of circumstance as of conscious public policy in favor of public enterprise.

During the Depression, for example, the federal government established the Reconstruction Finance Corporation (RFC). During 1932, the RFC made loans totaling $2.3 million—mostly to banks, but in some cases to railroads as well so that they could repay loans extended by banks. The activities of the RFC were kept secret; many loans were made to banks with which its directors were connected. The RFC was authorized only to make loans; it was not permitted to purchase stock. For many banks, RFC loans were of little help; their problem was lack of capital, not the availability of loan money.

Under the New Deal, the RFC became more aggressive. Roosevelt appointed Jesse Jones, a wealthy Texas entrepreneur, as its head and sponsored legislation to expand its size and powers. Roosevelt and Jones wanted the RFC not just to protect the nation's credit institutions but to serve as an instrument of economic stimulation.

The RFC was authorized to extend loans to corporations of all types. In addition, as a pseudo holding company, it became the corporate vehicle under which a number of subsidiaries were created. The Commodity Credit Corporation supported the prices of agricultural commodities. The Electric Home and Farm Authority financed the purchase of electrical appliances, particularly in rural areas. The RFC Mortgage Company and the Federal National Mortgage Association bought up mortgages to pump money into the construction industry. The Export-Import Bank, another subsidiary, provided financing for exports.

In addition, the RFC helped to finance flood control and other public works projects, and offered loans for agricultural marketing and rural electrification. In the process, it helped put into business such firms as Tennessee Gas Transmission and El Paso Natural Gas.

By January 1934, less than two years after its creation, the RFC had pumped more money into the American economy than had the House of Morgan from 1919 to 1933. By 1938, the RFC had disbursed $10 billion.

With the onset of World War II the RFC, through its subsidiary, the Defense Plant Corporation (DPC), became the holding company for industrial expansion. The DPC loaned more than $9 billion, nearly half of which went to the nation's largest corporations. By 1945, the DPC had financed 2,098 plants;

920 of these were owned outright by the corporation. After the war, most of the plants were sold at bargain prices to private corporations.

Another large RFC subsidiary, the Defense Supplies Corporation, disbursed an additional $9 billion; among other things, it helped to foster the synthetic rubber industry. Yet another subsidiary, the Metals Reserves Company, spent almost $3 billion to purchase strategic minerals and finance the necessary processing and extraction plants. A smaller RFC operation, the Defense Homes Corporation, spent about $75 million to construct housing for government employees. During the years 1932-46, the RFC spent approximately $50 billion, a massive amount at the time.[19]

The RFC was an exceptional occurrence, however. The most common form of public enterprise in the United States at the federal level has been what Professor Lloyd Musolf calls "the mixed enterprise." This vehicle is generally used to subsidize or bail out the private sector, or to undertake a venture private enterprise is unwilling to finance alone.

During the nineteenth century, state governments invested in hundreds of mixed enterprises with private capitalists. The most well-known example of mixed enterprise at the national level is the Union Pacific Railroad, which enjoyed huge land grants, government loans, and other privileges in the name of developing the continent. The government held five seats out of twenty on the board of directors; inspected the company's books and records; and filed an annual report with the secretary of the interior. According to studies of this experience, the government directors were not invited to meetings, were rarely listened to, and were "treated as spies or antagonists by the rest of the board."[20]

Examples of mixed enterprises currently in operation include Amtrak, the federal rail passenger transportation corporation; Conrail, the federal freight rail corporation; COMSAT, the Communications Satellite Corporation; the Corporation for Public Broadcasting; the Federal National Mortgage Association ("Fannie Mae"); and the Federal Home Loan Bank.

In his study of mixed enterprise, Musolf concluded: "Scrutiny of the anatomy of mixed enterprise in our business society has confirmed the expected strong development of the private sector side as well as a corresponding weakness of the government side."[21]

The largest existing government corporation is the U.S. Postal Service. It is cited regularly by business spokesmen as an argument against government ownership and was used as a whipping boy during the public hearings over the proposed creation of a federal oil and gas corporation. A word needs to be said about the Post Office, if only to clarify the facts in the matter. The Post Office is run not to make money, but to deliver the mail—a public service; its rates subsidize businesses more than individuals.

In 1974, the *Washington Post* ran a series of articles on the operation of the Post Office that revealed a number of "horror" stories about the lack of modernization, backward manpower policies, and unsophisticated rate structures. The new post office corporation—the U.S. Postal Service—was established to depoliticize the Post Office, so that it might be run in a more businesslike manner. According to the *Washington Post,* the management board appointed by the Nixon administration failed miserably to "rationalize" postal service. In 1971, Nixon named Elmer T. Klassen, former president of American Can Company, to head the new post office corporation. Klassen took little interest in the post office, spending long weekends at his summer home. Under the structure established by Congress, Klassen reported to a board of governors, whose members are appointed to nine-year terms by the president. Nixon, not surprisingly, appointed conservative businessmen and professionals to these positions. The *Post* series depicted the board members as uninterested in improving service; they appeared to pay little attention to the way in which Klassen was running the corporation.

It is almost as if conservatives have a vested interest in seeing that a public enterprise does not serve the public well. Appointment to the board of a public enterprise of directors who have little if any incentive for seeing that the enterprise operates effectively and in the public interest (they own no stock and do not represent consumers or labor) almost guarantees poor management and fuels the myth that the "public can't run a business."

Advocates of a federal oil and gas corporation have cited the Tennessee Valley Authority as a working example of a successful public enterprise. From a business perspective, the TVA has been run efficiently. It produces relatively low-cost power and engages in a host of other activities, including flood control and regional planning. The experience of the TVA shows that a public enterprise can be run without corruption and without a drain on the public treasury—but there are other points to be made about the TVA.

The TVA was not demanded by the inhabitants of the area. Rather, it happened to them, because of the existence of the former munitions facilities at Muscle Shoals, which the government had not sold off and which Senator Norris and others fought to keep in public hands. The TVA, even at its birth, was not a public enterprise with clear public goals.

Rexford Tugwell, one of Roosevelt's key aides at the time, described how the newly appointed directors of the TVA called on him shortly after being appointed to inquire just what the TVA was supposed to do: was it a government planning agency? or a government power corporation? or something else? Tugwell replied that the president really had no firm ideas about the matter, and that it was up to the directors to work it out. Of course, if a political uproar occurred, the president could not bail them out.

Because of this lack of explicit goals, the TVA almost immediately accommodated itself to the local power structure in the South, which meant working with local white businessmen and farmers instead of promoting land reform and a better deal for share-croppers, both black and white. It also meant that the TVA saw itself primarily as a producer of low-cost power to stimulate the development of private enterprise in the region. Being in the power business, private or public, leads to a certain set of mind.[22]

Forty years after its creation, the TVA was attacked by environmentalists as being too development-minded—too committed to more dams, power, and industry, and to nuclear power.

David Freeman, appointed head of the TVA by President Carter, told the *New York Times:*

Low-priced power is a religion with them. That puts them in conflict with the Government on environment. Isn't it time for TVA to have a new yardstick, a new mandate—energy conservation and environmental protection—to show the country how to use the least number of kilowatt hours?

Freeman called the TVA "the most successful New Deal agency—regional government that worked." Now, he said, "when it comes to fighting over environmental legislation, they're just like the other utilities."

The TVA never became the standard in power production, as its advocates hoped, for its range of operations remained limited to one geographical area. During the 1930s a series of regional TVAs were planned, but these did not pass Congress. The TVA did, however, serve as a kind of yardstick by providing the government with the data which led to the uncovering of the GE price-fixing scandals.

The TVA was never a *redistributional* agency; it was and is a *developmental* one. As a public enterprise fostering growth, it has been a huge success. If different goals are required of a public enterprise, they will have to be made explicit and built into its structure and operation.*

Public enterprises at the state level were established earlier in the century in times of intense political change. In 1917, for example, the Progressive movement was at its high point in Wisconsin. One of the many industries which the Progressive movement criticized, led by Governor Robert La Follette, was life insurance. The state legislature enacted tough regulations and created a State Life Fund—the only state-run insurance program in the country. The goal of the act, according to Herman L. Ekern, insurance commissioner at the time, was to provide "guaranteed insurance at cost."

Supporters of the program predicted that thousands would flock to the plan. Efforts were made to publicize the State Life Fund. Brochures and applications were sent to banks, city clerks, and the treasurers of every county, city, and village in the state. The press followed the plan closely—but few people signed up. Only a few hundred policies per year were sold. Nevertheless, the private insurance industry tried without success to have the fund killed in the 1919 session of the legislature. Such efforts have been repeated periodically, most recently in 1965. Each attempt to abolish the fund focused public attention on its existence and increased the number of policyholders.

The fund is administered by the secretary of state,

---

*In a June 26, 1978, interview with *Barron's*, Freeman declared that in the future the TVA would explore new energy sources such as solar power and wood; advocate conservation of energy; and use TVA purchasing mechanisms to promote electric cars.

the state treasurer, the attorney general, and the commissioner of insurance, who act collectively as an investment board. Investments are primarily in first mortgages on improved farm property in Wisconsin.

In 1975, the fund had about 10,000 policyholders and provided a total of some $60 million worth of insurance coverage; this represented only one-third of 1 percent of the more than 3 million life insurance policies held by Wisconsin residents.

Supporters of the fund argue that it should be allowed to advertise and believe it could act as "yardstick competition" for private firms. The fund employs no agents; all business is done by mail. The lower cost of its policies is due partly to low overhead and partly to the absence of private profit. State Life premiums are between 10 and 40 percent cheaper than comparable private policies.

Another state-level public enterprise born amidst political upheaval is the state-owned Bank of North Dakota. In 1917, the Nonpartisan League—a Populist farmer-socialist organization—captured the state legislature of North Dakota. It created a state Industrial Commission, comprised of the governor, attorney general, and commissioner of agriculture, to oversee three new state industries: the Bank of North Dakota, an experimental creamery, and a state mill and grain elevator.

When the Bank of North Dakota opened for business on July 19, 1919, the state issued bonds for $2 million to provide a capital account, but business interests obtained an injunction to prevent the floating of the bonds. The U.S. Supreme Court finally ruled in *Green v. Frazier* that the Industrial Commission and the state industries, including the bank, were constitutional. When the legal route failed, business organized a nationwide boycott of the bonds, but the boycott was broken by the sale of bonds to trade unions and sympathetic individuals around the country. (The Chicago Federation of Labor and the

Minneapolis Trades Council, among others, voted to deposit their funds in the Bank.)

Deposits, which initially included the mandatory depositing of school district and government agency funds, amounted to $13 million. By May 1920, over $2 million in loans to farmers had been made at an interest rate of 6 percent. The bank also financed the state mill and grain elevator and a Home Building Association, and loaned money to other countries to buy seeds and feed from farmers suffering drought losses.

The league faded from the scene, but the Bank of North Dakota still functions today, though not in competition with private banks. It is run efficiently and makes a profit for the state. It accepts savings and checking accounts from individuals and corporations, but is prohibited from making direct private and commercial loans. Instead, the bank participates with other banks in commercial loans; direct loans are limited to state agencies, school districts, and counties and cities. The bank does a large business in GI, Federal Housing Administration (FHA), and Small Business Administration (SBA) loans through co-sponsorship. It also serves as a correspondent bank for banks throughout the state.

In 1978, the Twentieth Century Fund released an in-depth study of public enterprises in the United States. The author, Annmarie Walsh, studied the Port of New York Authority, the many New York state authorities created during the Rockefeller administration, several of Pennsylvania's municipal corporations, the New Jersey Highway Authority, the Lower Colorado River Authority of Texas, the Metropolitan Council of Minneapolis–St. Paul, and public enterprises in the Municipality of Seattle.

The study found that such public enterprises undertake only projects that appear to provide a safe and quick financial return. This orientation has been encouraged by the bankers and businessmen who make up the boards of the enterprises and by operating managers who seek organizational autonomy "largely insulated from public debate." (Robert Moses was a classic example of a public manager who himself defined the public interest.) Public officials pay little attention to the operations of the authorities except when a crisis occurs.

These public authorities favor highways over rail transportation, water supply and power production over pollution control and recreational use of water resources, school construction over expansion of student counseling, sports arenas over open space, industrial parks over small business assistance, middle-income and luxury mortgage finance over rehabilitation and low-income housing construction.

The study recommended: government coordination and control of the prices, subsidies, and surpluses of public authorities; a broadening of the boards of directors of the authorities to include representatives of various constituencies affected by the authorities' operations; the disclosure of internal operations; and the establishment of public investment banking institutions as an alternative to private money markets for the financing of public enterprise.[23]

The economic downturn of the mid-1970s led to public debate in Congress over the possible creation of new national public enterprises.

When the Franklin National Bank was on the verge of bankruptcy in 1973, the Nixon administration considered a $1 billion bailout scheme; this prompted Congressman Henry Reuss (D-Wis.), chairman of the House Banking and Currency Committee, to propose that instead the bank be nationalized and run as a competitive public enterprise. Reuss made the following arguments in support of his proposal:

—The New Franklin National Bank (as the nationalized bank would be called) would make more desirable, less inflationary loans. It would concentrate on socially desirable loans—for productive capital investment, low- and moderate-income housing, small businesses, and state and local government needs— rather than waste the nation's credit resources or grant inflationary loans to finance conglomerate mergers or help speculators bid up the prices of scarce inventories and real estate.

—The New Franklin Bank would rely on demand and time deposits from the savings of moderate-income customers.

—The bank would avoid speculative loans and investments in currency speculation.

—The bank would give average-income customers better deals by pioneering in new savings instruments that offer small savers the same high interest rates that wealthy savers now enjoy.

—The bank would be free of conflicts of interest caused by interlocking boards of directors.

—The bank would make profits for the public.

Reuss's proposal was not received favorably by the Nixon administration, and the notion of nationalizing banks, failing or otherwise, has not become part of Carter's economic policy. However, Professor William Shepherd, in a paper entitled, "Public Enterprise and Accountability," argued that public ownership of a national financial institution should be given priority in any strategy of significant economic reform. Shepherd, one of the country's few experts on public enterprise, noted:

The main need is for a new Public Investment Bank, with funds on a scale comparable to the largest private commercial and investment banks. It would take holdings in those large industrial firms which offer large capital gains, reaping these gains for the public purse while influencing the firms toward more socially acceptable performance. The main targets would be (1) sluggish firms which can be shaken up and turned around, with resulting large capital gains, and (2) monopoly firms in new fast-growing markets (recent examples are IBM, Xerox, etc.). The main objective is to increase banking competition, exert influence on a variety of sensitive cases, and provide capital for a range of outsiders presently excluded by capital markets. Much of the funds could come from taking private savings and deposits in competition with private banks.

The whole effect would be progressive, partly because the Bank would exploit the usual expert and inside-information sources which presently are available mainly to the rich.[24]

Rising energy prices in the 1970s prompted some liberal Democratic senators to propose that the federal government go into the oil and gas business as a way of counterbalancing the power of the multinational oil companies. Senator Adlai Stevenson III (D-Ill.) introduced legislation to create the Federal Oil and Gas Corporation, which would be funded by $500 million in appropriations in equal annual installments over ten years. The corporation would issue government-backed bonds to finance capital needs. Its mission would be to explore federal lands and offshore waters for gas and oil. It would set up production operations in competition with private oil companies and sell crude to competing American refineries. In addition to increasing the supply of energy, the corporation would serve as a standard against which to judge the performance of private firms with regard to operating costs, prices to the consumer, and other variables.

The corporation would be directed by a five-member board appointed by the president and confirmed by the Senate; members would serve staggered five-year terms. The proposed legislation would grant the corporation first choice in the lease of public lands, but would limit its holdings to no more than 20 percent of the total acreage. It would also allow the corporation, if necessary, to engage in refining, transportation, and sale of oil products, so that it could become an integrated public oil company.

Supporters of the measure, who included Senators

Kennedy (D-Mass.) and McGovern (D-S. Dak.), Ralph Nader, Lee White (former chairman of the Federal Power Commission), and the United Auto Workers, argued that foreign dependence on oil has grown, while existing energy reserves in the United States have remained undeveloped because of the cartel nature of the industry. Much of the existing reserves in the United States are on public land. "They are owned by the people," noted Senator Stevenson. "They should be developed for the people."

The oil industry opposed the measure in testimony before the Commerce Committee of the Senate. Frank Ikard, president of the American Petroleum Institute, asserted that "under a Government-owned oil and gas corporation it would be impossible to escape the inefficiencies, the hidden or covered-up additional costs, the political influences, and the mistakes that have occurred elsewhere." Industry argued that at least ten years' start-up time would be required before oil could begin to flow.

A spokesman for the Exxon Corporation declared that the public corporation would represent unfair competition because of the preference it would receive with regard to federal lands. Ikard contended that a federal company would siphon staff from private companies and weaken their ability to compete. In a letter to Senator Stevenson, M. A. Wright, president of Exxon, declared, "It is likely that creation of a Federal Oil and Gas Corporation would be the first step towards a total nationalization of the industry."

John Lichtbau, an oil economist, told the *New York Times* that the corporation would be too small to have any noticeable effect on production and prices. "If the government wants to know what the oil companies know, it should require wider disclosure of industry records and information—even the geological records," said Lichtbau. "Ultimately they would get all the information needed to regulate the industry intelligently—and they can take that step immediately, with no lead-time to worry about."

At the request of Representative Michael Harrington (D-Mass.), a report on the Federal Oil and Gas Corporation was prepared by the Economics Division of the Congressional Research Service. Economist Ken Hughes examined the experience of public energy corporations in Western Europe as well as the performance of the TVA, and reached the following conclusions:

The corporation could be staffed quickly and with well-qualified people. Initial financing is no problem if Congress will appropriate the necessary funds, as was done with the TVA. The potential market is there. "In sum," noted Hughes, "the federal oil and gas corporation appears to be economically viable."

Congressional hearings, new legislation, and a steady hand on the purse strings all kept the TVA under public control. "There is no reason," according to Hughes, "why the new corporation should have a different experience."

Stricter environmental standards, economic development missions, public employment responsibilities, countercyclical capital constraints, and the constant pressure of the press and politicians are a few of the factors that may be different for a public corporation.

The indications from the foreign experience and the record of the TVA are both encouraging. Despite the political pressures and the added responsibilities many of the ENI (Italian national oil company) subsidiaries have been able to compete on a worldwide basis. The TVA successfully cut prices, grew, prospered, and made a significant contribution to the economic development of an eight state area. Efficiency in the new corporation?—probably.

For many purposes, the rough comparisons that can be made between public and private operations should be a considerable aid to decisions on the true cost of production, regulation, tax incentives, or the need for price controls. In this sense, the public corporation would provide a valuable measurement tool.

Finally, Hughes observed:

The evidence suggests that a Federal Oil and Gas Corporation would certainly be economically viable. There is no reason why it could not run at a high level of technical competence and general efficiency. It will not necessarily provide an exact yardstick by which to measure the performance of private corporations, but should put the government in a position to make "ball park" judgments about the operation of the industry.

In communications, a true fourth network—a public television system—could function efficiently and greatly improve broadcast programming. "The talent is here and the determination to use it," noted David W. Rintels, former president of the Writers Guild of America, in hearings before the Carnegie Commission on the Future of Public Broadcasting. "Give us the chance to prove that we are the equal of the BBC or anyone in the world and we will not disappoint you."

The major problem is money. In 1978, public television and radio received just over $100 million a year in federal appropriations and about $300 million a year from grants and donations, mostly from large corporations such as Mobil and Exxon.

"Public broadcasting is gradually turning into nothing but a carbon copy of the commercial networks," testified Chester Migden, executive secretary of the Screen Actors Guild. "If it continues at its current pace, we will have turned public television into corporate-advertiser television."

As has been pointed out by Geoff Cowan, professor of communications law at UCLA, the pioneers of the broadcasting industry believed that radio and television should be free of commercials and financed by a sales tax on television sets. The notion that commercial television is free—one urged by the networks—is false. Citizens pay for the advertising through higher prices—at the rate of approximately $5 billion annually. The present commercial system, according to Professor Cowan, costs the average American family between $200 and $300 a year.[25]

In England, the public broadcasting tax runs about $28 annually for each color television set and $16 for black and white. If Americans paid a fee equivalent to that in England, over $2 billion would be available for public television. The revenues could be collected through an independent agency and allocated to stations according to a fixed formula. According to a 1970 CBS-sponsored poll by Columbia University, one-half of the viewing public would prefer television without commercials and about 30 percent "would be willing to pay a small yearly amount to have TV without commercials."

A Public Enterprise Strategy

Most public enterprises in democratic mixed economies are run efficiently. They are well managed, technically advanced, and just as productive as private enterprise. Examples of mismanagement are certainly no more frequent than in the private sector.

In practice public enterprise in the postwar period has not significantly threatened private enterprise. Public enterprises in monopoly areas such as the utilities have subsidized and promoted the growth of private business through pricing policies. Public enterprises in sectors competitive with private business have worked comfortably with the leading firms in each industry. Where public enterprise has taken the lead, it has served to rationalize and modernize industry in the interests of overall national growth.

Efforts have been made to see that this growth is relatively balanced throughout the given country, but they have been only moderately successful.

Public enterprises have not redistributed wealth and income in any significant way. Previous private owners of most nationalized firms received fair if not generous compensation. The distribution of wealth and income in most mixed economies has shown no tendency toward greater equality; however, a combination of public enterprise and government social programs probably has managed to offset any trend toward greater inequality.

In labor relations, public enterprises have tended to be more progressive than old-line private firms, particularly in France and Italy. Public firms have a good record in such areas as health and safety and workers' benefits. They have not, however, advanced programs for industrial democracy in any significant way. Management personnel and techniques in public enterprises are scarcely discriminable from those in private enterprise.

Overall, public enterprises have met the *development* needs of economies dominated by private business and increasingly by large corporations. Most economists have recognized that government management of the economy is a necessity in advanced industrial societies and that public enterprise is one of the forms taken by government policy.

The potential does exist, however, for a more progressive—that is, redistributive—use of public enterprise. As economist John Sheahan has written:

Public enterprise seems in general most likely to be helpful when it constitutes an additional decision center within an oligopoly that learned too well to minimize competition. When an industry consists of only three or four firms, all of them concerned with avoiding drastic upsets, the odds become high that they will fail to see or to explore all the possibilities for change that become open to the field.

Public management, with a different mixture of concerns, may act differently and reveal new openings. The equivalents of Renault and Finsider, if added to the American automobile and steel industries in the 1950's, might have made highly constructive differences.[26]

Proposing outright and complete nationalization of any industry or group of major firms would be both politically infeasible and unduly costly, given Americans' genuine concern about big government and the courts' recognition that propertyowners must receive just (and in many cases immediate) compensation for property purchased by government. It would also make little sense given our goal of democratizing economic life, for the same managers and technocrats who have run the company or industry before nationalization would have to be relied upon to run it under government ownership, or else the new public companies would face economic ruin.

Public enterprise does have a role to play in our strategy. It is a structural reform we advocate; but it must be used selectively and as part of an overall set of reform policies, including those discussed in later chapters.

A strategy of selective and competitive public enterprise involves the following elements.

Creation of a new government holding company. Unlike the RFC of the 1930s and 1940s, the new holding company would be used to reform and gradually democratize corporate capitalism. The company would purchase the requisite number of shares (between 10 and 20 percent should be sufficient in most cases) in at least one major firm in each major industry dominated by a few companies. These would include the automobile, drug, chemical, and computer industries, as well as others. Empowered by its share interests, the government holding company would place public members on the boards of these corporations—members who represented consumers, labor, and the government itself; in some cases, management changes would be made.

These competitive public enterprises would, in many instances, affect the behavior of the remaining private firms by engaging in proconsumer commercial practices and, through competitive pressure, inducing these companies to follow their lead in producing, for example, a longer lasting light bulb, a safer, high-mileage car, or a readable insurance policy. The public companies would also provide vital information to the government on the actual costs and processes involved in the industries, and thus serve as a standard for social responsibility in areas such as product safety, worker health and safety, labor relations, and community relations. If requested by the government holding company to undertake any activities that were excessively uneconomic yet necessary for social reasons, the public firms would be compensated by direct grants.

The second major task of the government holding company would be to help finance and encourage new public enterprises at the municipal, state, and regional levels by engaging in joint ventures and mixed public-private enterprises together with state and city governments, pensions funds, and other sources of capital such as universities and churches. These mixed enterprises should have a clear social purpose, such as the development of new labor-intensive technology, for example, solar or other nonpolluting equipment; the creation of *permanent* jobs in underdeveloped rural areas and in the inner city (here joint ventures with community-owned development corporations would be important); the production of publicly needed goods such as school textbooks and mass transit equipment; and development of "new communities," both urban and rural, through public purchase of land and public planning of the new community and with a mix of public and private ownership of the new industries as well as stores and other services located in the community. The government holding company might create special-purpose subsidiaries to carry out these functions, just as the old RFC established the Commodity Credit Corporation, the RFC Mortgage Company, the Electric Home and Farm Authority, the Defense Plant Corporation, and the Defense Homes Corporation.

Finally, the new government holding company, through an investment bank subsidiary, would serve as a source of financial support and consulting talent for major experiments in worker-owned and worker/community-owned enterprises, as well as for the construction of nonhierarchically designed factories such as the Volvo plant at Kalmar, where teams of workers build entire cars from start to finish.

The government holding company would also establish a major school of democratic management to train men and women in the skills necessary to run enterprises in both an efficient and a democratic manner. (The Italian holding company IRI has a training school for managers of its various concerns.)

Creation of a public energy corporation. Given the importance of energy policy to the entire economy, we advocate the establishment of a publicly owned energy corporation separate from the government holding company. The energy corporation would be a completely integrated firm with producing wells, pipelines, and gas station outlets; in addition, it would be active in other nonfossil fuel areas of energy development. The firm would be created partly anew and partly through purchase of the assets of a few smaller oil firms. As proposed in Senator Stevenson's original legislation to create a Federal Oil and Gas Corporation, the public firm would be given special rights with regard to energy on publicly owned lands and would be free to engage in joint ventures with other public firms (such as the national oil companies of Canada, England, Norway, Mexico and other countries) or, in some cases, with other private firms.

Support for public ownership in energy is growing, particularly among organized labor. At a national meeting in August 1979, the AFL-CIO Executive Council declared that the government should seriously consider nationalizing the oil industry.

Creation of a fourth network—an adequately funded public television and radio system. Through a tax on the sale of television sets and radios, adequate funding could be made available to transform the existing public broadcasting system into a genuine national fourth network. Local stations would be democratized by providing for the election of board members by citizens of the counties in which the stations are located. Local public stations lacking VHF channels would be awarded them, so that the public network could compete with the private networks on equal terms.

Creation of such a fourth network is a critical element in our reform strategy. The existing networks will neither support nor encourage open debate and reporting on the nature of the American economy. Only a fair and open-minded public network, free of any control by owners of capital, will make possible national discussion and reporting on the problems and prospects of democratizing the economy.

The report of the Carnegie Commission on the Future of Public Broadcasting, titled *A Public Trust* and released in early 1979, recommended a tripling of funding for public television by imposition of a fee on commercial broadcasters for the use of the airwaves. The study also recommended a reorganization of the public system using a public telecommunications trust to serve as fiduciary agent. William McGill, chairman of the commission, told the press: "The Commission's faith is that public broadcasting in America is a radical idea whose time is at hand."

The commission declined to call for a fourth network—mostly, it appears, from the fear that such a reform proposal would overly anger both private broadcasters and existing public stations, which enjoy a high degree of local autonomy.

We agree with the Carnegie Commission on the importance of increased funding, but the report ignored the need to democratize existing public stations by requiring the election of board members and providing access to programming for a wide variety of community groups.

Our public enterprise strategy relies on government ownership of selected, *healthy* firms, which can use their economic power and resources to produce more balanced and equitable economic growth and to assist in the democratization of the economy. Unhealthy or declining firms and industries should be handled by other entities and policies, not by public enterprises. We do not intend to bail out the losers of American capitalism. Where private enterprise has failed and vital public services are concerned, as with the northeastern railroads or possibly the steel and coal industries, separate public enterprises should be designed and created to run these utility-type enterprises in an efficient manner (though not necessarily one that is commercially profitable).

New public enterprises can and should be created at the state and city level without waiting for the establishment of new national public enterprises. City- and state-owned banks and insurance companies are crucial, given the key role that such financial institutions play in the investment process. Exerting democratic control over investment, rather than nationalizing major firms outright, is the strategic route we believe holds real promise for significant reform in the United States. (This issue is explored in detail in the next chapter.)

By Western European standards, our public enterprise strategy is a moderate one. We believe that it must be. In some areas, such as energy and television, past experience and polling data show public support for new or expanded public enterprise efforts such as we propose. Of course, creation of a public oil and gas corporation and increased funding for a public fourth network face opposition from corporate interests—but there is also a base of support among the public that makes these political battles possibly winnable.

As we have noted, nationalization of an entire industry is alien to American political experience and is an entirely unworkable strategy—one that is doomed to failure. Creation of a government holding company, as we propose, provides a vehicle for selective and, in many cases, partial public ownership without the immediate financial and ideological burdens that large-scale nationalization efforts would entail. Once the vehicle is in place and a competent staff has been developed (no small problem in itself), strategic interventions would be carried out in particular sectors of the economy as fruitful opportunities arose. For example, a request by a corporation for a government subsidy, loan guarantee, or tax break (as has been made by Lockheed, Pan Am, American Motors, and other firms) might be met with an offer to purchase stock and place a few public directors on the firm's board. Or, firms convicted of criminal behavior or simply exposed publicly for grave misconduct (bribery, deliberate marketing of unsafe products, extreme pollution) might become prime candidates for purchase by the government holding company, since a good case could then be made that public management was a necessary remedy for the firm's antisocial behavior.

The development of a trained and competent staff for the government holding company would also provide the necessary talent to take advantage of plant closings by large firms and successful antitrust actions by the Justice Department. In both cases, opportunities for converting existing plants into worker-owned, worker/community-owned, or mixed public-private enterprises would not be ignored; most important, such opportunities could be critically evaluated as to their actual chances of success. "Lemon socialism" is a danger that should be avoided.

What we are seeking, over the long run, is not greater government ownership of the economy, but greater democratization of economic decision making. Public enterprise is only a means to that end, not an end in itself. What we would like to see is an economy with, in Crosland's words, "a diverse, diffused, pluralist, and heterogeneous pattern of ownership"—in our own words, a truly *democratic* economy. Ownership of productive wealth in the United States is unfortunately neither diverse nor diffuse; it is highly concentrated in a few hands, with actual control resting in the grip of a corporate and financial elite. In the next chapter, we examine some possible remedies for this unhealthy situation.

CHAPTER THREE

Democratic Control of Investment*

American society is characterized by extreme concentration of private ownership and control of capital. A study by the Joint Economic Committee of the
Congress in 1976 found that the richest 1 percent of
the U.S. population accounted for nearly 26 percent
of total net worth, owning more than half of all
corporate equity as well as more than half of all
outstanding debt (60 percent of bonds), including
corporate and government debt. Half of even this
small group—or just over one million people—owned
50 percent of the total value of all outstanding corporate stock in 1972.[1]

Direct purchase and ownership of securities issued
through capital markets has increasingly been dominated by financial institutions. Individuals have been
more likely to place their savings with a financial
intermediary than to invest directly in corporate
stocks or bonds. This does not change the picture for
the top wealth holders, however, for even if they are
not purchasing new securities directly, they still control these new assets through their continuing ownership of the institutional purchasers.

The tendency toward the concentration of ownership and control can be noted among financial institutions; interlocking directorates between the most

*With Marc Weiss.

powerful of these and the large nonfinancial corporations also serve to concentrate control in a few hands. For example, in the life insurance industry, which is the most important source of corporate long-term debt financing as well as a major source of mortgage financing, the eleven largest companies held 55 percent of the $220 billion worth of total life insurance assets in 1971. Just two companies— Prudential and Metropolitan Life—held 27 percent.

At the end of 1974 there were more than 14,000 commercial banks in the United States with total deposits of $754.7 billion; yet just four banks—Bank of America, First National City Bank, Chase Manhattan, and Manufacturers Hanover Trust—held 20 percent of these deposits. Moreover, congressional hearings conducted in 1968 by Representative Wright Patman demonstrated that, in addition to their own asset holdings, a small number of the largest commercial banks controlled huge blocks of corporate stock through their trust departments. The earnings of the trust funds belong to the beneficiaries (including many billions of dollars' worth of pension plans), but power over the investment of the funds resides with the bank trustees.

In 1969, these same four banks plus twenty-eight other giants had a total of 514 interlocking directorates with the 220 largest corporations. This represents but one aspect of an entire complex of interrelationships whereby the top wealth holders in the United States maintain their substantial control over the economic life of the country.

As long as financial control of capital remains so tightly concentrated and interwoven, competition for funds will be heavily weighted in favor of the needs and priorities of the large corporations.

There are and will continue to be losers in the competition for capital. The flight of individual investors from the stock market and their replacement by large institutional investors has led to the development of what most economists and business analysts agree is a "two-tier" market, in which insurance companies, pension funds, trust funds, investment companies, and universities concentrate their stock buying in a small number of favorite blue chips, to the virtual exclusion of medium-sized companies also traded on the exchanges. Smaller companies are completely frozen out. And with the collapse of the new issues market in the late 1970s, it became almost impossible for new enterprises to raise capital through public offerings of common stock. They were hurt further by the decline of venture capital investment companies, which have also been affected adversely by the collapse of the new issues market.

Most important, there are a number of unmet public needs in this country: better and more universal health care, low-income housing and neighborhood revitalization, rebuilding of cities and economic rebirth of rural areas, pollution control, transportation upgrading, environmental enhancement, energy retrofitting, and many other projects whose costs run into the billions and even trillions of dollars. Given the stacked deck of capital competition, the question is not whether "private enterprise" will do the job, but simply whether or not the large financial institutions and corporations are planning to do it. State and local governments do not currently control enough sources of revenue to expand significantly their indebtedness and capital spending. The federal government, of course, has relatively unlimited spending powers, but it is constrained by the priorities of the top wealth holders, who exercise inordinate political power, and by the need for price stability.

These unmet public needs will be given a higher place on the list of capital priorities only when the distribution of wealth itself has changed. One way this can be done is through greater assertion of public *control* over assets and sources of funds that workers collectively and public citizens generally already "own" or to which they hold claims. These include: federal, state, and local government funds now controlled by private financial institutions, and employee retirement funds now managed by private financial institutions. If public and private pension funds, federal trust funds such as unemployment insurance and Social Security, and state and local government bank accounts are put to work under a different set of priorities than at present, an *effective* redistribution of wealth could result. One of the ironies of the emergence of the large institutional investor is that a considerable portion of the half-trillion dollars in workers' pension funds are now invested in the equity capital of American industry. Assertion of ownership and rights of control by the worker-beneficiaries could turn capital investment in new policy directions. This movement could form the beginnings of a more equitable distribution of wealth, a genuine full-employment economy, and greater democracy at the work place and in the community.

Labor Banks

In many countries, particularly in Western Europe, trade unions have employed commercial means to attain political ends by operating banks, using their members' money in an attempt to democratize the investment process and bring it under the control of working people. In Germany, for example, in the period after World War I, almost all trade unions founded banks; these grew into the Bank für Gemeinwirtschaft—the labor-owned Commonwealth Bank—which is now a well known and powerful national and international bank. These banks helped to finance cooperative housing for workers and, in some instances, provided credit to cooperatives, primarily in the consumer goods sector. In Israel, the labor movement—the Histadrut—owns many of its own banks, which, in turn, help to finance a number of labor-owned enterprises.

In the United States, in the period after World War I, a strong workers' bank movement developed. More than thirty banks were established by trade unions to put to use the funds accumulated by the strong unionized skilled trades during the war and in the immediate postwar boom. Many union leaders of the period, particularly the president of the Brotherhood of Locomotive Engineers, viewed workers' banks and investment funds directed by trade unions (by means of holding companies) as a suitable instrument for controlling at least a portion of the country's industry in the interests of the working class.

In 1920, during a strike of shipworkers at Norfolk, Virginia, a newly founded workers' bank—the Mount Vernon Savings Bank—extended necessary credits to a major firm that had agreed to the unions' demands but was being pressured by capitalist banks. The action allowed the company to remain open and to keep its union agreements. The Mount Vernon Bank had been founded that same year by the Trade Union of Mechanical Engineers (later the International Association of Machinists). The Railway union's president euphorically declared that the strategic use of workers' banks could even end all strikes. All the workers had to do was gain control of existing stockholdings—that is, take ownership of the companies where they worked.

The most important workers' bank of the period—the Brotherhood of Locomotive Engineers' Cooperative National Bank—was established by the Locomotive Engineers Union at the end of 1920 in Cleveland. The brotherhood opened a second bank in Hammond, Indiana, at about the same time.

The move toward workers' banks was fueled by the private banks' support of the open-shop movement during the depression of 1921. For example, a workers' bank was established in Tucson, where the private banks and the Chamber of Commerce openly fought unions by refusing credit to firms employing union labor.

During 1922 and 1923, the Brotherhood of Locomotive Engineers founded four more banks with the help of the Brotherhood Investment Company—a trust established for this purpose. The trust would take majority stock of the newly founded bank and appoint leading local trade union officials to the bank's board. Such banks were established in San Bernardino, California; Minneapolis, Minnesota; and Three Forks, Montana. Without assistance from the trust, a railway workers' local founded its own bank in Spokane, Washington. Altogether, fifteen banks were established by the Locomotive Engineers trust. The Amalgamated Clothing Workers Union established banks in Chicago in 1922, and a few months later in New York.

Workers' banks often operated as yardstick competition for private banks by offering better consumer services to working class and small business customers. They paid higher interest on savings than private banks (4 percent compared to 3 or 3.5 percent), offered lower service fees on checking accounts, inaugurated banking by mail, facilitated the transfer of funds to relatives overseas in Europe (an important service for immigrants), and created life insurance programs through monthly set-asides at a time when many working men and women could not obtain life insurance from private companies.

In their loan policies, the workers' banks provided credit to companies that employed union labor and/or treated their employees decently. They helped to finance a number of consumer cooperatives and invested heavily in farmers' banks and farmers' cooperative institutions, as part of labor-farmer solidarity. The workers' banks refused to loan money for "speculative" purposes or for the production of luxury goods. They pioneered in the provision of small consumer loans to workers.

Finance companies affiliated with workers' banks often invested in firms as a way of influencing their labor policies. For example, the investment company affiliated with the Locomotive Engineers acquired the mines and coal lifts of the Coal River Company of West Virginia, when workers went out on strike. The strike was quickly settled and model labor policies were adopted. Local consumer societies sold company coal direct to users, reducing middleman profits.

At the end of 1925, there were thirty-six workers' banks in existence. The AFL, originally skeptical of the idea, finally had endorsed the concept. Beginning in 1926, however, the workers' bank movement began to collapse, and by 1932 only six of the thirty-six banks founded between 1921 and 1926 were in operation. While several thousand private banks also closed during this period, special circumstances contributed to the decline and almost complete disappearance of the workers' banks. One factor was the decreasing power and membership of the AFL craft-based unions—a decline brought about by a combination of the rise of mass industry, the strong open-shop and company union movement pushed by employers in the 1920s, and the post–World War I "red scare" and political repression carried out against the most militant members of the trade union and working class movements. By the height of the Depression, *only 4 percent* of American workers were organized in the AFL. Such a weakened labor movement could scarcely afford the luxury of running its own banking system.

The management of the workers' banks also contributed to their decline. Some union locals insisted that the bank provide jobs for union officials who were ignorant of banking practices. At the same time, many professional banking employees refused to take jobs with workers' banks for ideological reasons, and the workers' bank movement failed to establish its own school to train a cadre of managers who were both technically proficient and pro-working class. Personnel problems and inefficient operations in turn soured working-class depositors on their own banks.

Another problem was the inherent contradiction in the principles that a pro-working-class bank should follow in a society dominated by capitalist enterprises. "Neither in their credit policy nor in their interest and dividend policy did workers' banks follow the rules of the money and credit market," commented one historical study.[2] Too many small unsecured loans were given out on the basis of the debtor's "honest face" and working class background. Often loans were made to shaky but prolabor commercial enterprises. For political reasons, the workers' banks helped the farmers' banks, and when agricultural prices fell in the 1920s, the workers' banks suffered great losses.

The workers' banks also paid premature and overly high dividends to worker-depositors that were not backed by sufficient reserve funds. An almost overwhelmingly hostile capitalist press trumpeted and exaggerated the internal difficulties of the workers' banks and hastened their demise.

Even without these problems, workers' banks were miniscule compared to private capitalist banks. At its height, the largest workers' bank, the Brotherhood of Locomotive Engineers Cooperative National Bank in Cleveland, had capital of less than $1 million. By comparison, the capital of the National City Bank of New York at that time exceeded a billion dollars. The postwar movement toward concentration among private banks destroyed most small banks. Only a close business partnership among all the workers' banks might have allowed the formation of a few larger, stronger banks and ensured their survival. The craft system of union organization, however, prevented such a development. The elite members of the AFL skilled trade unions isolated skilled workers whose unions had established workers' banks from the mass of unorganized unskilled workers. The workers' banks were decentralized and, even among themselves, largely autonomous, in spite of the key role played by the railway workers' union. Most workers' banks had vanished by the time the militant CIO began to gain millions of new members for the American labor movement.

At present, only a few workers' banks remain in operation in the United States. The strongest is the Amalgamated Bank of New York, founded in 1923 by the Amalgamated Clothing Workers. The second largest is the Amalgamated Trust and Savings of Chicago, a product of the same union. Amalgamated of New York survived by being one of the most conservative banks in the country. More than 90 percent of the bank's assets are liquid. Five years is the bank's limit for mortgage loans, and it makes almost no commercial and industrial loans. It does offer low rates for consumer loans and was the first bank in New York City to provide free checking. By New York standards, the bank is tiny, with only $270 million in assets at the end of 1977 and four offices. The bank has, on occasion, provided bail money for arrested union picketers and loaned short-term money to the NAACP. The bank manages the pension and welfare funds for the union and carries over its conservative investment policies.[3]

The United Mine Workers own 75 percent of the National Bank of Washington, which has operated for many years as the union's in-house bank. The bank has not distinguished itself as particularly pro-consumer nor proworker, which is not surprising given the corrupt and undemocratic leadership that ran the union until a reform group recently won control. The new head of the mine workers, Arnold Miller, has shown little interest in the possible progressive uses of the bank, however, and suggested that the union sell its interest in the institution.

The decline and almost complete disappearance of workers' banks in the United States is understandable given the historical development and depoliticization of the American labor movement. In Europe, many workers' banks begun in the 1920s have survived and play a supporting role in labor movements that are much stronger than that in the United States.

Interest in reviving workers' banks in the United States has been almost nonexistent. Only the women's movement of the 1960s has produced a drive toward such special-interest banks. Women's banks have been established in New York, Los Angeles, San Francisco, and other major cities, but with mixed results. The operation of the successful ones has not differed greatly from that of any other private bank.

The use of labor's financial clout as a political weapon has again—as in the 1920s—become a public issue, however. Now, it is the massive workers' pension funds, which came into being as a result of collective bargaining agreements between the industrial unions and large corporations, and between public employees and government in the post–World War II period, that are the object of political struggle.

"With pension-fund capital, the American economy has entered a new stage. American workers are now a major new ownership class," wrote Jeremy Rifkin and Randy Barber in *The North Will Rise Again—Pensions, Politics, and Power in the 1980s.* The book, published on Labor Day, 1978, caused a stir in the investment community. Rifkin and Barber argued that America's industrial and public employee unions can and should use the financial clout of the massive employee pension funds they have negotiated as a political weapon to transform American capitalism into a worker-controlled economy. The book's authors are, we believe, overly optimistic about "pension fund socialism" as a strategy for democratizing the U.S. economy. Pension funds are but *one* source for increasing democratic control over the investment process. In the following sections, we examine the problems and potential of this approach.

Pension Funds

History

The earliest pension plans were established in the United States after the Civil War. The American Express Company started one in 1875. Most of the early plans were in railroads and related industries, with some of the giant industrial corporations forming plans around the turn of the century. By 1925, approximately 4 million workers were covered by 400 plans. More than 40 percent of these workers were employed by railroad companies, and roughly 1.3 million worked for just four corporations: U.S. Steel, American Telephone and Telegraph, Pennsylvania Railroad, and New York Central.

The principal reasons for establishing pension plans were to promote loyalty to the corporation (the worker would be less likely to quit his job if it meant sacrificing his retirement benefits) and to make it easier to squeeze out older workers when they became less productive. The employers did not feel they "owed" anything to their employees in the way of retirement benefits; rather, the pension plans were viewed as a bonus that could be given or taken away at the employer's discretion. In his comprehensive study *Pension Funds and Economic Power*, commissioned by the Twentieth Century Fund, Paul Harbrecht described these plans:

The early attitude of employers toward pension plans was [that] pensions were gifts to their workers in recognition of "long and faithful service" and that no legal rights were thereby given to employees who became beneficiaries of a plan. Plans at this period were extremely informal, often consisting of mere statements that the employer expected to pay certain benefits to those who fulfilled certain service requirements. In general the employer did not set up a special fund to provide pension benefits and the text of the plan was carefully worded to relieve him of all liability.[4]

This legal view was underscored by the U.S. Supreme Court in 1889 when it ruled in *Pennie v. Reis* that, even though two dollars had been taken out of a policeman's pay each month and put in a pension fund, that money did not belong to him and he could not claim it as his property if he did not qualify for pension benefits.

Organized labor maintained a very skeptical attitude toward pension plans during this period. Samuel Gompers of the American Federation of Labor argued that if workers were paid a decent wage they would be able to save for their retirement without being dependent on their employers. This arms-length attitude on the part of labor leaders is one reason why pension plans did not become more widespread.

The first real impetus for pension plan growth came from the federal government. In 1921, Congress exempted the income earned by pension funds from the payment of income tax, and also excused employees from paying income taxes on the contributions made to the fund on their behalf. (They must pay income tax when they actually receive the benefits during retirement, but at this time they are generally in a lower tax bracket.) During the 1930s and 1940s, the Congress and the Internal Revenue Service tightened the regulations so that employers could not divert the money in the fund for any purpose except paying out pensions; but the basic seed for expansion was planted when employers were allowed to deduct their contributions to pension funds from their gross income.

The second major impetus was the Great Depression of the 1930s. Millions of people lost their savings in the bank failures and stock market crash. Concern for financial security in old age became a principal issue of the New Deal, leading to federal takeover of the bankrupt Railroad Retirement funds and the passage of the Social Security Act in 1935.

The establishment of federal Old Age and Survivors Insurance (Social Security) legitimized the need and desire of American workers to receive an adequate retirement income. Yet the benefits paid by Social Security were far from adequate. As a result labor leaders, particularly in the newly emerging Congress of Industrial Organizations, began pushing for pension benefits from industry to supplement Social Security. This push dovetailed nicely with the situation during World War II, when high corporate income tax rates made the tax-deductible contributions to pension funds suddenly look very attractive to the large corporations. By contributing a portion of their earnings to the retirement funds, corporations greatly reduced taxable income and were able to save millions of dollars. The fact that the pension contributions could then be reinvested in the company by the fund managers made these plans even more lucrative. In addition, the exclusion of pension plans, which were considered a "fringe benefit," from the tight wartime wage freezes created an added incentive in the eyes of both the unions and the management.

All that was needed was one final step, which the Supreme Court provided in 1949 when it ruled that Inland Steel was obligated to bargain with the United Steelworkers Union over a pension plan because pensions were part of the structure of wages as defined by the Taft-Hartley Act. As unions pressed their demands and corporations became convinced of tax and other advantages, pension plans grew at a fantastic pace in the 1950s.

Legislative Reform

As plans proliferated in the 1950s and 1960s, so too did books and articles describing the many cases in which workers, either individually or collectively, failed to receive the retirement benefits they had been promised after many long years of employment. For example, while it is true that a pension fund can receive tax advantages only if it is used for the sole benefit of the eligible recipients, the fund can always be terminated and no further benefits paid. This is exactly what happened in South Bend, Indiana, in 1964, when the Studebaker Corporation closed its doors and left thousands of workers and retirees with virtually nothing in pension benefits. Other widely publicized abuses include the use of the large Teamsters Union pension funds to finance Las Vegas gambling casinos and other pet projects of organized crime.

In 1958, Congress passed the Welfare and Pension Plans Disclosure Act, which required all plan administrators to file financial reports with the Department of Labor, so that management of the funds could be monitored. While this law helped curb some of the more flagrant abuses, many workers in covered plans were reaching retirement age without ever receiving their promised pension. Finally, after a long legislative battle in Congress, the Employee Retirement Income Security Act (ERISA) was passed in 1974.

ERISA dealt with several of the existing problems (for *private* pension plans only) by requiring minimum standards for plan eligibility and the vesting of benefits (the nonforfeitable right to receive a pension once certain age and service requirements have been satisfied, even if the worker is no longer with the company at the time of retirement); by requiring employers to insure themselves with a Federal Pension Benefit Guaranty Corporation, so that benefits would be paid in the event of a plan termination; and by establishing standards for reporting and disclosure, fiduciary responsibility of fund trustees and portfolio managers, requirements for fully funding plans, and other such provisions. No employer is required to have a pension plan, and in fact many smaller employers have since terminated their plans in the face of the higher costs and more stringent requirements of ERISA. But any private plan that does exist must conform to these standards.

Types of Plans

In the early days of pensions, most plans were financed on a pay-as-you-go basis, with the employer simply funding the contributions out of his current operating budget. Some small, informal private plans still use this method today, as do some state and local governments. It has become common practice, however, for most plans to have an actuarially calculated, separate and permanent fund into which contributions are made and from which pension benefits are paid.

This fund is held in a kind of trust on behalf of the plan participants. Managers of the fund invest the money in government or corporate securities or some other type of debt or equity instrument that will either pay interest or appreciate in cash value. As of the end of 1976, the total book value of all assets held by pension funds was $443.4 billion. Of this, federal pension funds amounted to $87.7 billion. These funds are invested exclusively in U.S. government or agency securities. State and local government accounted for $117.2 billion. At one time these funds were invested primarily in U.S. government securities or state and local government bonds, but an increasing proportion is being put into corporate stocks and bonds.

Private pension funds had total book-value assets of $240.5 billion at the end of 1976. Some $80.1 billion of this amount was in insured funds; in such funds, the employer pays the contributions to an insurance company, which is contracted to pay the pension benefits according to eligibility requirements and the benefit schedule. The insurance company generally places the funds together with the rest of its investment portfolio, though in some cases it does maintain separate accounts. A large portion of its portfolio is invested in corporate bonds and stocks; various types of mortgages also take a large chunk.

The remaining $160.4 billion are in private noninsured pension funds. Single-employer plans are generally administered exclusively by the employer through appointed trustees. The funds can either be managed in-house or, as is more common, turned over to bank trust departments or independent asset managers. Bank trust departments manage the bulk of these funds.

There are also a number of funds that are not solely corporate-administered, but are administered jointly by employers and union representatives under Section 302 of the Taft-Hartley Act. Such funds are found primarily in industries where there are many employers but one large union, such as the Teamsters, Maritime Union, Ladies' Garment Workers Union, or the various building trades unions. Together these funds represent about $35 billion of the total $160.4 billion of all private noninsured funds. Some of these "union" funds were originally established through the members' own contributions and were later converted to employer contribution pension funds. The overwhelming majority of all private pension plans are financed exclusively by employer contributions, which are deductible from the employer's taxable income.

While almost all federal and most state and local government employees are covered by pension plans, only about 48 percent of all full-time employees in the private sector are covered. Labor union collective bargaining has been one of the most important forces in the establishment of private-sector pension plans. The areas with the least coverage tend to be non-unionized, low-paying, marginal-type occupations and industries.

Of the roughly 500,000 private pension plans covering 38 million active and retired workers, more than two-thirds cover ten or fewer employees. At the other end of the scale, the seventeen largest plans cover more than 20 percent of all private sector workers, and the twenty-five largest plans, each with assets of more than $1 billion, amount to nearly one-fourth of all private noninsured funds.

The total amount of assets in pension funds is indeed huge, and can be expected to continue growing at a very rapid pace. The question that is becoming more and more important in light of this massive growth is: who owns the pension funds, and who should control them?

Ownership and Control

At the turn of the century, pensions were viewed largely as a gratuity or "gift" by the employer. This idea, like so many others, began to change radically during the 1930s as more and more people claimed retirement security as a "right." Still, its provision was viewed primarily as the responsibility of the government; only in the postwar period were private employers pushed to provide retirement benefits. Even then, CIO unions, particularly the UAW, adopted the position that pensions were a form of "human depreciation" a corporation was bound to pay for retiring worn-out workers, just as it set aside depreciation funds for the eventual replacement of worn-out equipment. The UAW argued that the level of benefits should be based on the worker's needs rather than his wages, and that all workers should be included equally. This argument for management's responsibility was still essentially a moral argument; it has gradually been replaced over the last thirty years by the position that pension benefits are really a form of deferred wages. As one labor pamphlet explained:

A pension plan is not . . . a conditional or discretionary gift by the employer, but a deferred wage earned by current labor services, and required by the terms of the contract . . . the worker's interest in the pension fund is not established solely by reason of advanced age and "long and faithful" service with an employer. That interest is established by reason of the work performed by all the members during the term of the contract.[5]

This viewpoint got its biggest boost in the Inland Steel case of 1949, in which the Supreme Court upheld and quoted with approval the contention of the National Labor Relations Board that

realistically viewed, this type of wage enhancement or increase, no less than any other, becomes an integral part of the entire wage structure, and the character of the employee representative's interest in it, and the terms of its grant, is no different than any other case where a change in the wage structure is effected.[6]

Subsequent Supreme Court decisions, while not directly addressing the question of ownership of the funds, have also taken the position that pension contributions by employers must be viewed as part of employee wages.

The tax laws have contributed to this argument by stipulating that a pension fund must be for the sole benefit of the employees in order to qualify for tax-exempt status. Once a contribution has been made to the fund, that money no longer belongs to the employer. While no taxes are paid at the time the contribution is made, however, retired employees must pay income tax when they receive their pension benefits, which again reinforces the deferred wages principle.

This idea, in fact, has become so respectable recently that even conservative social commentator and business consultant Peter Drucker has enthusiastically endorsed it. In his book, *The Unseen Revolution: How Pension Fund Socialism Came to America,* Drucker declared:

If "socialism" is defined as "ownership of the means of production by the workers"—and this is both the orthodox and the only rigorous definition—then the United States is the first truly "Socialist" country. Through their pension funds, employees of American business today own at least 25 percent of its equity capital, which is more than enough for control. . . . Indeed, aside from farming, a larger sector of the American economy is owned today by the American worker through his investment agent, the pension fund, than Allende in Chile had brought under government ownership to make Chile a "Socialist country," than Castro's Cuba has actually nationalized, or than had been nationalized in Hungary or Poland at the height of Stalinism.[7]

If the money contributed to the fund belongs to the workers, then the workers own the fund's assets, which include among other things a huge block of stock in America's largest corporations. In a case such as this, however, "ownership" means very little. The worker cannot borrow the money, trade it, use it as collateral, or do any of the other things ownership normally allows. Moreover, with few exceptions the worker has absolutely *no control* over how the funds are utilized. These decisions are made on the worker's behalf by the trust departments of America's giant banks. Paul Harbrecht described the situation:

In the end, the anatomy of control of the pension trusts may be described quite simply. In general, financial control has been delegated by the employers to the banker-trustees, which exercise considerable power in the capital markets as a result. The employer controls the day-to-day operation of the plan itself, in many cases in accordance with a basic agreement arrived at with a union. It is the employer who, either unilaterally or in conjunction with a union, fixes the amount of pensions and usually alone determines how a plan is to be financed. The employee himself, without his union, has little or nothing to say about the pension plan which, ultimately, is financed out of his earnings.[8]

Not only do many corporations turn over management of their pension fund portfolios to asset managers or bank trust departments, but many Taft-Hartley joint union-management funds also follow this same practice. As a result, at the end of 1975, the one hundred largest banks controlled over $145.6 billion in pension funds, and the top ten banks controlled $80 billion. Bankers Trust and Morgan Guaranty Trust each control nearly $15 billion in pension funds.

Where do the trustees place most of this money? A study by the congressional Joint Economic Committee revealed that, at a time when individual investors have been bailing out of the stock market to the extent of $5 billion a year, pension fund trustees have been pumping into the New York and American exchanges a major portion of their $12 to $20 billion annual increase in investable funds. "In fact, for the last decade, only the retained earnings of industry have been a larger source of funds for capital formation," noted the committee.[9] Individual investors' share of equity ownership declined from 91.5 percent in 1945 to 64.7 percent in 1975; institutional investors made up this difference: private noninsured pension funds accounted for 11 percent of equity ownership;

state and local government trust funds, for 3.2 percent; insurance companies (which hold $80 billion in pension funds), for 3.2 percent; the rest was distributed among other institutional investors, including some pension funds. The Joint Economic Committee estimated that pension funds hold approximately 20 percent of the market value of all outstanding stock and predicted that this figure would increase to 50 percent ownership by 1985.

A more extensive investigation into these problems was held in the spring of 1977 by the U.S. Senate Subcommittee on Private Pension Plans and Employee Fringe Benefits and the Select Committee on Small Business. These hearings, entitled "Pension Simplification and Investment Rules," probed a situation in which "a mere two dozen private financial managers have responsibility for managing over $130 billion in pension assets."

The concentration of such a large amount of financial power in relatively few hands leads to all sorts of problems and abuses. Many of these have been documented by the House Banking and Currency Committee in its 1968 report, "Commercial Banks and Their Trust Activities," as well as in a 1975 study by Professor Edward S. Herman for the Twentieth Century Fund. The abuses go both ways: banks exert pressure on the big corporations through their ability to buy and sell large blocks of stock; various conflicts of interest arise, as when bank pension fund managers invest in the stock of the bank's best loan customers, or hold onto stock in declining companies when the bank fears large loan losses; corporations turn over their pension funds to the trust departments of banks from which they hope to obtain favorable loan terms—a whole host of other examples might be given in which the earnings of the pension fund are sacrificed to other priorities.[10]

Of course, the problem is not only with bank trust departments. The Twentieth Century Fund also has conducted studies of abuses and conflicts of interest in pension fund management carried out in house by corporate directors, by large labor union trustees, or by state and local government investment boards. The point is that, when the workers have no say in how the funds are invested, not only may the financial integrity of the fund be sacrificed but, more importantly, other key economic and social priorities will be ignored or even put directly into conflict with the workers' own goals. Thus, in a region of declining industrial employment, pension fund managers may be investing in corporations that are closing plants in that region and moving overseas; or a union may be fighting to organize a nonunion employer while the union's pension fund managers are buying stock and loaning money to that employer; or public employees may be passing resolutions opposing investment in South Africa, while their pension fund managers are purchasing securities of companies investing in that country. The problem is thus, in our view, that control over the funds lies in the wrong hands.

Asserting Control

Workers are not going to give strong support to innovative or politically desirable investment policies unless they are assured of the overall security of their pension plans. This is not a problem with defined-contribution plans, of course; the majority of plans, however, are defined-benefit plans, in which the worker is owed a pension, but the amount of money in the existing fund may not cover all present liabilities. As the situation now stands, all *current* retirement benefits are being paid, but the vast majority of funds are in arrears in putting aside money for future benefits owed—to use the appropriate financial terminology, they have unfunded liabilities. Conservative estimates of the unfunded liabilities of 1500 large U.S. corporations at the end of 1976 came to more than $48 billion. The unfunded liabilities of federal, state, and local government retirement plans were even larger.

Recent studies of the actuarial assumptions behind pension contributions indicate that the reported figures on unfunded liabilities may be significantly understated due to overestimation of the rate of return on investments of the fund (an increase of one percentage point can cut the cost of contributions by as much as 25 percent), as well as underestimation of the amount of future wage increases on which retirement benefits are based.

Some corporate investors are now concerned about the trend toward unfunded liabilities, for ERISA provides that, if a company's pension fund is unable to pay benefits, up to 30 percent of the net worth of the company may be claimed by the government for pension beneficiaries. This claim has the status of a tax lien; that is, it takes precedence over the claims of other creditors, including stockholders. If the corporation's pension obligations exceed 30 percent of its net worth, then the rest of the money comes out of the insurance fund of the Federal Pension Benefit Guaranty Corporation (PBGC), which charges premiums on all corporate defined-contribution plans. In other words, other corporations must pay. A study by Investors Management Sciences, a subsidiary of Standard & Poors, revealed that many corporations have unfunded benefits which exceeded 30 percent of corporate net worth, including such giants as Westinghouse, Lockheed, Uniroyal, Chrysler, and Bethlehem Steel. In 1977, *Fortune* magazine wondered what would happen if the stock market were to show a general sharp downturn, since pension funds are invested so heavily in common stocks. In such an extreme situation, no corporation would have enough assets to meet the obligations of the others, and the whole system would collapse into the hands of the federal government. *Fortune* noted that even Lloyd's of London refused to underwrite the PBGC insurance plan for unfunded pension liabilities on the grounds that it amounts to "insuring the profitability of the American economy." The magazine suggested that each company should be liable for only its *own* pension obligations, and contended that such a step would encourage greater management "responsibility" in trying to hold down wages and retirement benefit increases.[11]

Professor Mordecai Kurz of Stanford University argued in an unpublished paper, "Economic Power and the Functional Distribution of Income," that the major U.S. multinational corporations are deliberately underfunding pension plans to gain bargaining leverage: workers will be forced to accept lower wage increases in order to safeguard their pensions. This strategy seems aimed, in particular, at dividing the older workers from the younger with regard to wage demands.

. . . as of 1976 General Motors' corporate pension plan had unfunded vested benefits amounting to 3 billion dollars which represents 21% of GM's net worth. If we take into account all unfunded prior and/or past service costs then the amount rises to 7.3 billion dollars which is 51.1% of GM's net worth. Now, although it appears that GM's workers have a good pension plan the natural question which arises is why has GM not funded its plan in spite of the very significant tax advantages which the company may gain if it decides to fund. Depending on the method of finance, GM can save some 150-300 million dollars annually by funding.

Kurz pointed out that in 1977 the airline pilots of Pan American Airways, who had the largest pension plan, "led the move to *cut* wages in an effort to ensure that the company would not go under." At the end of 1976, Pan Am had $209.5 million of unfunded vested benefits, which represented 59 percent of its net worth.

The growth of employee pension funds is a

double-edged sword for labor: workers' reliance on future pension benefits closely links their personal interests to the health and stability of the corporate economy; however, pension funds as a collective pool of capital over which workers, through their unions, might exercise control is a potential source of politico-economic power. Union funds and Taft-Hartley labor-management funds already are partly controlled by union leadership, as are most teachers' pension funds and some other state and local government employee funds. This is not the case with defined-benefit pension funds that either are controlled directly by corporations or are turned over by them to insurance companies, money managers, and bank trust departments. Here workers will have to use the argument of "deferred wages" and the other positions advanced earlier to make a case for direct ownership rights over the fund itself. A long and protracted battle in the federal courts and in Congress is likely.

One consequence of asserting control would be that plan beneficiaries might actively attempt to influence the policies of the corporations in which they hold stock. In current practice, fund managers generally give passive support to management in matters of internal corporate policy. This is beginning to change, however. For example, some unions, non-profit organizations, and other employee retirement funds have voted on behalf of stockholder resolutions condemning corporate investment in South Africa.

An area where unions have occasionally asserted their pension power is in union recognition drives. Teamster pension funds purchased $1 million in Montgomery Ward stock during a crucial proxy fight in the 1950s and gained a long-sought recognition contract from a previously adamant union foe, Ward president Sewell Avery. The United Mineworkers Union forced Duke Power Company to settle a labor dispute after fifty other unions pledged to not invest any pension money in Duke securities until it recognized the Mineworkers.

The success of this tactic has led to another type of boycott: union threats to withdraw their pension funds and other accounts from large banks that support recalcitrant corporate foes. The Amalgamated Clothing and Textile Workers Union, stymied in its unionization drive by many unfair labor practices on the part of J. P. Stevens (well documented by the National Labor Relations Board), launched a campaign to pressure Stevens' management by forcing Stevens directors off the boards of other large corporations. The ACTWU focused on Manufacturers Hanover Trust (fourth largest commercial bank in America), whose board of directors included Stevens' chairman, James Finley. An affiliate of the International Ladies' Garment Workers Union withdrew a $6.4 million health and welfare fund account managed by Manufacturers Hanover; the International Association of Machinists threatened withdrawal of a $160 million retirement fund; and other unions threatened to withdraw a total of $1 billion in union deposits and pension funds. Finley finally resigned his post as director of the bank, declaring that he had decided "not to go where you're not wanted."

In Seattle in early 1979, the Retail Clerks Union threatened to withdraw $2 billion from the Seattle First National Bank unless the bank negotiated a contract with the union.

In Hawaii, when trustees of the Employees' Retirement System discovered that the system owned 16 percent of the stock of Hawaiian Independent Refinery, Inc., they successfully elected to the company's board of directors their own candidate, who represents the interests of the pension fund and its beneficiaries on matters of company policy.

Direct representation on company boards could become even more significant in cases where pension funds hold stock in the employing firm. ERISA now limits the amount of corporate stock a pension fund can hold in its own company to 10 percent of the outstanding shares and 5 percent of the total pension portfolio, but this is still a sizable amount (and no limit is set on profit-sharing plans). If, as Peter Drucker has suggested, the workers really do own a substantial portion of their own company, they could exert considerable influence over the management of the enterprise, including policy in such areas as the organization of work and employee relations within the plant.

Union Initiatives

Pension funds directed by workers can be invested in equities and securities that finance projects and endeavors of economic and social value to the plan participants as well as the wider community; not only the financial return, but the social return on investment can be taken into consideration in investment decisions.

Walter Reuther, former head of the United Auto Workers, for example, raised the issue of housing in 1958 negotiations with the Ford Motor Company. Pension fund trustees had been investing in the construction of luxury high-rise apartment buildings in Houston; Reuther argued that it would be far more beneficial if workers' pension funds were invested in moderately priced housing and other community facilities in the areas where Ford workers actually lived. The company rejected this claim on the grounds that the only thing the fund owed the workers was their retirement benefits.

The use of pension funds to finance low-cost housing for workers is common practice in West Germany, France, Sweden, and other European countries. Some Taft-Hartley pension funds in the United States, such as that of the International Ladies' Garment Workers Union, have also invested in housing. Former Congressman Wright Patman, as chairman of the House Banking and Currency Committee, introduced a bill in 1970 that would have required pension funds receiving federal tax exemptions to invest up to 2.5 percent of their total assets in a federally funded bank which would provide home mortgages for low- and moderate-income families.

A number of the AFL-CIO building and construction trades unions have for many years used their pension funds to promote jobs for union members in residential and commercial construction. For example, the million-member International Brotherhood of Electrical Workers (IBEW) puts 40 to 50 percent of its $900 million pension fund into FHA-insured and VA-guaranteed home mortgages. Testifying before Congress in 1970, IBEW international secretary Joseph Keenan declared:

The international officers also believe, as a matter of principle, that it is not always a requirement that the highest possible rate of return be realized. Given the choice between an investment in an AT&T bond paying 9 percent, and in an 8½ percent investment in an FHA or VA home loan for a young couple starting out in life, the IBEW will select the home loan.[12]

To qualify for IBEW financing, homes must be built entirely with union labor. The same is true for direct construction loans made by the IBEW as well as other building trades unions. Some of the direct construction loan activity has been curtailed since the passage of ERISA, whose provisions prohibit the loan of union funds to employers who contribute to the fund. Many of these unions are also involved in direct real estate investment, such as "purchase-leaseback" arrangements, mostly on commercial property whose development with union labor promotes the employment of union members as well as earning income for the pension fund.

The AFL-CIO maintains a $100 million Mortgage Investment Trust—a pooled trust for investment in federally insured or guaranteed construction loans and mortgages—for unions whose Taft-Hartley or union pension funds are not large enough to handle the administrative costs of servicing home loans directly. Recent yields on investments have averaged between 8 and 8.3 percent. All of the trust's investments are in projects built by union labor. The AFL-CIO convention in December 1977 adopted a resolution urging all unions to put at least 10 percent of their pension portfolios into guaranteed mortgages or into the Mortgage Investment Trust.

While union-controlled pension plans and some nonprofit organization and public employee plans invest substantial amounts in housing construction, the bulk of the massive corporate-controlled, private, noninsured pension funds have shunned such investments. Of the $160.4 billion in book-value assets at the end of 1976, less than 1.5 percent was in mortgages, and most of the latter was in large commercial properties or multifamily developments rather than single-family homes. Kenneth Rosen, who authored the study, "The Role of Pension Funds in Housing Finance" for the Harvard-MIT Joint Center for Urban Studies in 1975, argued that large, corporate-controlled plans shy away from real estate and housing not because of risk or relative yields, but simply because of the preference of bank trust departments and money managers for corporate stocks and bonds. He noted that even life insurance companies, with financial requirements similar to those of pension funds plus more than $80 billion in pension reserves, play a much larger role in housing finance than do noninsured corporate funds. Rosen's study as well as a similar study conducted for the California Employment Development Department in 1975 concluded that yields on federally insured FHA mortgages compare favorably with AAA-rated corporate bonds and carry a lower risk because of the federal guarantee.

For pension fund managers concerned about the administrative problems of acquiring mortgages, a number of mortgage-backed securities are now available which are no more difficult to handle than any federal agency security or corporate bond. The most prominent is the Government National Mortgage Association ("Ginnie Mae") "pass-through." Ginnie Mae (a part of the Department of Housing and Urban Development) began selling these securities in 1970, primarily as a way of attracting large institutional investors and pension funds into the market for FHA-VA single-family home mortgages. Back in 1957, in fact, the National Housing Conference had recommended

exploration of a broadened financial base for housing through investing a portion of Social Security reserves in a Federally-guaranteed bond-type security which would be attractive to pension funds and to the general bond market.[13]

As yet, no Social Security reserves or other federal trust funds have purchased securities from Ginnie Mae but the private market now holds nearly $50 billion worth of these securities which are sold in various denominations and backed by large pools of FHA-VA mortgages. The principal and interest are "passed through" to the security holder, and monthly payments are guaranteed by the federal government, regardless of whether or not they are collected. Current yields run between 8.3 and 8.4 percent. A similar security issued by the Federal Home Loan Mortgage Corporation ("Freddie Mac") pools conventional nonguaranteed mortgages and guarantees monthly interest payments to the security holder, but pays principal only as collected. Because of the greater risk, yields are somewhat higher. In addition, pension funds can also purchase the bonds of various state housing finance agencies.

There are two problems with the indirect investment approach. First, the purchaser has no control over which mortgages are backing the security. This becomes an issue if a fund wants to target its mortgage investment to a particular geographic area. Since the amount of pension fund money available for this purpose is potentially large, some experts feel they can insist that Ginnie Mae or Freddie Mac assemble targeted pools. In 1978, the State of Washington Retirement System arranged for the packaging of $50 million in FHA-VA mortgages entirely from Washington state. Others could presumably do the same.

A second problem is that pension funds may be investing in housing, but not necessarily in housing that benefits low- and moderate-income people. The finance agencies would have to be pressured to assure that a certain proportion of mortgages benefited these groups.

In addition to investing in housing, pension funds can also provide capital for job creation and economic development in targeted areas such as high-unemployment urban and rural communities. The financial requirements of pension funds are for stable and long-term growth; liquidity is of little concern. As was argued earlier, this puts them in an ideal situation to make the long-term loans and equity investments that would enable new enterprises, community development corporations, and neighborhood revitalization programs to grow and plan for the future. Many of these investments, while ignored by bank trust departments and asset managers, have quite competitive yields for a given level of risk.

There are a host of loan programs that carry practically no risk because they are guaranteed by the federal government. One congressional publication lists 164 federal loan guarantee programs that involve minority communities.[14] A pension fund could either make direct loans using the guarantee programs or purchase the guaranteed portion of a previous loan from the lender, thus freeing funds for further use. State loan guarantee programs could be utilized in the same two ways.

A good example of the latter approach—purchase of the guaranteed portions of loans from another lender—is the involvement of the Kansas Public Employees Retirement Fund in the secondary marketing of the guaranteed portion of Small Business Administration loans by the Kansas Development Credit Corporation (KDCC). A campaign by the KDCC known as "Kansas Funds Promote Kansas Jobs" convinced the pension fund in 1971 to commit $5 million annually of its $270 million assets to the program. Previously, all of the pension fund's investments were located out of the state. The KDCC program has made millions of dollars in additional money available for medium-term expansion financing of small businesses in Kansas.

The participating banks and the KDCC each receive ½ point for servicing the loan while SBA receives a ¼ point fee. Hence, the incentive needed by KDCC to engage in secondary marketing operations is a one and one-fourth point spread between the interest rate on the SBA loan and the interest rate acceptable to a KDCC buyer. At the end of 1975, KDCC was purchasing 10¼ percent SBA loans and selling them in $250,000 packages at a yield of 9 percent.

Sixteen other states have followed or are planning to follow Kansas DCC's pioneering efforts in the secondary marketing of the guaranteed portion of SBA loans. *This technique has become so widely diffused that banks have begun to develop direct links to state pension funds, by-passing the DCC's.*[15] [Emphasis added.]

Another example of the economic development approach to the pension portfolio is the $6 million loan (at 8.5 percent for fifteen years) made by the Pennsylvania state employees' and teachers' pension funds to Volkswagen as part of the package by which Governor Shapp convinced that company to locate in the Keystone State. In this case, the fund managers took into account not only the yield but the overall climate of economic growth in the state and the fiscal health of the state government, which of course is of direct concern to the union membership.

The Ohio State Teachers' Retirement Fund invests $13 million of its $3 billion assets (.4 percent) in seven venture capital firms. While it represents only a small percentage of the fund's total assets, this is still a large amount of money for venture capital markets, which are currently starved for funds to promote new business development, as testimony at 1977 Senate hearings indicated. While the Ohio Teachers' investments are based on yield and are located throughout the nation, such investments can be targeted geographically in order to promote state or local economic development.

One possible approach to economic development on a state level is to combine state-owned banks with public employee pension funds. Because of the "deferred wages" interpretation of pension benefits, and especially because public employee retirement plans generally involve substantial employee contributions, it would not be politically acceptable for the state to mandate particular pension investments. The state bank, however, could act as fiduciary agent and manage the pension portfolio. This is done in North Dakota, where the Bank of North Dakota manages state employee retirement funds and tries to maximize yield while still considering state economic development goals. Proposed legislation to create a state-owned bank in California contains a provision that would allow the bank to manage the portfolio of state and local government employee retirement funds.

Another area in which pension funds can play a major role is state and local government finance. At one time a large percentage of the portfolios of state and local government retirement systems were in municipal bonds; there has been a trend away from this in the last ten years, however, because tax-exempt pension funds derive no income advantage from holding tax-exempt municipal bonds, which generally pay several percentage points less interest than comparable taxable corporate securities. As of 1978, more than 80 percent of all public pension fund assets were in corporate stocks and bonds. Some retirement systems still hold municipal bonds, either because they do not wish to sell them and are waiting for maturity, or because they want to help bail out the local government from bankruptcy and save their own jobs, as in the case of the New York City public employee unions, which bought $3.1 billion worth of bonds in 1975 to rescue the city from default.

Senator William Proxmire introduced a bill in 1972 to allow states and municipalities to issue taxable securities at interest rates competitive with those on corporate bonds; the federal government would subsidize one-third of the interest costs. He argued that, since tax exemption already involves a substantial federal subsidy, the alternative of a direct subsidy of interest payments would cost the Treasury no more and would be much more effective for local governments because it would enable public and private pension funds to purchase the bonds. Adding this massive pool of capital to the municipal bond market would greatly expand demand and therefore probably lower overall interest costs. Proxmire's bill was defeated, but many experts in development finance continue to advocate such a measure.

"Prudent Man"

The Employee Retirement Income Security Act raised a potential problem in the area of "socially oriented" investments by placing all fund trustees and asset managers under fiduciary responsibility subject to civil suit by the U.S. Department of Labor (in addition to private lawsuits by plan beneficiaries). The basis for this fiduciary responsibility is the famous "prudent man rule," first expressed by Justice Samuel Putnam in 1830: a trustee "is to observe how men of prudence, discretion, and intelligence manage their own affairs" and to do likewise in the management of the trust.

Unfortunately, in most cases it is considered "prudent" merely to do what everyone else does, such as invest heavily in blue-chip corporate stocks. During the 1950s and early 1960s stocks were appreciating rapidly in value, and this was a good area for pension investments—so much so, in fact, that many state and local government retirement systems which were legally prohibited from purchasing equities lobbied successfully to lift this ban and have been investing heavily in the stock market ever since. The only problem is that, since the late sixties, the average rate of return on stocks, including capital gains (or losses) and reinvestment of dividends, has been abysmally low compared to other types of investments. As *Fortune* pointed out:

During the five years ending in 1975, the total return (i.e., including dividends, which are assumed to be reinvested) on the Standard & Poor's 500 ... was at a 3.2 percent annual rate. The figure for ten years ending in 1975 was 3.3 percent. The median rate of return for managed pension-fund stock portfolios over those ten years was only 1.6 percent.[16]

The 1977 Senate hearings on "Pension Simplification and Investment Rules" dramatized the way in which the "prudent man rule" has been used as a justification for portfolio managers to turn their backs on investments in all new enterprises and indeed in any firm with annual sales of less than $100 million. Senator Lloyd Bentsen's response to this problem was a proposal to suspend the fiduciary responsibility clause for investments of up to 2 percent of a pension fund's assets. Others argue that such a step is unnecessary; what is needed is simply for employee-beneficiaries to insist that their funds be more diversified. This is one element, of course.

The most significant problem in adopting any "alternative" investment policy is that it introduces another set of assumptions into investment decision making in addition to consideration of rate-of-return within a given risk class. The question of the *use* to which the money is put becomes critical. Evaluating investments on the basis of the social benefits generated may prove extremely difficult and conflict-ridden. In cases where beneficiaries of a plan can adopt a policy that is democratically conceived as *directly* benefiting the membership—such as building trades unions' creating construction jobs for themselves—then there may be no problem as long as yield is sufficient to insure adequate retirement benefits. But institutions such as public banks or development banks will have a hard time formulating standards of measurement and priorities for decision making to achieve the multitude of goals falling under the heading of "unmet needs." The geographic disparities in economic growth, jobs versus environment, public versus private or mixed enterprise, distributional effects, and hiring and labor policies will be joined by a host of other issues that can becloud any large-scale efforts to alter investment patterns.

Related to this is the question of scale. Many successful alternative economic institutions in the United States, such as community development corporations, producer and consumer cooperatives, and worker-owned and self-managed enterprises, have tended to be rather small in size. Opportunities do not even exist for large-scale capital shifts at the present time—at least not into businesses that *already* are democratically operated or community controlled.

Given the current concentration of capital and of political and economic power noted throughout this book, it should be obvious that those on top will not relinquish their place without a battle. The possible effects of severe economic disruption on the lives of large segments of the population act as a strong conservatizing force. Whether this force can be overcome and workers can gain more confidence in their own ability and/or that of representatives they have chosen to manage huge portfolios and large-scale enterprise is a significant psychological and political problem.

Enterprise management becomes an important point: were pension investments to withdraw from corporate debt and equity markets, these businesses would face such a severe capital crisis that workers might be forced to reinvest in the company and assume major management responsibilities in order to save their own jobs. Should this situation arise, problems of intersectoral and regional wage differentials, productivity and international competition, the retention of jobs and traditional prerogatives versus the introduction of new technology, and democratic work place decision making would have to be faced by the unions in a new and different context. For the individual worker, the problem of control over the excessive concentration of power in the union hierarchy would have to be confronted. After all, some unions already do control their pension portfolios—and not necessarily to the benefit of their membership, as the Teamsters have repeatedly demonstrated.

A related matter is the quality of administration and leadership of the people who would staff the alternative investment institutions. Two points are at issue: competence and integrity. Corporate critics like to cast doubt on the ability of public agencies or unions to handle intelligently the decision making associated with large-scale financial investment and management. The easy answer is to point out that big bankers certainly have no monopoly on wisdom, as the disastrous performance of bank-held real estate investment trusts (REITs) and pension asset management by trust departments has shown. Similarly, federal loan guarantees, bail-outs, and subsidization of corporate cost overruns demonstrate that businessmen as a class possess no innate powers of wizardry. The problem of competence, however, is still a serious one, which argues powerfully for experimentation in incremental stages to enable a new class of managers, "public and worker financial entrepreneurs," to develop and test their skills and abilities before large-scale responsibilities are placed in their hands (or full confidence is given to their efforts).

The Patman hearings and the Twentieth Century Fund's "Conflicts of Interest" series marshaled a wealth of impressive evidence that the present concentration of financial control does not lend itself to clean and pure transactions. The solution is strict accountability, and this can be built into the institutional framework and applied as vigorously to "public and worker entrepreneurs" as it should be to their corporate counterparts. The Bank of North Dakota has maintained a record of integrity throughout its fifty-eight years. The elimination of corruption requires the efforts of the people involved, of course, but it depends even more importantly on the framework for accountability and control.

One final question is whether changes in capital flows are to come about on a voluntary or a mandatory basis. Arguing that people who already hold claims to capital should exercise greater control is different from proposing that the government should exercise greater control over private claims. This issue, sometimes termed the problem of "credit allocation," has long been debated in this country. A great deal of credit, however, is already "allocated" by a small number of large *private* institutions. Perhaps the issue is not public versus private, but centralized versus decentralized. Certainly, one priority that continues to occupy a high place among the unmet needs is how to maximize freedom and opportunity. Even those who argue that it is "countervailing powers" or "checks and balances" that need most to be preserved, should agree that control over wealth is currently so highly concentrated that *many* measures are necessary before a better balance can be found. These include the assertion of claims over capital resources by pension and trust fund beneficiaries, social experimentation with alternative economic institutions, and greater assertion of public direction and control over capital by government institutions.

The basic elements of our strategy for democratizing investment are: the creation, from both private and public employee funds, of city- and state-owned banks staffed with trust departments competent to handle large pension fund accounts; the establishment by the labor movement itself of a national pension fund investment advisory service to assist unions in fashioning strategies for using this "pension power" (a step that has already been taken by unions in England); federal purchase of at least one healthy national bank-holding company and one nationally active insurance company to be operated as "competitive" public enterprises in the nation's capital market, as a means of providing the public with greater knowledge of the actual operation of major financial operations and giving the government a stronger position from which to influence the activities of the remaining private banks. Such publicly owned financial enterprises would also help to develop expertise among public-minded financial managers—entrepreneurs in the public interest.

CHAPTER FOUR

Democratizing the Work Place

Reforms such as public enterprise and the redirection of pension funds are national or at least statewide in scope. They require mass political movements or a socially conscious political leadership willing to shape public opinion toward reform. Reforms at this level are necessary for any structural change: they shift control over investment capital from privately held banks and other corporations to the public, or, at least, to "representatives" of the public. Such measures may, and usually do, result in greater equality of income and wealth, and give greater collective control of economic resources to workers and consumers. Socialist and social democratic societies are labor oriented; much more than the United States today, they tend to emphasize and achieve full employment, safe working conditions, old-age security, comprehensive health care, and—when taxes and public expenditures are accounted for—a more equal distribution of wages and salaries.

But a change from private to "public" control of capital is not *necessarily* more democratic than corporate capitalism. A labor-oriented public investment policy can be, and generally is, decided by a small group of people, whether they be the elite of a government bureaucracy, union leaders meeting with the heads of nationalized industries, or technocrats developing plans for legislative committees. To a lesser or greater degree, such "representatives" of the public must answer to a worker/consumer constituency. In capitalist democracies, we are accustomed to exercising this control through periodic voting. This is certainly a valid form of political expression. Even when firms are publicly owned, however, the change in ownership does not guarantee control over production and investment decisions at the work place. Furthermore—and this is a more subtle point— without that direct democracy, the nature of participation in state- and national-level economic and social decisions will probably be different, if for no other reason than the smaller amount of economic information available directly to workers in any industry or to consumers.

Nationalized firms are usually just as hierarchical as private capitalist firms, although smaller public salary differentials between workers and managers, where they exist, may change hierarchical relations in subtle ways. In economies where workers and employees know that they have considerable collective political power over national economic policy (as in Scandinavia), their relations with management seem to be very different (even if workers do not control decision making directly) than in economies where private capital has great influence over governmental policies. Yet the nationalized firm or the state bureaucratic firm (as in Eastern Europe) retains significant elements of capitalist relations even if the ownership of the means of production has passed out of capitalist hands. It makes sense, from our knowledge of human behavior, that the maintenance of hierarchical relations in production should have a significant effect on *overall* political participation: the two are logically intertwined. Changing the ownership of production (to public or social ownership) is not sufficient to change relations in production; in particular, to shift the control of production from an elite managerial group to the workers themselves. Public enterprise is an important reform in and of itself; so are reforms that shift power over investment decisions to workers and consumers. But power relations within firms (and, by implication, power relations in the society as a whole) may remain hierarchical and relatively undemocratic even after such reforms.

Worker control at the plant level is therefore a crucial element in developing democratic decision making in a society. But such worker control gives rise to a number of questions: Does it mean giving up economic "efficiency" in terms of product per worker input? Does it really produce more participation by workers, or does it degenerate for various reasons into new hierarchical structures? How does worker control occur? What forms does it take? What effects does it have on employment and income distribution?

There have been many attempts to establish worker-controlled production both in the United States and in other countries. The most common form has been the worker-initiated producer cooperative, but recently worker control has been used to preserve employment in declining industries —a worker reaction to layoffs and bankruptcies. By studying some of these cases—even though each case separately seems somewhat idiosyncratic—we can get some answers to the questions surrounding worker-controlled production.

At the same time, we can assess the political role of cooperative production and worker takeovers in the context of reform of the American economy. It is important to deal with both issues, since worker control almost always occurs in capitalist societies on a plant-by-plant basis. Do such cases have meaning in a political-strategic sense? Even if we discover that workers can be better off psychologically by forming a producer cooperative, and that they can be socially efficient producers, achieve a more equal income distribution, and so on, can we view isolated producer cooperatives and worker takeovers as contributing to an overall economic reform movement in the United States?

Before turning to the case studies, we need to clarify a fundamental point that consistently confuses the discussion of worker control. Is the "efficiency" of the capitalist organization of production greater than that of any other organization? An inherent part of American ideology is the belief that, for all its faults, the capitalist division of labor and its resultant hierarchy represents the most efficient way to produce goods and services. Even Eastern European socialist economies seem to have accepted this argument. Managerial elites in Hungary, Poland, and other countries avidly study American management "science" and eagerly await the arrival of each new issue of the *Harvard Business Review.*

Capitalist Work Organization

If we could choose a single feature to characterize capitalist production, it would have to be the control of production decision making by capital owners and their appointed managers. The control of work is separated from work itself. Those who actually manipulate the tools to produce goods and services are not the ones who decide what tools (technology) should be used nor the way these tools should be employed.

There is controversy about why this separation occurred and why it is essential to the capitalist system. In the view of orthodox economists and historians, technology and efficiency demand that decisions about the way things are to be manufactured, investment policy, sales, and so on, be made by those who risk capital. In their model, profit maximization requires capital owners and managers to make the "most efficient" decisions or else lose out to the competition. Put another way, those owners and managers who *made* the most efficient decisions were the ones who *did* survive. So the hierarchical structure of production, the technology used, and the division of labor now in existence have survived the test of time and competition. If firms remain competitive (are not allowed to become monopolies), the most efficient ones produce the most goods, realize the highest return to capital, can charge the lowest prices and pay the highest wages, and employ the greatest amount of labor.

But there is another view: the capitalist organization of production is geared not to maximize output, but to extract more labor from workers at the lowest possible wages. The *difference* between wages and productivity, not the maximization of product, is the key variable. This requires the development of technology that cheapens labor as well as increasing labor productivity. Semiskilled workers must be substituted for skilled, women for men. Work must be divided so that it can be better *controlled.* In this view, the hierarchical structure of production, the technology used, and the division of labor are chosen by employers for their efficiency in maximizing the productivity-wage difference—not production, employment, or even productivity itself.

The controversy is important because the two sides have very different views of capitalist "efficiency." According to one view, the organization of production under the present system of capitalism is the most "efficient" we can devise, and this efficiency offsets the alienating aspects of capitalist hierarchies; therefore, it should not be abandoned for a new form of organization even if workers are not very happy in their jobs. Management consultants of this persuasion, such as Peter Drucker and others, argue that changes can be made in the work place to improve worker satisfaction without altering either managerial/private-owner control of decision making or the production hierarchy.

But the other, radical view insists that the present system is efficient only in the sense that it maximizes the return to capital. Maximizing return to capital, however, has meant in practice choosing capital-intensive technology and reducing employment per unit of output. More importantly, worker dissatisfaction emanates from the very maximization of the return to capital that lies at the basis of capitalist decision making. So the capitalist definition of "efficiency" includes worker well-being, fuller employment, and higher output only when these are consistent with increasing returns to capital. In this view, improving the "quality" of working life without giving workers control of production and investment decisions might make job conditions better, but it would not eliminate the process by which managers try to keep wages low relative to productivity.

In the capitalist production process, decision making by employers is a *right*. The ownership of property carries with it legal control over its use. This poses a fundamental dilemma for the American concepts of individual freedom and democracy: if a person is employed (does not own the tools of production), he or she is governed *without recourse* by others' decisions about work. To the worker, it makes no difference whether these decisions are logical or arbitrary; they govern absolutely the conditions of work in that enterprise. Theoretically, of course, workers can change their employment: if one firm has better working conditions than another, workers who are sensitive to the difference in work environments will shift to that enterprise. In turn, they may receive lower wages, since a pleasant work environment has positive value in and of itself. But theory is not practice. Few capitalist economies have high enough rates of employment to enable workers to pick and choose among jobs. Choice is necessarily limited, especially for production workers and less-skilled white collar personnel. And what of the trade-off between working conditions and wages? Most of the higher wage jobs, such as manager, technician, and professional, are exactly those that have the healthiest and most pleasant working conditions, including the greatest choice in working hours and job location. Low wages and poor working conditions usually go together, although there may be some trade-off within a certain level or kind of work.

Worker control of production and the accompanying alternative organizations of work (such as a greatly reduced division of labor) could well result in greater output, more employment, more efficient use of labor, and less intensive use of capital than the present hierarchical arrangement. Workers might also enjoy their work more if they had greater say about how it is organized and what they produce, and participated directly in productivity increases.

Political rights have been extended to an increasing fraction of the American population—blacks, unionized workers, women—all of whom fought for this extension throughout the nineteenth and twentieth centuries. The principle of one person/one vote in the political arena, however, confronts the reality of unequal economic rights and an unequal distribution of economic power. The two cannot be separated. The "free speech" of a General Motors is obviously greater than that of any individual. We cannot speak of political power distribution as unrelated to economic power and rights, even though the two may not be the same. Economic democracy is a crucial ingredient in political democracy and vice versa. Under the capitalist organization of production, political democracy is an imperfect concept and can be achieved in practice only through a democratization of the economy.

Worker Participation and Worker Decision Making

In the seventies, worker participation and the conditions of work have become important issues for both workers and management. This is a logical outgrowth of the dissatisfaction of workers even in the face of relatively high wage rates, a dissatisfaction accentuated by political disillusion. People are told to vote for change; they do, and little changes. Higher consumption does not seem to solve these problems either (though it improves people's material well-being). Young workers with a relatively high level of education who have not suffered the low incomes of the 1930s and 1940s demand more from their jobs than increased wages.

Management has had to react to these demands in some way or face rising absenteeism, higher worker turnover, sabotage, low-quality output, and wildcat strikes. But management is interested primarily in increasing productivity without raising wages, or at least in increasing productivity *more* than wages rise. Traditionally, recessions and work-saving technology have served to "discipline" the labor force—to remind workers that they and their jobs are expendible. "Cheaper" labor, such as foreign immigrants, rural workers pushed off farms by new technology and drawn to the cities by higher wages, women and, most recently, illegal aliens, are also brought in to substitute for more skilled and higher paid workers. Firms can also relocate in search of cheap labor to Taiwan, Mexico, or South Korea. These measures are still available to managers and owners in their drive to maintain and increase the return to capital. It is in this context that management is willing to improve work conditions: better working conditions can be substituted for higher wages. From a management/owner standpoint, worker participation in decision making can become part of improved work conditions only if it increases productivity more than wages and does not remove control over investment and profits from management and owners.

This is *not* what we have in mind when we advocate worker participation and worker control. An increase in participation that does not address the fundamental relationship of workers to their bosses does not alter the inherently undemocratic nature of capitalist production. Participation in decisions about the height of a workbench, the size of the parking lot, or the availability of a coffee machine may make the work place more pleasant and may make workers feel better about their jobs, but they do not change the fact that workers can be fired with two weeks' notice without explanation or discussion, or that they must answer to the whims of the foreman or manager. Changes in the "quality" of working life that lead to greater output—either because workers are more satisfied with their work and so produce more or because "participative" work arrangements use worker time more "efficiently"—should result in higher wages for workers, or at least a choice in how the higher productivity is to be allocated between present and future wages. This can occur only if workers themselves are involved directly in the firm's production and financial decisions. So worker control means decision power over how work is to be done, how work is to be allocated, and how much workers are to be paid.

We must also distinguish between worker control and worker "ownership." Profit-sharing plans and pension fund "socialism" make workers partial "owners" of firms through direct or indirect stock purchases without giving them much, if any, control over wage, employment, or investment decisions. Typically, through a profit-sharing or stock-option plan, workers own only a small percentage of their company's shares, which they would have to vote collectively and almost unanimously to have any influence at all over company policy. With stock options, managers have a ready source of direct investment capital in workers' wages without any need to relinquish control of the firm to workers. Productivity may rise if workers feel they have a stake in the firm's profits; and pressure on wages may decrease because worker-stockholders may be willing to forgo wage increases in favor of higher profits (and greater stock dividends). Thus, employee stock ownership plans or other stock-option plans turn workers into stockholders ("capitalists"), but do not, in practice, give workers ownership or management decision-making rights; rather, they put part of workers' wages at the disposal of management and owners without forcing them to divest control of profits.

Pension funds invested in various firms are also a potential source of worker control; but again, in practice, they have served as a ready and large source of investment capital without increasing workers' participation in decision making. Such pension funds are often legally separated from their owners; they are invested and controlled by trustees (usually bank directors). Even when this is not so, the funds may not be permitted legally to purchase shares of the company where the workers who own it work, and union bureaucrats who control the fund might not make it a practice to consult the rank and file in its use. As we discussed in the previous chapter, unions have used their control of pension funds to pressure anti-union firms. This may herald a new aggressiveness by unions in utilizing their investment power, but it is far from rank-and-file worker control over investment and production decisions.

Worker control involves both ownership and decision making. Workers can "own" a firm by having direct control over its shares, or by being citizens of a society whose government owns productive enterprises. Democratic, participatory decision making takes more than ownership, however. At the same time, workers can share in decision making without owning a firm, though there are important limitations on just how much they can influence corporate policy without direct ownership or public control (see chapter 6).

"Quality of Work" Reforms

A number of American firms—Gaines Dog Food, Corning Glass, and others—have initiated small-scale experiments aimed at improving the "quality of work life."

Some "quality of work" reforms are management responses to particular productivity problems. The change to be made is generally determined by technical specialists such as industrial psychologists and sociologists, or human factors engineers. These specialists redesign a job so that it is less tedious, healthier, safer, or more pleasant (in terms of the work environment). Other reforms cover more than individual jobs; they deal with groups of workers or even with the entire firm. Such reforms attempt to improve communications and human relations within the organization and to "manage conflict." If the reform is successful, workers are more satisfied and productivity and profits rise. We have already mentioned the example of profit-sharing plans. But these reforms can also result in redesign of the organization of production on the shop floor. Both Volvo and Saab-Scandia in Sweden have experimented with non-assembly-line production in automobile or auto engine assembly. At Saab, the engines are assembled by three teams of four women workers who cooperatively organize production and rotate particular tasks. The production schedule is set by management, but workers can vary how they carry out the assembly operation. Volvo has carried team assembly even further by constructing a plant in which the assembly line has been eliminated completely. In its place are a number of subassembly shops where teams of workers carry out functions similar to the assembly operations at Saab. Both firms claim improvements in productivity, quality control, and work force stability. A few smaller firms in the U.S. auto industry, such as a mirror manufacturing plant in Bolivar, Tennessee, have engaged in similar experiments in team production with the cooperation of the United Auto Workers.

Some companies have shifted control of decision making on certain tasks or jobs within the firm from management to workers, while leaving untouched the overall decision-making process in the enterprise, as reflected in decisions on the choice of products or services to be produced, pricing policies, investment plans, distribution of profits, and organizational structure. Job enrichment approaches assume that workers can be more highly motivated if their responsibilities on the job are increased, for example, by assigning them to plan, organize, and evaluate work in addition to performing it.

One of the most important applications of this concept is the autonomous work group. Developed by several researchers at the Tavistock Institute in London and the Work Research Institute in Oslo, this approach distributes organizational functions among relatively small work groups that make decisions on how their work will be performed. The assumption is that most employees can relate better to a small and identifiable member group than to a large, impersonal organization. While the group is accountable to a higher level of management for its performance, it controls internal assignments, scheduling, training, and innovation.

The shift from assembly lines to work teams in Swedish automobile plants is based on organizational technical redesign, but it also represents substantial internal change. Groups of workers in those plants can determine, within limits, the organization of their work.

There are other forms of participative management. Worker councils or committees elected by workers or appointed by workers and managers can be used to resolve jointly with management some of the major policy issues concerning the work setting. This is the *de facto* approach used in British industrial relations: shop stewards represent unionized workers in management-worker conflicts and decisions on changes in employment and work practices. In the British case, the process evolved as part of normal industrial relations practice, but the use of worker councils as a participative mechanism is being considered increasingly in U.S. and Western European enterprises. In Jamestown, New York, for example, joint labor-management councils have been established in a number of companies, with support from a grant by the U.S. Department of Commerce.

The specific features of any work-related reform are crucial in determining the nature of the results. We have already reviewed nationalization as a means of transferring decision making from private enterprise to public control. Such a transfer has obvious implications for the governance of work organization, but in nationalized firms traditional corporate management is usually replaced by other management that is just as hierarchical. Decision-making remains in the hands of a small group of individuals. The principal effect of nationalization is *public* control of surplus, allocation of production and investment, technology, wages, and pricing. Insofar as the workers identify with the government and its policies, this has its rewards. But at the enterprise level there are few differences in worker participation between private and public enterprises. Public firms may present greater possibilities for worker participation, however, because of their public nature: it is in such firms that the contradiction between economic hierarchies and political democracy is greatest. For better or worse on productivity grounds, public employees already are granted employment guarantees, grievance rights, and nonwage benefits that are less likely to be given in private firms. Wage differentials between the highest- and lowest-paid workers, between women and men, and between blacks and whites are smaller in government jobs than in the private sector. But nationalization also poses problems for worker action against management: once the traditional worker-management conflict is shifted to the public sector, whom are the workers striking against? Thus nationalization can be a boon or a constraint with regard to improved work conditions and worker participation depending on the nature of the nationalization process and the political context in which nationalization takes place.

There *are* many examples of worker self management in nationalized (public) firms, examples we did not discuss in chapter 2, on public ownership. The Yugoslav version of worker self-management is the most highly developed in Eastern European socialist economies. It is based on workers' councils, which make the major policy decisions for the firms. In small enterprises (less than thirty employees), all of the workers are members of such councils; in larger firms, the councils are elected by the work force. The council holds all formal power, and it makes decisions regarding hiring and firing, salaries, investment, and other firm operations. Unlike some of the forms of worker participation instituted in American companies, where workers and worker councils are still accountable to management, under the Yugoslav model the management is accountable to the workers. Managers are appointed by the elected representatives of the central management board.

Various versions of worker self-management are also found in China, Cuba, and Israel. In China, workers participate directly in shop floor decisions as part of the general emphasis in China on worker control. Mao's death may mean much greater hierarchy and specialization in Chinese industry but, for the last generation, worker participation at all levels of management has been a principal feature of Chinese society. Managers, on the other hand, have had to put in time as common workers to prevent the separation of a managerial elite from production itself. Cuba, too, has dealt extensively with the problem of managerial elitism and the separation of managers from manual work. Although worker participation in decision making in Cuban enterprises has not been notable, moves toward political democratization have had their counterpart in production. In the Israeli kibbutz, all decisions as to production as well as to the distribution and use of productive surpluses are made by the membership. The traditional work hierarchy is eliminated in favor of a democratic mechanism for making collective decisions in production and consumption.

The Yugoslav, Chinese, and Cuban cases can teach us about the possibilities and problems of worker control, but these problems all exist within the political context of relatively underdeveloped socialist states. This context includes national planning, the absence of property rights for individual producers and, at least in principle, national emphasis on cooperation for achieving collective social goals.

The Israeli kibbutz exists within a capitalist society; as an ideological island representing only a small (and declining) fraction of Israeli workers, it has lessons to teach about collective, worker-controlled production units trying to survive in an ideologically ambivalent environment. On the other hand, the kibbutz has a traditional and important place in Israeli society— particularly in the pioneering of development and in border defense—that producer cooperatives and worker-managed enterprises do not have in the United States or Western European countries. Thus it has only limited relevance for a reform movement in the United States.

There is another work governance reform that we leave for a later chapter: the inclusion of worker representatives on corporate boards, a reform especially important in Western Europe. For example, the Federal Republic of Germany has adopted a policy of co-determination *(Mitbestimmung)* requiring that from one-third to one-half of the places on firm governing boards be delegated to workers. In 1976 the Commission of the Common Market recommended co-determination and workers' councils in companies operating in two or more member countries. A British Commission on Industrial Democracy has also recommended recently that the governing boards of all British firms employing more than 2,000 persons be required to include elected worker representatives. This approach would be equivalent to placing a significant proportion of worker representatives on the corporate boards of large U.S. companies.

The structural reform with which we are concerned here is direct employee ownership. In some ways, this would seem to be the most far-reaching of these reforms, since ownership should give the employees the right to govern their own work organization and the nature of the work situation. In practice, however, ownership may have little to do with employee participation in management or worker control of production.

There are at least two general forms of employee ownership. The first is management-initiated, and the second, worker-initiated. Management-initiated types of employee ownership usually consist of a program in which part of the remuneration of employees is offered in the form of stocks or options to purchase stock on the basis of seniority, salary, or position. In other cases, the employees acting as a group purchase the firm by obtaining a loan that is repaid out of profits. Perhaps the best-known plan for effecting such a transfer is the employee stock ownership plan or ESOP.

Management will choose the first of these plans as a means of supplementing wage and salary benefits while building a mechanism to increase employee motivation and productivity. The second form generally is adopted primarily as a means for increasing the amount of capital in the firm, an intrinsic attribute of the ESOP approach. It should be no surprise that management-initiated plans to increase employee ownership construct no mechanism whereby employees might participate in the management of the firm. Indeed, in a majority of such cases employees seem content to leave these decisions to traditional managerial hierarchies, tacitly assuming that professional expertise is necessary to obtain maximum growth and returns to their stock.

Employee-initiated ownership plans, in contrast, almost always result in direct or representative participation in the governing of the work enterprise. The most typical approach is that of the producers' cooperative in which the members both own and manage the organization. Such organizations can be created from the beginning in cooperative form, whereby members or employees are required to invest in the enterprise, or they can emerge from the conversion of conventional firms into producer cooperatives. In both these cases, workers enter into a voluntary association for the production and sale of some good or product. As a general rule, responsibility for the formulation of overall production and sales policy resides in a general meeting of the cooperative's membership. It exercises control of the internal organization of work as well as levels of remuneration, product planning and development, marketing, pricing, and other functions. In capitalist societies, the producer cooperative represents the most complete form of structural reform of the traditional capitalist relationship within enterprises.

Cooperatives provide an opportunity to examine how production relations change—if at all—when ownership is not divorced from those who produce and decision making is (potentially) centered in the labor force. Since producer cooperatives are idiosyncratic to capitalist development (representing only a miniscule percentage of capitalist production in industrial economies), it is difficult to generalize from their experiences to decide whether they should form an essential part of a strategy of worker control at the plant level. Each case seems so different that there are only bits and pieces of analysis to put together for any political conclusions. The same can be said of our understanding of why cooperatives survive or not. But we are on firmer ground in analyzing differences between the behavior of workers and firms under worker control and under traditional capitalist ownership, particularly with regard to the possibilities and limitations of democratic life within the work place and the effects of such democracy on employment, income distribution, and productivity.

We have examined five case studies of producer cooperatives in four countries. Some of these experiences have more relevance to the United States than others; two are not even cooperatives in the true sense of the word, but present interesting data that add to our understanding of worker control. Many other subtle problems, which we shall not cover here, are faced by co-ops. Ultimately, as we conclude, the success or failure of a co-op depends both on market conditions, including the availability of credit (which often are out of the members' control) and on the relations between its members. It may be impossible to draw up universal formulas for success in the area of relations between co-op participants, and we do not have enough information at the moment to develop such formulas even were they to exist. But the legal structure of the co-op may strongly affect the possibilities for cooperation and participation; here we may be able to draw some important lessons from our examples.

The Producer Cooperative Experience

Worker associations have existed in the United States and Europe since the early 1800s. But, in the United States, only in the 1850s and 1860s, with the growth of a sizable industrial labor force, did the producer cooperative develop into a significant economic movement. Even so, the number of cooperatives was historically a cyclical phenomenon, declining in the early part of this century and then increasing in the period between 1910 and 1930. This pattern was repeated in Great Britain, but there the growth of cooperatives was more gradual (until 1897) and the subsequent decline somewhat slower as well. As a number of historians have shown, producer co-ops have never employed more than a small percentage of the labor force in either England or America. The same is true for other countries such as France and Sweden, where co-ops have had greater success.

Why have democratically managed and operated, employee-owned industrial firms done so poorly in democratically oriented countries like England and America?

Many of these worker cooperatives were formed during depression years and served primarily to provide jobs for unemployed workers. Once the depression was over, the usefulness of the co-op to the workers declined. According to one labor historian, producer cooperatives failed largely for internal reasons: management was not democratic and degenerated into an authoritarian type of leadership; managers were not well educated and had poor business qualifications; and because managers relied on workers' votes for reelection, administrative discipline was very limited, contributing to low productivity.[1]

Another historian, Derek Jones, argued that there were waves of co-op creation during boom periods of U.S. history, or at least during periods of increasing demand for the product in question. He also cited data showing that co-op managers were well trained in business practices and that many co-ops were well run. Some cooperatives, he found, survived for long periods of time. Using British data, Jones demonstrated that producer co-ops were longer lived than small private firms in that country.[2]

The popular notion that producer cooperatives did not (and do not) do well in America, Britain, and other countries because of the inherent tendency of democratic management to degenerate is thus open to serious question. To the contrary, there is "fragmentary evidence to support the importance producer supremacists attach to the role of forces beyond the control of producer coops in explaining the demise of producer coops."[3] These forces include the hostility of the business community, of political groups, and of the unions. Most important, producer cooperatives faced more unfavorable legislation and hostile capital markets in comparison with private businesses. As we saw with the workers' banks, both sets of factors—internal and external—led to the demise of worker-owned financial enterprises.

In the seventies, interest in producer co-ops rose around the world. In the United States this interest has taken the form mainly of substantial numbers of small retail service cooperatives in major urban areas: bookstores, auto repair firms, food outlets, nursery schools, and so on, largely in the consumer coop tradition. A few medium-sized industrial producer co-ops also exist, notably plywood firms in the Pacific Northwest, a furniture factory in New York, an asbestos mine in Vermont (no longer a co-op), and others. Producer co-op movements have continued to be much more developed in Europe than in the United States. Britain, France, Spain, and Sweden all have well-known and highly productive producer cooperatives, supported in some cases by national co-op organizations or the union movement.

These industrial cooperative experiences can be divided into two broad categories: cooperatives formed by workers as new firms (job creation), and cooperatives arising out of corporate divestitures (job preservation). The U.S. plywood factories and the Caja Laboral Popular of Mondragon, Spain, fall into the first category. The Vermont Asbestos Group, Triumph Motorcycle in England, and the Lip watch company in France fall into the second. These examples give us insights into the cooperation process and the problems of and prospects for cooperatives in industrial production.

Worker-Owned Plywood Firms

Eighteen plywood firms in the Pacific Northwest are owned and controlled by their workers. These companies produce about 12 percent of American plywood. They range in size from 80 to 450 worker-owners, and each one grosses between $3 million and $15 million annually. Some of the firms have been in operation more than thirty years.

The first of these companies was established in the 1920s by Scandinavian immigrants steeped in the cooperative culture; three more were formed before World War II in response to the growing demand for this relatively new product. In each case, for a $1,000 subscription, a worker received one share of stock in the company; the share entitled him to employment, an equal share of the profits, and an equal vote in deciding all company matters. But the big expansion came in the early fifties. Twenty-one cooperatives were formed between 1950 and 1955, with promoters helping to raise money for the worker-owners. The success of previous plywood cooperatives contributed directly to their proliferation. Although a few companies have sold out to corporations or closed down, most were still operating in the 1970s, despite large fluctuations in the price of plywood.

Worker-owned firms have shown amazing resiliency in the face of severe price swings in the plywood market. Workers in the co-ops take wage cuts in hard times and divide the decreased work, which enables worker-owners to find part-time employment elsewhere. Despite the swings, the price of shares has risen from $1,000 to $40,000 (as of 1973-74).

According to sociologist Paul Bernstein, who visited these mills in 1973, and Edward Greenberg, who studied them in 1977, the firms are genuine cooperatives: the workers hire the manager, set his salary, and make all major decisions on company expansion, modernization, diversification, and so on. All shareholders receive the same hourly wages, and only working shareholders receive a portion of the surplus. The directors are elected by their fellow workers, receive neither deference nor extra pay, and continue to work in the plant. Most managers feel that as many workers as possible should serve as directors in order to better understand the finances of the business and the type of long-term financial decisions that have to be made.[4]

Much of the success or failure of the mills depends on the general manager. He must persuade the worker-owners to make the proper long-run decisions, often in opposition to their short-run interests of realizing as high an income as possible. His relations with the members affect their productivity. Either these managers have been very successful or the relatively high productivity in the worker-owned mills (as compared to conventional firms) has outweighed the inefficiencies of poor management. This higher productivity is evidenced by:

—the ability of worker-owners to take losing private firms and convert them into successful enterprises;

—the higher output per hour worked (115 to 120 square feet of plywood vs. 80 to 95 square feet in conventional firms in the 1950s and 197 square feet vs. 130 square feet in the 1960s);

—a ruling in the tax courts that worker-owned firms, because of productivity 25 to 60 percent higher than the industry average, could pay their members higher than industry-level wages;

—the ability of the firms to keep workers on the job even during slumps.

One of the greatest problems faced by the mills has resulted from their success. As older workers near retirement, they have to find someone to buy their shares, each worth $40,000 to $50,000. Since most members were about the same age when they organized the mill, they can find it more attractive to sell to a private corporation all at once than to try to sell their shares individually. With the difficulties caused by a declining building industry, this option becomes particularly interesting. Paul Bernstein noted:

There has been no great resistance from the workers to these sales because of the members' implicit priorities. The worker-owners view their companies not as specimens to be preserved for their own sake, but first of all as means for their own livelihood.[5]

Most members joined the cooperatives for financial reasons, not on ideological grounds.

Even so, these same members later came to appreciate the special environment the enterprises offer to those who own and work in them. And the environment *is* significantly different from that in traditional private firms in the same industry. Declared Greenberg:

What this suggests, in our view, is that these differences in collective mood between the plants (traditional vs. coop) is reasonably traceable to differences in the organization of power and authority within them, one set characterized by self-governance, the other by hierarchical authority, and superordinate-subordinate relations.[6]

Despite the limitations placed on complete self-governance by the technical, machine-based process, the work is organized in a way that allows considerable individual initiative, work cooperation, and self-management. There is much less supervision than in conventional plants, jobs are rotated frequently, and workers participate directly in changing the manufacturing process if production can be improved. They also participate fully in decisions at the enterprise level, and through their board members, who remain in jobs on the shop floor, obtain any information they need regarding any aspect of the plant's operation. There is also high turnover on the board of directors. Greenberg concluded that the plywood cooperatives are

without question examples of "direct" democratic institutions in which the rank and file is decisive in the decisions which give direction to overall enterprise policy, and in the development of those informal arrangements by which the social processes of production are carried out in the workplace.[7]

Yet, the plywood cooperatives have generally been units unto themselves. They have not attempted to create additional plywood co-ops or to develop cooperative production of other goods and services. Neither have they faced up to the problems generated by the spiraling costs of their shares and the rising age of their work force. A few efforts have been made by the firms to organize joint activities—including a joint marketing association of five companies—but these are limited (antitrust laws also set restrictions on such activities). While each firm is democratic and cooperative, members reveal little awareness of being part of a movement that is larger than the individual enterprise.

Mondragon's Cooperative Network

While the Northwest's plywood industry shows the success of a number of cooperatives in the same industry, the Basque cooperatives of Mondragon, a town in northern Spain, represent an integrated network of eighty-two finance, industrial, and service cooperatives spread over a fairly small area and linked by common practice and their own bank. The group, which exists alongside capitalist enterprises in the area, consists of a nucleus of sixty industrial cooperatives with a combined sales of about $400 million. The group also includes agricultural and service cooperatives, a graphic design company, and a chain of shops. About 14,000 people work in the industrial sector, another 1,700 in the agricultural sector, and 45,000 in the shops. Within the Mondragon movement there are five schools with 1,500 pupils as well as a polytechnic with 2,000 students, a co-op factory run by students to provide a link between study and remunerative work, leisure clubs, and five housing cooperatives. A social security co-op covers members for social benefits. Spanish law provides few such benefits to co-op members, since they are self-employed.

All of this grew out of a technical school founded by a Basque priest, Don José María Arizmendi, in the mid-1940s. Ten years later, in 1956, five of the school's former pupils, advised and encouraged by Arizmendi, founded Mondragon's first cooperative, which produced oil stoves. During the next three years, other co-ops were started and in 1959 they set up their own bank, the Caja Laboral Popular, whose role was to attract savings and lend money to new and expanding co-ops. The bank now has seventy branch offices. The Franco regime's legislation governing co-ops and savings banks, and its policy of keeping interest rates down, helped the Mondragon movement. But so have the ingrained savings habits and nationalism of the Basques, who are loyal to their own institutions, including banks and cooperatives. By 1977, sixty industrial co-ops manufactured a variety of goods ranging from electronic components, dishwashers, and car parts, to excavators, equipment for steel mills and refineries, and even small ships. Their sales rose from $47 million in 1966 to $336 million in 1975.[8]

Fundamental to the operation and financing of the co-ops is their central bank, the Caja Laboral Popular. The Caja serves to acquire capital for the other Mondragon co-ops. Its ownership is shared fifty-fifty between its employees and the other cooperatives in the movement. All the other co-ops are owned entirely by their own workers. The Caja is not the only source of capital, however; upon joining a cooperative, a new member must pay the equivalent of almost $2,000. Of this, 25 percent goes into a collective fund and 75 percent forms the beginning of the members' own capital account. In each cooperative, at the end of the financial year approximately 60 to 70 percent of the net profits are paid into the capital accounts of the members in proportion to their pay. The rest is divided between reserves and educational and social welfare projects in the community where the co-op is located. Earnings differentials in the co-op may not exceed three to one. The index for unskilled workers is 1; for foremen, 1.6; for middle-level executives, 2; for "important executives," 2.3; and for top management, 2.5 to 3. Members receive interest on their capital account at a rate of up to 6 percent annually.

Every cooperative has an annual general assembly of its worker-owners, each of whom has one vote. To become a voting member, a worker must be accepted from a list of applicants, work for a probationary year, and then pay $2,000 dollars for a voting share (this amount can be borrowed and repaid out of salary). The assembly elects a twelve-member board, the *junta rectora,* which functions much as a board of directors in each firm. The board meets monthly and makes senior managerial appointments; these managers, in turn, appoint middle management. In addition, each group of 200 workers is represented on a social council, whose task is to communicate ideas between workers and management and reach agreement on matters such as working hours and conditions.

The assembly can sanction workers for various antisocial acts, absenteeism, and lack of consideration for other workers. A worker whose job is eliminated must accept any other job offered by the co-ops and undergo retraining if necessary. Strikes are rare but do occur. The largest firm in the group (3,000 workers) has had the greatest problems in industrial relations. In general, however, worker-management relations are good, and the management seems to be well qualified and dedicated despite much lower pay than in private industry. Because a high proportion of profits is reinvested, industrial co-ops are better equipped than their private competitors and have been able to fulfill one of their most important goals, the creation of new jobs. The co-ops state that their aim is not to create a privileged class of cooperatives by distributing much of the profits to present members; rather, they prefer "to extend the benefits of cooperation to as many workers as possible."[9]

The social structure in the region, including the long and widespread tradition of savings and small farmer cooperation, has contributed greatly to the success of the cooperative movement in Mondragon; these traditions are difficult to transfer to other places. The co-ops were originally established to forward the interests of the *community:* they were viewed as a resource created by Basques for their people. But there are also strong material reasons for joining the co-ops—the already proven financial and employment security in the areas of work and social benefits, backed by the Caja's technical expertise, and the slightly lower taxes paid by co-op members. These have attracted workers from outside the region.

Yet, there is serious question as to just how much direct participation exists in Mondragon. Although the general assembly elects the *junta rectora* and anyone can sit on this body, it *represents* the workers and does not have to answer to them on a day-to-day basis. The social councils are the direct link between management and the workers, functioning somewhat like unions in handling labor and wage problems. Workers may find this arrangement perfectly satisfactory, content with the equal income distribution in the co-ops and with their bonuses and steady employment; but this does not negate the possibility that the co-ops fail to promote participation. Some of these shortcomings are admitted readily by the management members.

The Vermont Asbestos Group

The development of a cooperative firm as an entirely new enterprise, as in the case of the plywood factories or in a movement like Mondragon's, apparently requires a set of conditions that make it obviously profitable to begin such an enterprise and/or an ideological motivation to work in a cooperative setting rather than a traditional capitalist firm. In the United States, a new situation has developed: plant closures, particularly in areas where there are few work alternatives, are sometimes met with worker attempts to run the business themselves. As Cornell sociologist William Whyte reported in 1977:

From all over came reports of employee owned firms arising out of corporate divestures: Byers Transport Limited in Canada, and in the United States, Saratoga Knitting Mill, Vermont Asbestos Group, Jamestown Metal Products, South Bend Lathe, Mohawk Valley Corporation, and so on. Now when plant closings are announced, workers are no longer willing to accept the catastrophe fatalistically. They organize themselves to try to buy the plant, with community support and with financing from government agencies and banks, whose officials are interested in maintaining or restoring employment.[10]

This new development can be traced to the unraveling of the corporate merger movement of the 1950s and 1960s. Many firms extended themselves— for the sake of growth or to acquire tax write-offs or companies with good cash positions—into the production of goods not entirely consistent with their overall expertise. When the economic situation deteriorated in the 1970s, conglomerates discovered that they had bought more than they could manage effectively and found it necessary to divest through plant closings and sales.

The asbestos mine of the General Aniline and Film Corporation (GAF) in Lamoille County, Vermont, became a variation on this theme in early 1974. GAF had decided that it would rather close down the mine and eliminate 178 jobs than invest $1 million in the equipment needed to meet new Environmental Protection Agency (EPA) standards. In 1973, the mill and the conventional open-pit mine supplied one-fourth of the nation's $16 million annual production of asbestos, used in mineral siding, gaskets, brake linings, and chlorine manufacture. The mine was the keystone of Lamoille County's economy; the mineworkers affected by the closing would have had to move or go on welfare.[11]

Though the mine was profitable, GAF balked at the cost of installing equipment required by the EPA to reduce potentially cancer-causing dust within the mill and to eliminate emissions from the plant. Company analysts judged that the mine would be unable to continue profitably in an uncertain asbestos market and with the possibility that other EPA requirements might be imposed in the future. Employees viewed the profitability issue in terms of continued jobs, rather than in terms of returns to capital. The State of Vermont also viewed it this way, particularly since the mine closing would have cost the state almost $1 million annually in welfare payments and drastically decreased freight revenues for its recently purchased St. Johnsbury and Lamoille County Railroad.

The state government therefore helped an employees' group interested in acquiring the operation by assigning an economic analyst to prepare feasibility studies and either to convince GAF to change its mind or to raise the capital necessary to buy the mine and install the new EPA equipment (the total package came to almost $2 million). In early 1975, nearly a year after GAF announced plans to close the mine, it agreed to sell to the miners for a salvage value of $400,000. The miners formed themselves into the Vermont Asbestos Group (VAG) and issued 2,000 shares; 78 percent was bought by mine employees, each of whom purchased at least one share. After great difficulties in obtaining further financing, VAG finally was able to borrow $1.5 million from a consortium of Boston banks, with the loan guaranteed by the state of Vermont. Another local bank financed the $400,000 purchase loan, which was backed by an 87.5

percent U.S. Small Business Administration guarantee. In March 1976, VAG assumed ownership of the mine and mill.

In 1976, the company's annual gross sales totaled about $8 million; profits were over $1 million, double those under GAF. A series of strikes in Canadian mines and increasing demand doubled asbestos prices and made VAG an extremely profitable venture. It was discovered that the deposits in the mine would last twenty years, not six or seven as first believed. The miners hired a well-known accountant as the company president; the board of directors included seven union men, seven management people, and a state legislator. An annual meeting of stockholders voted on management decisions. The distinction between blue and white collar workers did not vanish with employee ownership, however. Although 78 percent of the stock was originally owned by the employees, these included over thirty "white hats" (inplant management and foremen). One "white hat" alone bought 100 of the 2,000 shares. "White hats" continued to direct the operation, both through their supervisory roles on the job and through their dominance on the fifteen-member board of directors. For members of the United Cement, Lime and Gypsum Workers Local 338, bargaining for higher wages and benefits continued as usual. Even so, the union had supported the idea of buying the mine since the inception of the scheme. The payoff for hourly workers in the last three years has been great. Besides a fortyfold increase in the value of shares, from $50 to more than $2,000, working conditions have improved with the EPA-mandated equipment, and three one-year contracts have brought wage and benefit increases of about 15 percent per year. Workers now get 100 percent company-paid insurance, more paid holidays, and sick days. Most workers agree that their power as part owners is responsible for the good contracts.

Many workers, however, became dissatisfied and bitter about their lack of influence as shareholders over policy decisions by the board of directors. Twice in one year (1977), shareholders' votes failed to back company expenditures to build a new wallboard plant in neighboring Morrisville. The plant would have used waste rock from the mine. Most workers supported the plan but wanted VAG to supply only 50 percent of the $1.5 million cost of the plant. When the board could not get the desired financing from the banks or the state and went ahead with the project anyway, many shareholders were furious. Profits had fallen 44 percent in 1977 to $900,000 with an ease in the asbestos shortage, and the miners were concerned that, as new EPA demands were made and expenditures for the wallboard plant increased, the company could be caught short of cash.

Another bone of contention was the directors' rejection of an offer by a group of businessmen to buy VAG for more than $2,300 per share, despite an informal poll of shareholders showing that most were interested in pursuing the sale. The sparse minutes of directors' meetings did little to increase the workers' trust, and directors were reluctant to admit or defend their unpopular decisions face to face. John Lupien resigned as chairman of the board in March 1978, and the board fired John Hammang, the original president (apparently because he favored a go-slow position on the wallboard plant)—again, much to the disgust of many of the worker-shareholders.

The conflicts came to a head on April 8, 1978, at an eight-hour annual meeting. VAG shareholders rejected the incumbent directors, who supported a continuance of the original (1975) form of employee ownership, and elected a new slate headed by Howard Manosh, self-made businessman and owner of the construction company building the wallboard plant. Hammang was elected to the new board and named vice-president, while Manosh became chairman and president. Manosh had previously tried to buy all the stock of the company and had accumulated about 13 percent ownership. By the time of the stockholders' meeting, employees controlled only 58 percent of the stock.[12]

Although the election of the new slate appeared to be a rejection of employee ownership, the issue was more one of choice between two groups of management. VAG never operated as a cooperative, but rather as a largely employee-owned company with worker representatives on the board. That board apparently did not represent workers' wishes very accurately. It is likely that VAG will now function more like a traditional company, with Manosh making most of the decisions, but with a number of employees still sitting on the board of directors. The union will have to fight harder for gains in contract negotiations, but the power of top management will be limited by the large number of employee shareholders—shareholders already accustomed to participating in the reorganization of the company hierarchy.

On the one hand, the first three years of the VAG experiment were a great success: they demonstrated that in a *viable* industry (even if the degree of its viability came as a great surprise to all involved) employee ownership is a real alternative to a plant shutdown. As far as workers' control is concerned, however, the results are more ambivalent: the workers seem to have developed a pride in their right to know what management is doing and to have a voice in what happens to profits; but the experience of bickering and inconclusive meetings convinced many of them that a system with "180 bosses" cannot work. The experiment brought home the fact that employee ownership and work place democracy are not one and the same.

The Meriden Cooperative

With the decline of the British motorcycle industry in the late 1960s and early 1970s, a number of British motorcycle manufacturers began to go under. The industry was reorganized in 1973, and management, with government financial help, began to rationalize British bike production. As part of that rationalization, it was announced in September 1973 that the Triumph plant near Meriden would be closed, and that the motorcycles being produced there would be manufactured at two other plants. The 1,750 workers at Meriden were given no warning of the closing, and they did not go along with it even though other jobs were available in the Coventry area. Instead of allowing Meriden to be phased out over a five-month period, 800 of the workers occupied the plant and refused to leave. The Conservative government convinced management not to evict the workers, apparently because it feared such an action might provoke a mass walkout from factories in the Coventry area.

In October 1973, with no resolution of the occupation in sight, the workers began to develop an alternative to plant closure. Dealers in the United States felt they could sell 2,000 Bonnevilles a month, and the workers thought they could produce them more efficiently than the old management. So they suggested that a producers' cooperative be created. Negotiations between the workers, management, and government lasted for more than a year. Deals were almost completed only to fall through as management held out for more. When the Labour Party came to power, the workers—who had occupied the plant for eighteen months—were rewarded with a government loan to the cooperative to purchase Meriden Triumph from its owners for 4.2 million pounds. Ironically, the long delay in completing the transaction after the February 1974 elections was caused by union opposition to the scheme. Motorcycle production workers in other plants were especially opposed, since they felt such a move put their own jobs in jeopardy. Ultimately they agreed, and the cooperative was formed.

Meriden is an unusual cooperative arrangement. The workers do not own shares in the plant directly; instead, three shares are held in trust and are voted by three trustees on behalf of the worker "beneficiaries." For any action to be taken, at least half of the workers must meet, and three-quarters of those meeting must favor the action.

In 1975, everyone received the same pay—50 pounds per week—including managers, engineers, and office workers. Policy decisions are made by eight directors, elected from each of the eight unions in the plant. In addition, the plant manager sits with the directors to ensure harmony between everyday managerial decisions and board decisions.

The eight-person committee is responsible for all major decisions in the plant, though financial decisions customarily are referred to the workers' assembly. Each of the 280 workers who remained in the plant until the end of the negotiations has five votes in this assembly. New workers (the original 800 who conducted the September 1973 occupation were given first priority in hiring) get one vote after one year's work in the plant and an additional vote for every year they work, up to five years.

The fact that the workers themselves do not own individual shares allows employees to be hired and fired without the complication of determining their role as "absentee stockholders" after they leave the plant. In any case, the one-year probation period provides time to test the skills and attitudes of new members, and most workers believe that once their newer colleagues become members there will be little need to fire. In fact, unlike firms concerned primarily with return to capital, Meriden's management expanded the company slowly up to a "reasonable" long-term capacity of 750 workers precisely to avoid the necessity for personnel cutbacks in the future.

The management of the firm, though appointed by the directors, is responsible directly to the workers for its policies. The plant is operated on the honor system: workers punch a time clock only to comply with insurance requirements that there be a record of who is working on a given day. The demarcation between jobs has disappeared; workers clean up after themselves; jobs are rotated; some teach their jobs to others. The incentive to do a sloppy job in order to create more work is gone. Since jobs are essentially guaranteed and pay is equal, the incentive to perform higher quality work results from pride in the product, the desire for peer approval, and the idea that, if everyone does a good job, everyone will benefit.

The cooperative has survived a series of crises since it began operation in March 1975. The agreement that had been reached between the workers, the management of Norton-Villiers-Triumph (NVT) (who represented the plant owners), and the Labour government gave the co-op very little working capital and pinned it under a marketing arrangement that gave NVT complete control of sales at home and abroad. But by late 1975, only six months after the co-op started production, NVT was in serious financial difficulty because of the U.S. recession and Japanese price cutting. The British government's Department of Industry, which previously had backed the Meriden-NVT deal, now rebuffed NVT by withdrawing its export credits. The question became one of whether or not Triumph-Meriden would be dragged down with NVT.

By the end of 1976 the co-op was in desperate need of money. It had suffered a loss of 1 million pounds that year; NVT's distribution and sales operation was almost nonexistent once it ceased building the Triumph Trident; and NVT was not buying the motorcycles Meriden produced, even though it was contracted to do so. Financial difficulties raised another, divisive issue: were Meriden's problems caused by poor management? Was the cooperative too egalitarian? Were professional managers, hired from the outside on managerial pay scales, necessary to save the workers' jobs? Dennis Johnson and Bill Lapworth, two of the chief organizers of the Meriden occupation, thought not; eventually, both resigned from the board over the issue, believing that the co-op had made too many compromises with its fundamental cooperative ideology.

But financial needs settled the issue in favor of professional management. Geoffrey Robinson from Jaguar, an industry representative who had supported the co-op from early on, convinced the Department of Industry to buy out NVT's marketing operation for Meriden, and the General Electric Company (of England) to provide a 1-million-pound loan to purchase Meriden's stock of 2,000 unsold bikes. At the same time, the 700 Meriden workers voted to lay themselves off for six weeks while the situation was sorted out. All this occurred in February 1977. By May, the 2,000 bikes were sold on the home market, General Electric was repaid its 1 million pounds, and the Meriden workers were back on the job. GE's involvement was supposed to be marginal, but it provided free advice and had considerable influence on co-op policies, including the shift to professional management. Co-op members now hire five employees who are paid professional salaries and are not members of the co-op: a managing director, a chief accountant, an engineer, a quality control manager, and a sales manager. GE advisers also tried to institute a permanent wage break between highly skilled and other workers, primarily through a differential bonus scheme. While all workers would be paid an equal flat wage, the weekly bonus for skilled workers would be higher. The members rejected the differential bonus scheme in February 1978, however; all workers still receive the same weekly wage, including bonuses. The flat rate is now 68 pounds per week, and with some overtime—which is voluntary—as well as bonuses, members receive almost 85 pounds weekly, *every week.*

Thus, workers at Meriden seem to have compromised somewhat on the strong principle of egalitarianism to which they adhered when the occupation was first over. Whether the hiring of permanent management was necessary for production and marketing efficiency is still arguable. Workers participate less in management than they would have if Dennis Johnson had had his way. On the other hand, the co-op has survived some very bad times, and did so while maintaining considerable direct worker control. It is now the only motorcycle plant in Britain and, at least in the home market, the Bonneville is presently the leading make of bike in the 750 cc class, outselling both Suzuki and Honda in the first five months of 1978. The plant produces about 350 bikes weekly and employs 720 workers. As predicted in 1975, employment has slowly expanded: once workers are hired, they tend to stay and become co-op members.[13]

In view of the general demise of the British motorcycle industry and the withdrawal of broad government support, Meriden's survival is impressive. It can be explained largely by the commitment of the co-op members to their jobs and their product. It is also evident from the Meriden case just how important is government involvement in this type of undertaking. The co-op came about because the entire industry was brought to its knees by shortsighted, inept owners and managers. And when the government turned to an entrepreneur such as Dennis Poore, head of Maganese Bronze and the epitome of success in the private sector, his solution was shutdowns rather than revival. If anything, the workers saved the remnants of British motorcycle glory; but they could not have done it without public help.

This point is reinforced by the behavior of the Conservative government elected in 1979, which almost immediately demanded repayment of the government loans to Meriden. Geoffrey Robinson, chief executive of the co-op, sought financial backing from European motorcycle manufacturers, and the work force agreed to introduce early retirement for workers between 60 and 65. Lack of government support may, in the end, spell the co-op's demise.

Lip Watches

The original Lip watch factory in Besançon, France, produced high-quality watches; it employed skilled craftsmen and had a minimal internal hierarchy. In 1960, the Lip family opened a new plant; watch production was more mechanized, and the plant had two new divisions—machine tools and precision instruments for weapons. With the opening of the new plant, unionization increased. Two unions organized the plant: the Confédération Générale du Travail (CGT, close to the Communist Party) and the Confédération Française Démocratique du Travail (CFDT, aligned with the Socialist Party).

By 1965, Lip was doing badly. It had failed to respond to the competitive pressure of cheaper watches turned out by mechanized processes in Japan and the United States. Faced with increasing financial difficulties, Fred Lip sold shares in his business to a Swiss watch company. By 1971, the Swiss group owned 42 percent of the shares, and the Lips sold out completely. The new management planned to convert the factory into an assembly plant for parts made in Switzerland, and to eliminate the weaponry and machine-tool divisions. Such a move involved considerable layoffs. But at the first attempt to release workers, in 1971, the Swiss were met with resistance and backed down.

In April 1973, the new owners asked for the resignation of their own director at Lip and filed for bankruptcy. Two professional managers were designated, who in turn announced that there could be no employment guarantees and that the enterprise itself might be closed down. The workers reacted by forming their own internal organization, independent of both management and the unions, and by carrying out production slowdowns and partial work stoppages to force management into discussions. Finally, the population of Besançon and, later, of all of France became involved in the conflict. On June 12, to find out what management's plan was, workers confined the two administrators and several supervisors in their offices. Company files disclosed the proposed 1971 scenario, including the layoff of 500 workers. A general assembly of all workers was convened and voted to conceal the entire stock of watches "as guarantee of continued employment" and, later, to occupy the factory "to safeguard our tools." As one observer of *L'affair Lip* wrote:

> The conflict no longer had a single uni-dimensional structure. Although the employment issue remained very much at the core, the entire question of ownership and control—in particular the crucial issue of the relationship between property rights and the workers' right to information—came to be at stake. . . . It is for these reasons that in order to guarantee their employment, they had decided to "control by seizure" (but not to claim ownership of) their tools, the factory and the products of their past labor which they felt had been "invested" in the enterprise.[14]

On August 14, 1973, two months after the workers' takeover, 3,000 riot police broke into the plant to evict the workers. Key items of the factory's machinery had already been moved, however, and the workers used this equipment in clandestine workshops to continue production. At the same time, the French government began to negotiate with trade union representatives. These negotiations resulted in the Giraud plan, which proposed a layoff of 160 workers, closing of the machine-tool division, and elimination of most of the benefits won by workers since 1968. But the workers' general assembly rejected this compromise by almost four to one on October 12. The Giraud plan represented the government's attempt to use the unions as a means to divide the workers against each other and to weaken greatly the autonomous organizational structure in the plant. Although the workers rejected the plan, it split the two unions—the CGT and the CFDT—with the former urging adoption of the plan, and the latter opposing it.

The final negotiations were engineered by the trade union representatives under the direct supervision of their national leaders and "progressive" industrialists. On January 29, 1974, the compromise plan (known as the Neuschwander plan) was accepted overwhelmingly by the workers, although it called for the rehiring of only 300 workers. This plan, however, provided for a long-term, financially sound enterprise supported by two French industrial giants, and it stipulated that, if Lip's performance were satisfactory, 500 more workers would be rehired on September 1. Unemployed workers would receive education and training. No wage ceilings were specified, and the plan provided for workers' control over employment issues.

Ultimately, the major French economic actors were drawn into the Lip conflict: the big unions, industrial interests, and the government all had a stake in the settlement. Lip threatened to boil over into something uncontrollable, endangering basic French capitalist institutions. "These additional parties to the initial conflict—rather than the Action Committee and Lip management—dominated the game in the final phase and, of course, played an instrumental role in shaping the eventual settlement."[15]

By autumn 1975, Lip did, in fact, employ more than 900 workers and produced the same range of products as before the takeover (precision instruments for weapons and machine tools in addition to watches). But this "normal" situation was to be short-lived. The workers' victory in this single enterprise could not overcome the broader difficulties of the French watch industry. Solution of those problems would have required the support of the government as well as of financial institutions in rationalizing the industry as a whole; neither was forthcoming in sufficient quantity. There is also evidence that Lip's new management set its sights too high in 1974, attempting to produce an expanded line of watches and enter the car clock business, all at the same time. The recession of late 1975 and 1976 in France provided the final push; Lip's directors filed for bankruptcy in April 1976.

These were important reasons—though not the only ones—that influenced the workers' decision to reoccupy the plant on May 5, just two days after a Paris court approved the liquidation of Lip's assets. Unlike Triumph's workers, however, who saw themselves primarily as artisans committed to producing a great motorcycle, *les Lip* were much more politically oriented; they viewed their struggle as the struggle of the French worker against the large corporations and a central government which supports those corporations against worker interests. At Meriden, the occupiers were committed to saving their jobs, but were unwilling to tie themselves to a political movement for workers' rights or the reform of production relations; on the contrary, they saw their only chance for success to lie in separating themselves from any affiliation with the Left. In that sense, they were probably correct; but, at the same time, their achievement has had little impact on the British worker's consciousness, or on Britain's political configuration.

The Lip strategy was completely the opposite: the watch workers believed that their only hope lay in bringing the force of the French Left and the organized working class to bear on their own case. The months following the reoccupation were therefore marked by *la lutte*—the struggle. *Les Lip* opened their doors to the public (there were 60,000 visitors in May alone) and to union meetings, and themselves attended meetings all over France. They also undertook "actions" such as decorating the Belfort-Paris express train with posters, pamphleting vacationers at the nearby Swiss border, and—with workers from the Peugeot bicycle factory (who had also occupied their plant in protest of layoffs)—delaying the start of the famous Tour de France bicycle race at Valentigney. All this time, they were also holding press conferences and meetings with representatives of the government and the court-appointed liquidators.[16]

Living off unemployment insurance and the production of various articles sold to their sympathizers, the workers won what they considered to be important victories, including election of a Socialist mayor in Besançon and court delays in the order to liquidate Lip's assets. By the fall of 1977, the workers began to anticipate a victory by the left-wing coalition in the March 1978 legislative elections. With such a victory, they expected renewed support for a solution to their situation and to the decline of the French watch industry. In November, Lip's worker assembly, which had been meeting constantly during the occupation, decided to present formal plans for a cooperative, an association of workers who would buy the plant from its former stockholders.

Why did *les Lip* wait nineteen months to choose this alternative? The answer lies in political ideology: they had considered themselves fundamentally workers and, in a capitalist society, their principal undertaking was a struggle *against* owners and ownership, not a struggle to *become* owners. They wanted to preserve their jobs as *workers,* while at the same time curtailing the prerogatives and rights of their employers. As members of a cooperative, they feared a change of identity and perhaps a change in relations with the rest of the French working class. In the fall of 1977, two factors altered this strategy: first, no "acceptable" offer for Lip had been received; second, the impending victory of the left-wing coalition—which would put considerable government power in the hands of Socialists and Communists—meant that a worker-owned plant could be in the vanguard of a transfer of control to workers themselves. The cooperative could serve as an example for other worker takeovers within the context of rising leftist influence and power. In fact, in 1974-75, over 200 factory occupations were recorded in France, inspired in content and style by the Lip example.[17] At the same time, a leftist coalition government—to judge from statements by Mitterand and Marchais—would be committed to the reorganization and support of the French watch industry. Indeed, on March 9, just several days before the election, both the Socialists and the Communists presented their plans for the development of watch manufacturing in the region.

The cooperative plan presented put great emphasis on actual control of day-to-day and larger decisions by the workers themselves. This was a natural reflection of the type of decision making already in effect at Lip since the 1973 occupation. All directors were to be elected by the different sections of the plant, and subproduction units would elect representatives who would be directly responsible to these smaller groups of workers. The initial capital of the cooperative was set at 1 million francs. The city of Besançon (controlled by the Socialist Party) had already offered to buy the buildings and grounds of the plant, and the CFDT—the largest of the three unions at the plant—had filed against the liquidation of Lip's assets, pending since September. The name "Lip" could not be used for the cooperative, since that trademark was controlled by Swiss private capital, so the workers chose "Les Industries de Palente" (LIP). They began to raise the 1 million francs by subscription.

The Left did not win the election; the loss was a great blow to the Lip workers' hopes. The directors in charge of Lip's liquidation subsequently rejected Besançon's offer, arguing that "nothing solid had been proposed and no serious document had been introduced." But despite everything, the workers continued to search for a solution. When one of the authors visited the plant in June 1978, the workers were on the verge of presenting their second co-op proposal and were committed to that strategy even with a procorporate government in power. "We know that we have to be more economist than political, and we will not win under the flag of worker control. Without contradicting ourselves at all, we decided to show that we can handle all the economic and financial questions," a shop steward told *Le Monde*.[18] The proposal called for a relatively small plant assembling inexpensive watches, including quartz timepieces, and producing precision parts under subcontract to other firms. Algeria has already signed two contracts with the workers, the first to set up a watch factory as soon as the co-op is under way. Sixteen French firms have also ordered precision pieces, and Djibuti and Vietnam are talking about projects for the future. The proposed plant would ultimately employ 600 workers, beginning with 200 and adding 100 workers each year.

Both Lip and Meriden show that job preservation struggles clearly have strategic value: they may end up preserving jobs and they define the issues of production and property rights in a corporate society in ways that every worker can understand. They are basic grass-roots "revolutionary" movements to change worker-employer relations, and, as such, they have the tremendous advantage of local control and individual involvement in decision making—economic democracy from the bottom up. But the two factory occupations—carried out in two very different political situations—also show that such actions alone cannot achieve change, and may not even succeed at the plant level without organized mass movements able to gain at least some control of the government. In England, the initial factory at Meriden was predicated on the presence of an active Left in the Labour Party, with cabinet representation. Without the support of industry minister Anthony Wedgwood-Benn, it is doubtful whether the deal would ever have gone through. In France, *les Lip* triumphed and then survived because of the national power of the French Left, the direct support of Socialist and Communist unions, and the Socialist administration at the municipality level. This dependence was made clear by the results of the March 1978 elections: a divided and weaker Left put the Lip workers in peril.

Worker Control and Productivity, Employment, Income Distribution, and Worker Well-Being

Do worker-controlled firms maintain or improve worker productivity? A large body of data indicates that they can do as well as or better than individually or managerially controlled enterprises. The case of the northwest plywood factories, for example, shows that productivity in the co-ops can be higher than in traditional enterprises. This fact was recognized by the IRS when it ruled that co-ops could pay wages higher than the industry average (the IRS was concerned that the firms charged these higher wages as higher costs of production). And there is a consensus in existing studies that productivity is enhanced in firms where worker "participation" is introduced. The extent of the positive effects depends on the importance and intensity of worker involvement in the decision-making process.[19]

Poor management in marketing and the purchase of raw materials and other outputs could in practice offset this higher productivity. So it could be argued that co-ops may be more efficient in terms of worker productivity but much less efficient in terms of management. Yet all the cases we reviewed seem to indicate the opposite. The plywood co-ops have been able to take over failing private enterprises and make them pay; reports of management efficiency in Mondragon are all positive; even in a declining industry like British motorcycles, Meriden's cooperatively controlled management has been able to keep the firm ahead of its dying British competition; and in the deteriorating Vermont asbestos situation, management's principal shortcoming was not company inefficiency in the traditional sense, but failure to trust and carry out the decisions of worker assemblies as well as failure to communicate to members the decisions of the board of directors. If anything, management efficiency of co-ops is questionable in nonpecuniary areas rather than in the maximization of income and profits. Achieving cooperation among workers and between workers and their selected management is as difficult a managerial task as achieving high production and sales.

In one important way, cooperatives do not have to be as efficient in generating profits as do capitalist firms. Worker-owned and -operated firms can maximize *income*, not profits. This means that a co-op may continue to operate even when a capitalist firm chooses to close because the rate of return to capital is too low. The co-op has to make enough over the long term to pay its members a decent wage and cover capital depreciation and interest. A traditional capitalist firm is interested in reducing wages relative to productivity and investing where the return is highest. The co-op will maintain employment through difficult economic times, whereas the traditional capitalist firm will begin laying off workers at a certain point in the recession (where labor's marginal cost exceeds turnover cost). For corporations, recessions are periods of labor-capital rationalization; for co-ops, they are periods of devising ways to occupy the members and maintain their wages.

Yet, while worker ownership certainly would tend to stabilize employment in comparison with corporate capitalism, income maximization probably would produce a lower growth rate for individual firms and for the economy as a whole. The return to capital would be lower, since workers would continue to operate lower-return firms rather than close them and invest in more lucrative possibilities elsewhere. Capital would be tied much more to *groups of people,* less willing to move than a single entrepreneur and much less willing to shift capital around than the depersonalized centralized accounting system of a large corporation. One of the central tenets of capitalism—the movement of capital to the most lucrative prospect—would be fundamentally altered. The provision of stable employment in a particular geographic location is a principal use of capital under cooperative arrangements.

Other reasons why worker-owned firms may not expand as rapidly as private firms include the fact that workers tend to view capital investment in new machinery as detrimental to employment in general and their employment in particular; and workers tend to take profits in the form of increased wages rather than reinvest them, even if profits are as high or higher than in private capital firms. This was certainly part of the debate at Vermont Asbestos over investment in the wallboard plant.

Worker-owned firms should face no contradiction between investment and jobs: worker-owners are guaranteed work even if machines are introduced. An investment that maximizes worker income would be in the clear interest of the worker-owners even if it reduces the amount of work necessary in that particular part of the production process.

In Mondragon, investment is high; however, this is largely because of the initial agreements concluded between the co-ops and the Caja Laboral. These agreements were made by each co-op's workers assembly. Workers' preferences are less clear. Espinosa and Zimbalist, two researchers, found in Chile that "contrary to the hypothesis of those who assert that worker-managed enterprises will distribute more earnings in the form of wages and, consequently, underinvest, participation was found to be significantly correlated with investment."[20]

The possibly lower growth rate in a cooperative economy might expand employment less rapidly than in the present system. But the slower growth rate and its resultant effect on employment could be offset by the greater labor intensiveness of production under producer cooperative than under the present system, and the slower but more stable increase in employment (fewer and less intense downturns) in the long run. With worker-controlled firms, the possibly lower rate of capital formation could still represent as high a rate of *domestic* capital formation. Worker-controlled firms would be very unlikely to invest their capital overseas in runaway shops. Moreover, workers in worker-controlled firms are less likely to engage in strikes (against themselves) and other economically destructive actions.

The interest in job preservation and job stability may reflect a shift in American values. Workers may be tired of being relocated or of having to migrate to follow capital. Certainly, job stability and full employment have always been principal worker demands. There seems to be a subtle drift toward accepting lower growth rates in exchange for greater job security and more meaningful work. The Depression generation is gradually leaving the labor force to be replaced by a generation of workers who have known difficulties but not hunger and fear of long-term poverty. The need to increase consumption rapidly may very well be replaced by the need for stable but varied employment within the enterprise in worker-owned firms. Given the possibility of world resource shortages, slower growth in the United States appears likely, and worker-controlled firms promising stable, but perhaps slower, growth may have great attraction.

Even in an economy dominated by producer cooperatives, worker-owned firms would not be the only source of investment funds or investment decisions. As we outlined in previous chapters, our alternative economic policies include public investment either in co-ops or in public enterprises as well as some form of democratic planning. Worker ownership of enterprises would lead to slower growth rates only to the extent that the public sector failed to intervene in the cooperative market system or to the extent that co-ops fully controlled public investment. Further, even if worker enterprises did control public funds, in a cooperative society where investment was publicly controlled, workers could choose to expand *employment* rapidly even if this would be accomplished through projects that did not yield as high a return to capital as under the present system. In Mondragon, for example, given Basque social values, the choice *is* apparently for greater employment rather than maximization of income for those already employed.

Whether this would be true in the United States is

more doubtful unless cooperation led to a less competitive consciousness among American workers. Neither the plywood co-ops nor the Vermont Asbestos case *proves* how workers would behave given the choice between higher profits (income) and increased employment.

There is no doubt, however, as to the wage (income) distribution effect of cooperatives. In each of the cases reported here, if the worker-owned enterprises did not make wages completely uniform, they at least equalized them significantly compared with capitalist-owned firms and even with the public bureaucracy. In the plywood factories, Meriden, Mondragon, and Lip, the salary ratios between the highest- and lowest-paid workers or managers were very low compared with traditional firms. In some cases, everyone, including managers, was paid the same salary. In others, the manager and some specialized, nonmember workers were the only ones paid a higher rate—the rest had equal salaries.* Low managerial salaries in some cooperatives were compensated by participation in an exciting movement—a cause.

From all available evidence, worker ownership and operation of enterprises would definitely produce a more equal distribution of income than now exists in capitalist societies such as the United States, or even social democratic Sweden. The rules of distribution simply are different in cooperative production than in capitalist production. Apparently, the different rules do not have a significant negative effect on productivity. The experience of the plywood factories, Mondragon, and Meriden bear this out. It

---

*The Vermont Asbestos Group, which never took on a truly cooperative status, failed to deal with this issue, as well as with the issue of whether there should be directors separate from the workers. The results of this failure proved harmful to the continued operation of the enterprise under a worker ownership arrangement.

appears that, the greater the participation of workers in the enterprise, the greater the equalization of the wage structure.

The employment, income distribution, and productivity effects of producer cooperatives are all important positive contributions to workers' economic well-being. But what about the effect of producer co-ops and economic democracy—worker participation—in nonpecuniary areas? Do worker-managers obtain more social services on and from their jobs? Does self-management make workers feel better about their work and about themselves?

When workers own and operate enterprises, they consciously protect their health and safety, and generally contribute part of their surplus or potential surplus to investment in themselves. The Mondragon cooperatives contribute to worker social security and other benefits, as well as community education; the plywood factories retrain workers who are made obsolete by new machinery and provide free lunches, full medical and dental care, and company-paid life insurance. Meriden workers have voted themselves extensive benefits, including free life insurance; even at Vermont Asbestos, worker benefits increased rapidly under worker ownership. In the short-lived Chilean worker-operated enterprises, researchers found that typical investments in the area of social services (representing about 1 percent of total investments) included:

improvements in working conditions (e.g., ventilators, heating, elimination of gases, noise level reduction); acquisition of work clothes, gloves, goggles and so on for the workers; improvements in hygienic and sanitary conditions (baths, kitchens, etc.); construction of a new or expansion of an old cafeteria; formation of consumer cooperatives; rest homes or summer houses; building of sports grounds; construction of day care centers in factories with a sizable number of female workers; installation of medical, dental, or first aid clinics and the purchase of ambulances ...

initiation of various cultural activities . . . and the provision
of liberal arts, administration, and technical courses to the
workers.[21]

In worker-managed firms, workers are more likely
to teach each other skills because job security and
relative wage equality reduce the competition for
promotion. Meriden workers stressed this point repeatedly. Job rotation and cooperation among workers greatly increased responsibilities *within* the plant.
These general benefits add to the kinds of worker
training investments made in Mondragon and Chile.

Workers *do* feel better about their work if their
participation controls decision making in the firm. In
the cases of the plywood factories, Meriden, Lip, and
Vermont Asbestos, observers noted that workers were
generally enthusiastic about the participatory basis of
the firm. Various reports point out how much better
workers feel about working under a worker-own-
ership-participation system than in the traditional
capitalist firm. Workers in the plywood firms had
comments such as the following:

I don't think I'd ever give it up. . . . It's been good to me
and it's . . . There's a certain feeling to know that you own
part of what you're working for. I mean it's better than
working for somebody else. . . . I've always gone to all the
stockholders meetings and . . . I enjoy it.

I've never had so much fun!
Hell, we run this operation all by ourselves.[22]

The attitudes toward work of the 260 workers
interviewed in the co-op plywood factories contrasted
markedly with those of more than 150 workers interviewed in conventional plants. According to Greenberg:

This overall sense that we are our own bosses, that we are
the people who run the enterprise, and that in addition to

making a decent living at it, we are also enjoying ourselves, is a complex of themes mentioned spontaneously by many of the shareholders. . . .

Not surprisingly, while there remains a great deal of variation among the shareholders in their rates of participation, the pervasive participatory environment of these places fosters an extremely strong sense of collective responsibility and mutuality.[23]

The comments of workers at Meriden were similar to those of employees at the plywood plants, except that they also reflected an eighteen-month struggle:

Nowadays we've got no gaffers. You come in and start to work and there's nobody watching you. You seem to get more done. Of course, we have our little grumblers: it wouldn't be right if we didn't.

The comradeship was fantastic. We all felt we were fighting for an ideal of showing that we could make bikes and make a profit. Nowadays, if we have a problem, it is a common enemy for us all to solve. . . . A lot of management is about accepting the responsibility to make a decision, and that's not too difficult if you've got the facts in front of you.[24]

Although the feelings at Vermont Asbestos certainly are more mixed because of the strained relations between workers and management, even there at least some workers expressed positive feelings about worker ownership:

It's a good feeling to be able to say we own this company. . . . One share doesn't make much difference, but I feel a part of things.[25]

In writing of Chile's worker-controlled sector during the Allende regime (a somewhat, but not totally, different case from those in other capitalist societies), Espinosa and Zimbalist reported that informal conversations with workers revealed a clear preference for the new participative system as well as a strong sense of liberation, new-found dignity, and pride. They quote a foundry production worker:

In general there was a qualitative change in human relationships. The executives and technicians attended the worker assemblies with everyone else—and their vote wasn't worth more than that of a worker. We were all "workers" with different functions—but the difference in functions didn't define social privilege. It was a birth of a new sort of society—the reflection of our hopes and aspirations.[26]

Worker-controlled firms are as productive as—sometimes even more productive than—traditional capitalist enterprises. When workers own and manage production, they have more equal wage distribution and steadier employment, and they feel better about their work. These factors are obviously related: when workers have more equal wage distribution and steady work and pay, they tend to feel better about their jobs; and when they feel better about their jobs, they show higher productivity. Workers' feelings about their work and their productivity, however, are not necessarily causally related; that is, productivity can rise because worker ownership provides more direct material incentive to produce more. Working itself may be just as painful and unsatisfying. But improved satisfaction through even minimal increases in participation in nonworker-owned firms also improves productivity; a number of studies have reported cases in which a small degree of participation at the shop floor level has yielded positive results. Increased well-being and satisfaction do increase worker productivity.

Worker ownership or management tends to change the nature of supervision and to reduce absenteeism and time wasting. It has been alleged that, without rigid authority, worker discipline will deteriorate. But most evidence shows that worker management is perfectly capable of disciplining its co-participants or members. As one plywood worker told an interviewer:

And if somebody . . . is goofing off . . . you can holler over there and tell him, "Let's get going here." You know, frankly, we're all watching each other so that nobody else is goofing off too much.[27]

Once the sanction of immediate dismissal is removed, it has been argued, there will be a tendency for workers to stay out of work for the slightest illness, to remain home even when not sick, to hold meetings to discuss every problem—all with little fear of being fired. But, again, absenteeism seems to be lower in worker-owned and -operated firms, largely because the material incentives (albeit collective material incentives) and responsibility for higher output are great. Even *some* participation in decisions and profit-sharing seems to reduce absenteeism. The 400 workers at the luxurious Plaza Athenée Hotel in Paris seized control in 1968 to prevent its conversion into a Hilton-type operation. Once they settled with the new owners, elected their own manager, and obtained a profit-sharing plan, absenteeism and turnover—two of the greatest problems in the hotel business—practically ceased to exist.

Yet, like all organizations, worker-owned or -managed firms must face the difficulties of interpersonal conflict in a work situation. A study now under way by the Center for Economic Studies in Palo Alto, California, is finding that commercial credit and interpersonal conflict are the two greatest problems of small U.S. producer co-ops. No matter how much pride a worker may have in his or her work, personal conflict with other workers or managers does affect well-being on the job. Unlike in traditional capitalist firms, in co-ops such difficulties cannot be solved easily by firing or threatening to fire people. Co-ops must be effective in *settling* interpersonal problems rather than eliminating workers from the firm. In a larger plant this is part of efficient management. In a smaller group, where all members participate in management, an understanding of dynamic group relations assumes particular importance. Therefore, in a more democratic economy, the whole nature of management changes. Clearly, new schools of democratic management will be needed to help resolve questions of nonauthoritarian business enterprise.

Worker Ownership in a Capitalist Society?

A worker control movement is an essential part of economic democracy and of greater political participation in American society. But if such a movement is to be part of a strategy for reform, we must know how worker-managed firms can survive in the context of a U.S. corporate economy, and—even if they do survive—how they can contribute to a movement toward a worker/consumer-controlled economy.

The experiences of workers in the plants we have discussed give us important insights into the worker-control process in capitalist societies. Workers in each of these societies are, after all, a product of the society. When they form a cooperative, or take over ownership, or even occupy a plant for a long time, they are attempting to secure employment as well as material and nonmaterial benefits that are not provided by strictly capitalist firms.

In each society, however, workers do differ in their receptiveness to cooperation and in their political awareness of participation and of their overall social role toward other workers. In Mondragon, Basque nationalism, savings habits, and cooperative outlook play a crucial role in the success of the cooperative movement there. In France, Lip was just one—although the most important—of more than 200 worker takeovers in 1974-75. Lip workers are highly conscious of their role as members of a political movement to transform the French economy; to them, participation at the plant level is as much a political process as an attempt to preserve their specific jobs. U.S. workers have neither the cooperative outlook and nationalism of the Basques, nor the political consciousness of the French industrial worker. For this very important reason, worker control in the United States—either through the creation of co-ops or through worker takeovers to form co-ops—may be much more difficult to develop than in —Europe.

The key to positive results in worker-owned and -managed firms is participation in decision making. Participation does not guarantee financial success, which often depends on market conditions beyond the workers' control; but it does improve productivity, help workers solve production and financial problems, and increase their commitment to each other. The greater the emphasis on nonmaterial, or cooperative, goals by those engaging in the project, the greater the likelihood that a financially successful operation will continue as a co-op. This is easier to say than to do. Although the plywood co-ops began with workers steeped in cooperative traditions from another society (Sweden) and even though members today appreciate the advantages of cooperation, they have done little to continue that tradition in the next generation of potential workers. Vermont Asbestos, moreover, is an illustration of worker-owned enterprise that was successful in its primary objective of preserving jobs but rapidly degenerated into noncooperation and into a capitalist-worker hierarchy.

Participation itself is not easy to achieve. Espinosa and Zimbalist found that, in Chilean firms socialized during the Allende period (1970-73), the most important variables explaining worker participation were the ideology and attitude toward participation of leaders in the factory, and worker ideology regarding worker control. Variables such as the social and bureaucratic organization of the firm, the technology used in the firm, and workers' formal education were all statistically insignificant or weak correlates of participation.

The centrality of ideology in participation suggests the difficulty of establishing successful producer cooperatives within a capitalist society, particularly the United States. If long-term success is taken to indicate a strong consciousness of participation and a commitment to it, then the evidence shows that worker-owned and -managed firms which emphasize primarily job preservation or financial gain tend to degenerate. For one thing, each such enterprise or group of workers views itself in isolation from other workers engaged in worker-ownership ventures. Rather than relating to a common ground of cooperation, participation, or work-place democracy, they relate principally to other capitalist institutions—banks, wholesalers, suppliers. Managers tend to emphasize *only* financial success, since it is only such success which is demanded by these other institutions.

The process and context of job preservation take on special importance with regard to workers' ideology and the subsequent structure and operation of a firm that is converted into a cooperative. If workers simply *buy* the firm (even with some difficulty, as at Vermont Asbestos), the essentially capitalist nature of the transfer is preserved. The union can even continue to play its traditional role as bargaining agent for production workers. Workers are likely to press management for higher dividends (profit disbursement), since they view the enterprise largely in terms of wage benefits rather than as a long-term cooperative venture. Management focuses on profits rather than participation. But if, as in the case of Meriden or Lip, workers must confront corporate power in their efforts to preserve jobs, the quality of that experience may unite them as a *collective* entity with goals beyond their jobs or material gain.

This points to a second important element in the success or failure of worker control ventures: the way in which shares are held by the workers. Again, no matter how financially successful the firm, if each individual holds a transferable share, the tendency to sell those shares to outsiders is accentuated. Even if this is not allowed, as in the case of the plywood co-ops, the very success of the cooperative makes the price of the shares increasingly inaccessible to individuals. At the higher price, shareholder-workers view the culmination of their efforts to be selling out—to anybody. This makes it much more likely that the buyer will be a large, private corporation, able to purchase all shares at a price that benefits the present generation of co-op workers, but eliminates the possibility for the younger generation to work in that context.

European cooperatives generally do not grant shares or stock to members, but rather *rights* of membership, such as voting power and access to dividends. Retirement from the co-op may give the member accumulated savings, as in Mondragon, or retirement benefits based on a high percentage of the last years' salary level, as provided at Mondragon, Meriden, and in the proposed Lip plan. In Mondragon, new members are not even required to put up subscription money; shares are held in trust, and only the income of the trust belongs to the members. Membership may change, but the trust goes on. In spirit, this is the same concept behind Meriden and the proposed Lip cooperative.

It is not accidental that cooperatives in the United States (or an attempt at worker ownership, such as VAG) should make workers shareholders, not simply members of a cooperative. Much more than in Europe, American workers are still imbued with the wish to become capitalists, to see the value of their *capital* grow as a result of their efforts. Cooperation becomes a way of accumulating capital rather than merely assuring stable employment, good working conditions, decent wages, and control over the work place. As long as this capital-accumulation aspect is the central focus of the co-op and worker-takeover movement (every worker a capitalist), American cooperatives will face the type of problems encountered by the plywood firms and Vermont Asbestos: degeneration into private ownership in either the short or the long run. Ironically, the more financially successful the co-op, the greater the pressure on the workers to sell to private industry.

This does not mean that the formation of every producer co-op in the United States is motivated by the desire to accumulate capital. There are many smaller handicraft and service co-ops whose members entered into cooperative arrangements specifically to escape the strains of the conventional business world. According to Greenberg, who has studied these newer cooperatives:

Almost each and every one of these new cooperatives, whose business activities range from groceries, to woodworking, to baked goods, to health food outlets, to health clinics, and the like, were formed by small handfuls of people (several, with as few as *three*), almost all of whom were of upper-middle class and college educated background, active in either antiwar, ecology, or counterculture politics, with the explicit purpose of establishing businesses of a distinctly different type. That is to say, their motivations to form small cooperatives, businesses that would serve the community and provide a work environment devoid of the "hassles," hierarchy, and "rat race" of the conventional business world, were inherently political. While very few of these cooperatives hold to a specific and narrow political "line," each represents an attempt to create a work environment in which the normal internal politics and governance are altered into more democratic directions, and in which the goals of the enterprise include linkages to and concern for the surrounding community and its development.[28]

The principal drawback of these cooperatives is that their membership is rather transient, they tend to be very small, and they are hardly representative of the much larger, more complex enterprises employing most American workers. It is important that the cooperative emphasis of these small co-ops be transferred to the formation of industrial, agricultural, commercial, and service enterprises.

The third element in the success or failure of cooperatives is access to credit and good management advice. In Mondragon, this has been provided by the Mondragon co-op movement itself. The Caja Laboral provides a significant portion of the financing and technical assistance to groups of workers in the region wishing to form a cooperative. The bank is able to provide this service because of the capacity for savings in the region itself. (In this sense, the Caja Laboral operates in much the same way as the early savings and loan associations in the United States, except that savings and loan banks loaned to individuals for homebuilding.) In the plywood firms of the Northwest, worker subscriptions and loans from local banks (once the early co-ops showed success) financed the enterprises; professional managers were brought in to handle day-to-day operations. At Vermont Asbestos as well, worker-community subscriptions and private bank loans made it possible to buy the company, with the state of Vermont providing loan guarantees as well as help and planning advice. In all these cases, co-ops were formed in industries that turned out to have a viable market and growing demand (at Vermont Asbestos, this was a surprising aspect of the worker purchase). Even in such industries, however, credit lines and good management advice are important. With these two elements and a cooperative ideology, co-op firms can be as successful as traditional enterprises and can remain as cooperatives, even within a capitalist society. The question is more whether a capitalist society will allow cooperative movements to grow by providing that financing, particularly if co-ops are competing with traditional capitalist firms.

Meriden and Lip are examples of worker takeovers in troubled industries. To succeed, such ventures require not only government financing, but government involvement in the overhaul of the industry, as well as good management advice. While it might make good sense for a government interested in promoting cooperatives to make public funds available for co-ops in growing industries, does the same apply in industries such as British motorcycles, French watches, or American steel (Youngstown, for example)?* Yet it is in precisely such industries that worker takeovers tend to appear in capitalist societies. It is such industries that private capital seeks to leave, abandoning workers to their fate. If there is any chance that they are to survive, public financial and technical support is an essential ingredient.

Given these considerations, does it make sense to promote cooperative production in the United States without first changing the structure of American society? Co-ops can succeed given the same financial and demand conditions faced by traditional firms, and they provide much more secure employment, better working conditions, more equal wage distribution, and work that is more meaningful and less demanding. For these reasons alone, the promotion of

---

*In 1978, the Department of Housing and Urban Development granted $300,000 to the National Center on Economic Alternatives to study the feasibility of worker and worker-community ownership of the Youngstown steel facility.

cooperatives should be an explicit part of strategy for democratizing the economy. Even a handful of worker-owned and democratically run companies can serve as models of what a democratic economy would be like.

A cooperative movement faces tremendous obstacles in a capitalist society, however, particularly in the United States, where people are not educated to produce cooperatively and institutions are organized to function within corporate hierarchies. Not only are traditional capitalist banks and most government institutions less than friendly to worker cooperatives, but so are most unions (even though certain unions supported both Lip and Meriden). The International Woodworkers of America and the Lumber and Sawmill Workers Union in the Pacific Northwest have not opposed the plywood cooperatives, but they do not advocate worker ownership. The fact that worker-owners receive wages higher than union scale during good times leads to conflict, and, by lowering their wages in slow times, argue the unions, cooperatives make it difficult for unions to protect their contracts. Mondragon developed during a time in Spain's history when unions were controlled by the Franco government; but today's leftist unions oppose such cooperative movements because they tend to diffuse the workers' struggle with national capital. The ambiguity of the unions' roles in the worker purchases and takeovers at GAF, Meriden, and Lip was an important part of the process in each of these cases.

The source of the problem for unions in dealing with workers' control lies in the essential ambivalence of trade unionism itself. As labor historian Richard Hyman has pointed out, unions are

on the one hand, a protest and defense against the economic and human deprivations imposed on workers by their role in capitalist industry; on the other, a means of accommodation to the political economy of capitalist industry.[29]

This produces contradictory pressures in union organization and collective bargaining: though a basic conflict of interest exists between employers and employees on matters of pay, working conditions, and control of production and investment, the unions' acceptance of capitalist management forces them to support corporate growth and a stable, compatible bargaining relationship. So while ameliorating the terms of workers' subordination, they do not contest the *fact* of this subordination. To do so would be to challenge the very structure that gives legitimacy to the present unions and their hierarchy.

A worker control movement creates two fundamental problems for unions. First, when workers own and manage a firm in a truly participatory way, the union becomes redundant at the plant level. Unions are defined (and define themselves) in a collective bargaining role; this requires two conflicting sides, with the control of investment, work, and wage decisions formally in management hands. Once the dichotomy between workers and management is removed, collective bargaining is obsolete. Second, and perhaps more important, today's unions represent a particular form of workers' organization. If workers begin to gain control of production and participate in decision making, the nature of worker organizations will change. Democratic worker self-management turns power over to the workers, not to hierarchical worker organizations. The workers in each plant would gain power over many aspects of production that would not derive from decisions of national union offices. So were there to be a national worker self-managment movement, many unions would be likely either to oppose it or to try to control it.

This represents an important dilemma for producer cooperatives and other attempts at worker control. For if the worker ownership/management —economic democracy—movement is to transcend a few isolated success stories, it must become a workers' movement. To become a workers' movement, it must deal with union organization and union leadership, as well as with the power of industrial capital and management.

The Institute for Workers' Control (IWC) in Britain has attempted to work with union leadership and with the Labour government to push for increased participation in worker decision making. Is it possible to work within capitalist institutions such as the unions and the government to limit capitalist prerogatives? Is it possible to change the attitude of union leadership toward worker control without risking a union attempt to convert the worker control movement into an institutionalized compromise with traditional corporate capitalism (for example, stock ownership without direct participation or participation on boards without ownership)? The IWC thinks that it is. The institute believes that the development of workers' control will lead eventually to a crisis of "dual power"—a choice between the conquest of political power by the workers or a tremendous reaction by the propertied classes and the government. Workers' control in the trade union sense would sooner or later come up against the private ownership of industry, and that barrier will be surmounted only by political action and by a change in the law—the socialization of industrial property.

Richard Hyman disagrees. He argues that the development of consciousness is a *"collective* and *active* process," and this implies that a successful movement for self-management must emerge through "active struggle." This struggle should be carried out within and outside the unions and, according to Hyman, should include the development of an independent revolutionary political party. Increased awareness must go hand in hand with the organization and articulation of a physical challenge to capitalist domination. The trade union as such, "because of its very function of negotiation and accommodation within industry *as it exists*," cannot provide this challenge. This view, we think, is unduly pessimistic and fails to differentiate among unions and union leaderships. In France, some major unions (those associated with the Socialist Party) do advocate worker self-management. In the United States, the leadership of some reform movements within unions is potentially open to the idea of workers' control and ownership.

A worker control or cooperative movement in the United States (where unions are weaker and more limited in their combativeness than in Britain) faces great political difficulties even if there are some isolated instances of success. Yet, we still believe that it is important for *any* economic reform movement in the United States to include efforts to develop worker-controlled production as a basis for economic democracy. How can this occur if most private banks will not lend to a worker cooperative movement and if most unions are opposed, or at least will not serve as a source of organizing power for the co-ops?

We see the government—the public sector—as the primary source of financing and technical assistance for the worker control movement. While the government functions mainly in the service of private enterprise, both ideologically and financially, it is also an arena of conflict. Democracy is such an important aspect of American ideology in part because, first small farmers and artisans, and then an urban proletariat, blacks, and women fought for political rights. But, as we have emphasized, political democracy—particularly idealized democracy—is in contradiction with the limited rights individuals have in the work place. The government, then, must be included in the scenario of any worker control movement. It is the government which gives legality to private property laws and can legitimize and legalize drastic shifts in the meaning of those laws. Direct government loans to cooperatives (such as the British government loan to Meriden), and the use of pension funds are possible ways to aid worker ownership by making money available to co-op enterprises. Financial facilities do not guarantee participation or economic democracy (as Vermont Asbestos illustrates). But since participation is so vital to the economic success of worker-owned firms, it would be in the lenders' own self-interest to insist on a high-participation structure. This implies working through the government to develop and nurture worker-controlled firms.

There are two parts to such a policy: The first is the development of public financing for cooperatives through public banks that can use union pension funds for job creation and preservation, and through direct government loans to hard-pressed industries reorganizing under worker controlled production. The second is the development of a movement for economic democracy that coordinates information from various co-op and worker takeover experiences, provides technical assistance, helps government agencies and state banks plan their use of funds for loans to cooperative ventures, and promotes the formation of cooperatives in plants and communities. If public assistance to worker co-ops takes hold, it will become increasingly important to understand the conditions under which these cooperatives can be successful: what types of legal structures and organizations are more conducive to cooperation, and what types of industries—particularly among those that are in financial trouble—have a greater chance of success than others.

As financing and information become available, the interest in co-ops among groups of workers should increase. In a way, this is a top-down strategy: organizers and intellectuals push a particular idea, progressive elements in the government come to accept its validity and promote it and, finally, under this stimulus, workers respond. Given the ideological and financial difficulties confronting democratic work organizations, however, this is the only course to follow.

Michael Barratt Brown and Ken Coates of the Institute for Workers' Control consider legislation as a way to open the doors, "to advertise new standards and ideals, and to legitimize and encourage that truly social initiative which is so ruthlessly suppressed in our working people today." Hyman and other left-wing critics, however, feel that demands for legislative reforms should be subordinate to and derive from work-and-life organization and pressure. The government, according to Hyman, cannot be relied upon to develop worker-owned and -managed institutions without greatly increasing its level of activity in production units and worker organizations.

This is too static a view of government, however. Under certain circumstances, government in a democratic society can pass legislation that opens new political and social opportunities for citizens. Enactment of the legislation is often made possible by the lobbying and organizing efforts of a mass movement; the new legislation in turn helps the movement to grow by legitimizing the movement's goals and providing new legal and financial resources to it.

In recent years, some progressive work place legislation has been introduced, but not passed by Congress. In 1972, Senator Ted Kennedy introduced the Worker Alienation Research and Training Act which would have funded experiments and educational efforts concerned with work place democratization issues. In 1978, Congressmen Peter Kostmayer (D-Pa.), Stanley Lundine (D-N.Y.), and Matthew McHugh (D-N.Y.) introduced the Voluntary Job Preservation and Community Stabilization Act, which would have directed the secretary of commerce to identify endangered businesses, and to provide loans and technical assistance in those cases where a business could be profitably owned by employees or by residents in the affected communities. In England, a bill to create a Coop Development Agency was passed by Parliament in 1978; the agency will provide loans and technical assistance to worker cooperatives.

In 1979, a printing firm in Clinton, Massachusetts became the Colonial Cooperative Press with the help of a loan from the state's Community Development Finance Corporation, and the Small Business Administration provided a loan to a worker-owned poultry company in Connecticut—the SBA's first loan ever to a worker co-op. The new National Cooperative Bank, which began operation at the end of 1979, is empowered to loan money and provide technical assistance to producer co-ops, as well as to consumer-owned cooperatives.

This kind of legislation can help to open a public debate on work place democratization and provide vital resources for new worker-owned enterprises.

Worker ownership and democratic decision making in production can spotlight the contradiction between American democratic ideology and capitalist production. Worker-controlled firms act as a model for democratic production even if they are functioning in a capitalist society. Certainly, such firms can operate alongside corporate capitalist firms without necessarily threatening them, particularly when there is no organized movement to channel such experiences into meaningful political action against corporate power. But if there were to be such a movement, the structure and practice of producer cooperatives could very well serve as the beginning of a more democratic economy.

CHAPTER FIVE

A Democratic Technology

To what degree is a movement for economic democracy limited by the inherent technological nature of modern production processes? Some social scientists argue that industrial civilization *requires* publicly unaccountable experts, hierarchical work organization, private control of investment, and large-scale, centralized production and distribution units. Espousing a radically different view is a growing band of "ecotopians" who hope to usher in a new age of "appropriate" or "alternative" technology—a technology that is decentralized and on a human scale. What role, if any, does this "new age" technology have in a strategy for structural reform of the American economy?

These are complex questions, and we cannot hope to resolve them completely here. But they do raise issues that we passed over in our discussion of public enterprise, control of investment, and work place democracy. The daily lives of all of us are affected by "scientific progress"—by the development of new products such as the automobile, the computer, and the television set, to name but a few of the more dramatic examples. A price is frequently paid for this progress: a social cost that corporate capitalism passes along to society itself. With automobiles came greater mobility, but pollution and traffic jams also resulted; with computers came instant calculation and better planning for enterprises, but invasion of privacy, centralized credit, and other dossier systems also became more feasible; with television came instantaneous global communication and in-home mass entertainment, but the decline of social interaction outside the home and invasion of the home by commercial advertizing accompanied the new technology.

At times technology appears to *control* our society, to have an independent existence and to dictate society's living patterns; but this is a popular misconception fostered by those who actually control technology —the large corporations.

Even as liberal a thinker as John Kenneth Galbraith has fallen prey to this technological determinism. In his major work on the subject, *The New Industrial State,* Galbraith argued that large productive units are one of the prices we pay for modern industrial society:

Size is the general servant of technology, not the special servant of profits. The small firm cannot be restored by breaking the power of the larger ones. It would require, rather the *rejection of the technology* which in earliest consciousness, we are taught to applaud. . . .[1] [Emphasis added.]

Some critics of modern industrial society have questioned the wisdom of producing such items as nuclear power plants, jet planes, and even the modern automobile. We do not advocate a return to preindustrial society. Technology, however, is not autonomous; it develops within a context of economic and social institutions.

This becomes clear when the historical development of the large corporations is examined. David Noble, a scholar at MIT, studied the rise of such science-based corporations as General Electric, Du Pont, Monsanto, and AT&T. He found that the technological breakthroughs of the mid-nineteenth century were the work of a few creative inventors, who often worked alone in small laboratories or workshops. The new technologies, however, were controlled and guided by the large corporations and served as the basis of their economic expansion.

Noble demonstrated that the American patent system fostered corporate control over the process of invention at the expense of the individual inventor, that business leaders consciously shaped the universities into sources of engineering manpower, and that industrial research laboratories gave the corporations command over the flow of scientific investigation.[2]

Within the physical parameters of modern technology, there are a wide range of possibilities as to how technology can be harnessed and how the productive units in which it is applied can be organized. Modern technology does not require large corporations in order to be used efficiently in production. Industrial consultant Barry Stein analyzed the literature on technical efficiency and scale of production and concluded that "industries could be decentralized with respect to control structure, and thus more widely distributed across the country without loss of efficiency." Stein's examination of numerous studies led him to conclude that the level of *technical* efficiency (i.e., of realization of economies of scale) in the firm is the plant, which need not be of tremendous size—in most industries, approximately 100 to 150 persons.[3]

Stanley Boyle, in a study of the auto industry for the Senate Subcommittee on Antitrust and Monopoly, also found the level at which efficiency is realized to be the plant. Boyle concluded, "We have seen that the present size of the leading U.S. motor vehicle manufacturers is not dictated by the presence of economies of scale."[4]

John Blair, former chief counsel to the Senate Subcommittee on Monopoly and Antitrust, who spent twenty-five years studying the structure of the American economy, argued that modern technology actually offers great potential for decentralizing economic activity. Blair wrote:

With plastics, fiberglass, and high-performance composites (such as pre-stressed concrete) providing high-strength and easily processed materials suitable for an infinite variety of applications; with energy provided by such simple and efficient devices as high-energy batteries, fuel cells, turbine engines, and rotary piston engines; with computers providing a means of instantaneously retrieving, sorting, and aggregating vast bodies of information; and with other new electronic devices harnessing the flow of electrons for other uses, there appears to be aborning a second industrial revolution, which, among its other features, contains within itself the seeds of destruction for concentrated industries.[5]

Blair's hopes for a "second industrial revolution," however, rested naively on technology without reference to other forces in the society. This is not an uncommon outlook—the idea that somehow new technology will deliver us from the ravages of old, "bad" technology.

Over thirty years ago, Lewis Mumford wrote about technology and society. Mumford expressed many of the same feelings that Blair displayed later, but he approached the potential of modern technology for decentralization in a broader way. Mumford believed that electricity removed the advantages of size for factories. "The efficiency of small units worked by electric motors utilizing current from local turbines or from a central power plant has given small-scale industry a new lease on life," wrote Mumford. "Bigger no longer automatically means better: flexibility of the power unit, closer adaptations of means to ends, nicer timing of operation, are the new marks of efficient industry."[6]

Mumford continued: "So far as concentration may

remain, it is largely a phenomenon of the market, rather than of technics: promoted by astute financiers who see in the large organizations an easier mechanism for their manipulations of credit, for their inflation of capital values, for their monopolistic controls."

Mumford was not altogether correct in blaming the existence of giant corporations on the machinations of financiers. To be sure, large banks and investment houses have played a role in building corporate empires, but they played a facilitating role more than an entrepreneurial one. The managers of the large corporations were the ones who charted and carried out the expansion of their own enterprises. In building large business enterprises that sought a national market for mass-produced goods, these men as much as possible replaced the impersonal operation of the marketplace with planning and management by locating within the firm many of the economic exchanges and supply mechanisms that previously had been controlled by separate, smaller enterprises.

This process was neither dictated nor required by technology; rather, new technology such as the railroad, the telegraph, and electric power allowed access to a national market, and the expansionist drive of corporate capitalism—the imperative to grow—did the rest. Alfred Chandler of MIT pointed out that "career managers preferred policies that favored the long-term stability and growth of their enterprises to those that maximized current profits."

The professional managers became planners. "By the middle of the twentieth century," wrote Chandler, "the salaried large mass retailing, and the large mass transportating enterprises coordinated current flows of goods through the processes of production and distribution and allocated the resources to be used for future production and distribution in major sectors of the American economy."

The managers of the large corporations became, in Chandler's words, "the most influential group of economic decision makers" in the country.[7]

These economic decision makers today exercise what some economists call "market power." Professor William Shepherd of the University of Michigan, in his exhaustive study, *Market Power and Economic Welfare,* concluded:

In most industries, there is little or no apparent technical imperative for the present degree of monopoly, or for a further rise in it. Indeed, much market power arises purely in the pursuit of its own rewards and from the ability to acquire inputs at low prices and to secure various sorts of government sponsorship.

Shepherd criticized the market power of the leading firms:

Compared with the unproven, and perhaps modest, technical benefits of excess market power, its economic and social costs are large. The combined loss in efficient resource-use—internal inefficiency, misallocation, and external effects—may range upward toward 5 percent of national income. . . . Market power has also tended to sharpen economic inequality, and to accentuate racial discrimination in employment thereby causing no small economic and social loss and indirect repercussions. The various burdens of monopoly in this country do not seem to be shrinking.[8]

Other critics of the American economy have gone beyond the traditional market-power critique. Scientist-author Barry Commoner, in two widely read works *(The Closing Circle* and *The Poverty of Power),* attacked the energy basis of modern industrial technology. Commoner criticized the capital intensiveness of the energy inputs into the industrial system—above all, the use of nonrenewable fossil fuels—and the production of nonbiodegradable goods by modern industry. Commoner argued that this form of production uses up our natural capital—that is, the resources of the earth—and, at the same time, pollutes the earth, wastes energy, and causes unemployment by substituting capital for labor in the production process. Commoner called for the abandonment of capital-intensive, nonrenewable energy sources, particularly nuclear power, and the adoption of "soft" technologies such as solar and wind.

Another major critic, Harry Braverman, assessed the economy and the role of technology from a different perspective than Commoner. Braverman did not attack the nature of modern technology—that is, the processes themselves—but the *control* and *organization* of technology, which he viewed as inseparable from it. Braverman pointed out that the technical knowledge required to operate the various industries of the United States is concentrated in about 3 percent of the working population—mostly college-trained engineers and scientists. Modern management practices, he argued, are based fundamentally on the removal of technical knowledge from workers, so that such knowledge becomes the province of the corporation and its technical elite. Thus automation has led to the degradation of work in the twentieth century. Braverman cited such sources as the National Commission on Technology, Automation, and Economic Progress, which document that automation —particularly assembly-line production—has reduced the skill requirements of the factory labor force.[9]

Braverman argued that the organization of technology in business enterprises is based on the cardinal principle of control of the work force. Thus, it is inevitable that managerial capitalism will utilize technology in such a way that workers have little technical knowledge and little, if any, control over the organization of productive processes. Technology in the service of corporations is technology appropriate to hierarchical, management control of the work force. The imperative of industrial organization—even the choice of the kind of technology—flows not from the inherent scientific necessity of the technology, but from the control requirements of the corporations.

Other critics of modern industrial organization—particularly British economist E. F. Schumaker—have spurred a movement to develop alternative or "appropriate" technology. The movement, which began in the 1970s with publications such as *RAIN* magazine in the Northwest, the *Whole Earth Catalog* and now the *Co-Evolution Quarterly* in San Francisco, and *Undercurrents* in England, has expanded greatly, and small-scale government support is now being provided for research and experiments in appropriate technology.

The state of California, under Governor Jerry Brown, established an Office of Appropriate Technology, as did the government of Lane County, Oregon. The federal government has funded the National Center for Appropriate Technology, with headquarters in Washington and Butte, Montana.

California's Office of Appropriate Technology published the most detailed definition of this alternative technology. In a paper titled, "What Is Appropriate Technology?" by Jerry Yudelton and Sim Van der Ryn, the defining characteristics are described as follows:

An appropriate technology is small-scale: ecologically tolerable, human and community-scale; bioregionally based: diverse, using "informed non-uniformity" to design with local climate, natural energy flows and indigenous building materials; based on careful use of renewable energy and material resources, closing the loops of wide-open resource use through recycling of wastes; accessible to people; controllable at local levels; leading to more decentralized, autonomous, cooperative works, with a minimum of transport required; responsive to human needs, not culturally overwhelming; creative and regenerative in its effects on people and ecosystems providing a rewarding livelihood for people.

The criteria for appropriate technology are not applicable to the needs of a corporate-dominated economy. The very basis of the large corporation—national and international markets; national advertising; hierarchical chain of command; mass production; use of nonrenewable resources; little concern for environment—is almost the complete opposite of what is called appropriate technology. The two are quite incompatible.

Some advocates of decentralization and democratization of the economy object to the use of the term "alternative technology" or "appropriate technology." Peter van Dresser, in an interview with *Undercurrents* magazine, cautioned against the view that a new "good" technology will somehow magically deliver us from the old, "bad" technology. Declared Van Dresser:

I don't like the term "alternative technology" very much; it reflects the American hope that gadgets will solve problems. Much more is needed—the whole alternative rationale for restructuring society. Technology is only a portion of this, and to emphasize it misses a very large part of what has to be thought about and done. . . . We must be wary of leaping on the bandwagon of alternative technology as a panacea: I know of wealthy drop-outs who have bought an expensive wind generator and set it up on top of a dome while still running enormous four-wheel drive vehicles which use a hundred times more energy every day than the wind generator delivers.[10]

David Dickson, a British science writer, considered at length the relation between the development of an alternative technology and the sociopolitical context of technology. He concluded:

Only by realizing the extent to which technology provides an integral part of the ideology of contemporary society, at the same time as forming an essential element of the mechanisms by which the supremacy of existing political systems are maintained, can we see the extent to which the need to develop an alternative technology is both necessary and desirable. *To neglect the political dimension of this change is to support an idealistic concept of technology that does not coincide with the social reality of technology as it has been experienced.* Yet to imply that the problem involves merely the social relations of production, is to disregard the extent to which our current technology is permeated by the exploitative ideology of advanced industrialized societies, whether nominally capitalist or socialist. Only when we have created a viable *political* alternative shall we be in a position to perceive the real needs for a community science or an alternative technology. [Emphasis added.][11]

To understand more clearly the "political dimension" of technology, it is helpful to look at a few case histories demonstrating the politico-economic obstacles to the introduction of alternative technologies.

Solar Energy

A report of the President's Council on Environmental Quality, released in April 1978, stated that the nation could obtain "significantly more than half our energy from solar sources by the year 2020" if the government committed itself to that goal and to serious energy conservation. The council declared that a commitment to solar energy in the 1950s comparable to that made to nuclear technology at the time "would have led to the widespread economic feasibility of solar energy today."[12]

Of course, such a commitment—an available technological choice for the society—was not made because of the power of the energy companies that had a stake in the development of nuclear power, and the government's interest in developing nuclear technology for military use.

The report of the council recommended the following actions to advance solar technology:

—expanding government financial and tax incentives for the development of solar power;

—improving and increasing funding for federal solar research and development;

—pricing oil and natural gas at replacement cost levels instead of pricing these dwindling fuels at the lower levels now mandated by the government, so that the costs of alternative sources can be compared realistically;

—improving and expanding programs for the purchase of solar equipment for federal buildings.

The U.S. Department of Energy, however, continued to emphasize the increased use of coal and nuclear power, and President Carter's energy policy followed this route rather than the solar path.

Even what help the federal government has given to solar energy demonstrates that solar power, even if adopted, will not lead inevitably to a more decentralized, democratic economy. Tom Bender of *RAIN* magazine commented on government-sponsored development of solar energy:

Take a look at solar energy developments in the U.S. What's the pattern? You have a situation that clearly lends itself to decentralized, at-home application and local production and installation. You have individuals developing and refining the simple technology required and fighting the massive efforts of entrenched energy companies, financial institutions and government that have done their best to prevent the rapid conversion to solar energy. Now that the public has begun to demand application of solar energy, you find the government (ERDA in this case) giving massive amounts of our tax monies to pay large corporations to reinvent these already proven technologies. What is at stake is not inventing the technology but paying the corporations to develop their capabilities to produce it and also to receive credit from the government for inventing it. So the government promotes and pays big business to take over a new field that is developing quite well without its "assistance."

The next step is in process now. It is easier and more convenient for business to let government legislate the successful small producers out of business rather than have to compete directly against them. How to do it? Set up "performance" standards tailored to the capabilities of large corporations. The corporate approach to solar has consistently been biased towards exotic "high-efficiency" systems—ones that maximize the energy collected per square foot of collector but which produce less energy per dollar of expenditure. They know they can't compete on whole-system performance, so they try to push the issues to specific subsystems that can (but shouldn't) be maximized. The result is that an apparently innocent technical standard for thermodynamic efficiency clearly discriminates against simpler systems (homemade or local collectors, wood heat, passive solar construction) that are overall more effective and economical.[13]

The nation's largest energy companies have decided to protect themselves by getting in on the miniboom in solar research and development, and manufacturing. "A lot of the big companies are riding on big DOE (Department of Energy) contracts," Ralph Nader lamented to the *Washington Post* in October 1978.[14] For example, the federal government provided $50 million to the General Electric Company—nearly 50 percent of the company's total solar budget. GE has used the Department of Energy contracts to build a foundation in just about every area of solar development.[15]

In addition to utilizing government contracts, the energy giants have been getting into the solar market by purchasing small, innovative solar companies. Atlantic Richfield bought Solar Technology International and renamed it Arco Solar. Mobil Oil bought Tyco Laboratories, now Mobil Tyco. Shell Oil is the major stockholder in Solar Energy Systems. Exxon has set up its own solar company.

Arco Solar has big plans. "We feel we can become the General Motors of solar energy," declared Peter Zambas, vice-president of Arco Solar and manager of Arco's new business ventures, to a Los Angeles business publication.[16] Arco Solar is focusing on the development of photovoltaic cells, which convert solar energy directly into electricity—and a number of public officials are ready to assist in the effort.

"The only way we can get the cost of photovoltaic cells down is through government help," said Republican Congressman Barry Goldwater, Jr. Goldwater has co-authored a bill that would provide $1.5 billion for an accelerated program of research and development on solar photovoltaic technology leading to commercial applications. Mobil and Exxon are also deeply involved in photovoltaic research.

Solar power, originally championed by the alternative technology movement as a more democratic, decentralized, and environmentally benign alternative to the domination of energy needs by the powerful multinational oil companies, is fast becoming just another profit center for large corporations.

This process can be seen in California, where a political battle is raging over nuclear versus solar energy and the speed and manner in which solar will be introduced. In 1977, the California state government passed legislation providing tax credits for individuals who installed solar equipment in their homes (of course, tax credits are useful only to the relatively wealthy who can afford the initial capital investment). Interim eligibility criteria established by the State Energy Commission mandated expensive system testing by solar firms in order to become state certified, with a five-year warranty on parts and installation. To become eligible for the tax credit, the solar system must be certified. Requirements favoring solar systems produced and guaranteed by larger corporations such as Grumman, which has established a solar production unit in the state, will almost certainly drive many small solar firms out of business.

In addition, the existing California utilities have attempted to gain control of solar development. In 1978, Southern California Gas Corporation had pending before the State Utilities Commission a proposal known as Operation Sunflower, which involved an $11 million rate increase to finance a search for the best solar equipment package, to be rented to consumers at rates pegged to the price of natural gas. SCG's proposal amounted to consumer subsidy of the utility's efforts to win a solar distribution monopoly. Pat Shea, SCG's director for Operation Sunflower, told *New Times* magazine: "There's no way we want to charge for the sun. That's free. The equipment that utilizes the sun is not free. Never has been and probably never will be."[17]

The largest stumblingblock to the widespread introduction of solar energy is financial. As a June 1978 study by the U.S. Office of Technology Assessment concluded:

Utility conpanies have access to capital markets not available to an average homeowner. The utilities are also accustomed to operating with high debt-to-equity ratios and large ratios of investment to sales. This kind of financing capability would be required to produce on-site solar equipment calling for a large initial investment.[18]

The political struggle over solar and the key role of economic factors became highly visible in spring 1978 with the release of the report, *Jobs from the Sun,* by the California Public Policy Center, a public-interest research group. The report analyzed the outcome if a crash state program were undertaken to solarize most of the noncommercial space and water heating in California in the 1980s. Given such a program, the report found that a new solar industry in California would create almost 4 million jobs over a ten-year period, or 400,000 jobs a year, and that these jobs would be mainly in small firms with less than fifty employees.

The alternative for California, declared the report, is either liquefied natural gas from Indonesia and Alaska or nuclear power—both of which are capital intensive and would create far fewer jobs than solar energy. Both energy sources are controlled by large corporations. The obstacle to the development of a solar industry in California is not technology—which is available and which, according to the State Energy Commission, is competitive with that of alternative fuel sources—but capital and a market. Only through some form of government-backed financing will the necessary capital be available for small producers and for consumers; and only through a government-promoted solar development plan will the market be created to sustain a large number of small firms. In the absence of state financing and support for solar energy, the report noted, only large firms such as Arco, Exxon, or Grumman with sizable financial resources and the ability to wait for the market to develop slowly, will survive. Solar energy will become the province of a few large energy giants and manufacturing firms, and of private utilities, which wish to limit solar energy to a few demonstration projects and fancy supplementary systems for existing energy sources.

To head off corporate domination of solar energy, a coalition of environmental, labor, and public interest groups introduced a series of bills into the California legislature to regulate and stimulate the development of solar energy. These bills include the following:

Utility regulation: requires that the Public Utility Commission authorize any entry into solar marketing by investor-owned utilities following hearings and a finding that utility involvement will not hinder competition.

Small business loans: allocates $10 million to create a state-owned, nonprofit business investment corporation to provide up to $100 million in loans to small businesses that engage in the manufacture of solar systems or that need financing to convert to energy-conserving systems.

Job training: allocates $2 million in funds to the state CETA (Comprehensive Employment and Training Act) program to train low-income persons in solar and related fields.

Planning: instructs the state energy commission to establish a plan for "maximum feasible solarization" of California in space, water heating, and photovoltaics by 1990. Plan includes policy recommendations for achieving annual goals.

Antitrust: prohibits involvement in the solar industry by any major energy corporation selling a competing resource; restricts any one company from controlling more than 10 percent of the solar market.

The outcome of the solar energy struggle will be determined not by the nature of the technology, but by who controls it and how—in what organizational form—it is developed.

Agriculture

In the 1970s, America's food-producing and -distributing system came under criticism. Muckraking books such as *Eat Your Heart Out* by James Hightower and *The American Food Scandal* by William Robbins documented the growing concentration in the food system from ownership of land to middleman production, processing, and finally retail distribution. Concern over landownership itself (as in *Who Owns the*

Land? and *The People's Land* by Peter Barnes) led to political struggles over concentration of land, particularly in the fertile valleys of California. Books such as *Radical Agriculture* by Richard Merrill, *Food for People, Not for Profit,* by Michael Jacobson and Catharine Lerza, and especially *The Unsettling of America—Culture and Agriculture* by Wendell Berry, questioned the basic assumptions of modern agriculture. As Richard Merrill wrote:

There is a growing feeling in our culture today that the era of cheap abundant food is over, and that cornucopia has been a short-term marvel with long-term costs to society. These costs include the loss of good quality, the destruction of our rural culture and environment, the rise of centralized food monopolies, and the consequences of a vast migration of people from farms to cities. . . . In less than two generations there has been a revolutionary change in the means of food production and in the patterns of human settlement and food distribution in this country.[19]

The development of American agriculture was outlined and heralded by Earl Heady of Iowa State University in *Scientific American.* "Over the past 200 years the U.S. has had the best, the most logical and the most successful program of agricultural development anywhere in the world," wrote Heady.

Heady described how American agriculture has been transformed since the time when land was abundant and labor was cheap. At the beginning of American agriculture, capital inputs such as farm machinery, fertilizer, and food were relatively inexpensive, and most were produced on the farm. Energy was harnessed from the sun in the form of crops, and farmers generated their own fertilizer by rotating crops and using animal wastes. Rotation of crops also provided some control of insect pests.

In the nineteenth century, after the United States had expanded to its westward limits and the public land grants had been used up, the nation's agricultural policy shifted from simple expansion to the increase of productivity. The land-grant college system was created to encourage research and to extend new technical knowledge to farmers. With the application of technology, production approximately doubled in the period from 1910 to 1970, and by 1970 the nation was producing food on less land than it had in 1910. New technology became an effective substitute not only for land but also for labor. The result was that, between 1950 and 1955, more than a million workers migrated out of the agricultural sector into other sectors of the economy.

In the period 1950-70,

farms became larger and more specialized, handling either crops or livestock instead of both. Farms growing crops greatly increased their utilization of fertilizers, pesticides, farm machinery and other capital items . . . the use of fertilizer increased by 276 percent. . . . The use of powered machinery increased by only 30 percent, but in 1972 there were substantially fewer farms than there were in 1950. The result was that farm labor declined by 54 percent over that period as labor productivity quadrupled and total farm output increased by 55 percent.

Increased capital investment by fewer farmers and encroachment by the suburbs, combined to more than double farm real estate values between 1970 and 1973.

Heady pointed out certain side problems of this developmental process:

The change in the very nature of farming, with its higher productivity and greater degree of mechanization, has severely affected rural communities. . . . With the decline in the farm population the demand for the goods and services of businesses in the country has been eroded. Employment and income opportunities in typical rural communities have therefore declined markedly. As people migrated out of the rural communities, there were fewer people left to participate in the services of schools, medical facilities and other institutions. With the lessened demand such services retreated in quality and quantity and advanced in cost.[20]

Heady also acknowledged that this agricultural development has had a heavy impact on the environment. Larger, more specialized farms "are depleting the soil of certain specific nutrients and thus requiring larger amounts of fertilizer." The increased use of pesticides has polluted streams and lakes through runoff. The modernization of agriculture has also created new industries which together can be termed "agribusiness." Three major components are: the farm itself, which is increasingly large and specialized; the input-processing industry (machinery, fossil fuels for animal feeds, chemical fertilizers); and the food-processing industry. In recent years, the food-processing sector has come to represent a larger proportion of the total agricultural industry than farming itself. According to Heady, in 1975, 42 cents of each consumer dollar spent for food at retail prices went to the farmer and 58 cents to the food processor. "Even the typical commercial farm family," noted Heady, "now buys frozen, packaged and ready-to-serve foods from the supermarket rather than consumer products raised and prepared on the farm."

Heady predicted increasing concentration of ownership—that is, larger commercial farms—and fewer new farmers, given the high start-up costs. Prosperity for the small number of farmers will depend on international food sales, as well as the domestic market.

Critics of the current situation in American agriculture point out that there is nothing technologically determined about large farms. Numerous university and U.S. Department of Agriculture studies have concluded that most economies of scale are obtainable on well-run, modern, family-size farms.

Family farms face a number of nontechnical problems, however. In November 1977, the state of California released an extensive study entitled, "The Family Farm in California," produced by the state's small-farm viability project. The report concluded:

While well structured and properly run family farms may be able to compete successfully with far larger units in efficiency of on-farm production, they tend to be at a disadvantage in competing for resources and markets. The various task force reports detail the problems encountered by the small farmer in competing for outlets, information, land, financing, and other necessary resources. What is within his control, he does reasonably well, but he is vulnerable at those points where he must depend on others. Government rules and programs are very important in determining who shall have priority access to markets and resources, and as now implemented they often favor the large farmer rather than the family farmer.[21]

While professing to favor preservation of the family farm, federal farm policy for the past half-century has directly encouraged the concentration of farm ownership, mechanization of farm production, and increases in energy-intensive inputs in farming. This policy direction began with the New Deal, when the government intervened in the agricultural economy in a massive way through price supports and acreage allotments. New Deal legislation paid rhetorical homage to the family farm, but in fact the bulk of subsidies went to the rich farmer; this was particularly true in the South, where big landlords rather than their sharecroppers received most of the subsidies. As a result, millions of people, mostly black, left the South for the urban ghettos of the North and Midwest. An analysis of the New Deal farm policy by Sidney Baldwin concluded:

The New Deal's strengthening of individual and corporate, rather than cooperative or collective, agriculture had two dramatic consequences. First, it meant that the heavily capitalized, tax-subsidized enterprises of the future would view labor as a cost to be cut rather than as a productive factor. The New Deal thus led America not toward productivity and purchasing power on the land, but toward waste and welfare in our cities.

Second, the New Deal's strengthening of established institutions in agriculture was ominous politically. It was already apparent that the Farmer-Labor parties were disintegrating, that the National Farmers' Union would never win major influence, and that farmworkers were of marginal concern. Therefore, to rebuild agriculture without reconstructing it meant building power for the right-wing American Farm Bureau Federation and its allies. This second disaster, though less frequently noted than the first, may possibly rank close to it in importance.[22]

The New Deal price-support system not only benefited larger farmers more, it accelerated concentration in farm ownership:

Subsidies to retire farmlands, for bolstering profits in the face of low export prices, for storage of surpluses, and in the form of low-cost, government sponsored electrification, research and pest control projects, have combined to facilitate higher profits for the largest growers. These profits are invested in purchases of more lands from marginal farmers, used to diversify investments in processing and retailing and in the further mechanization of farming itself. In essence, government assistance programs have strengthened the monopolistic power of the largest firms.[23]

The land-grant college complex and the nation's agricultural extension service furthered concentration and mechanization through their activities. In California, for example, state researchers developed the "hard" tomato—a vegetable that would transport better for marketing purposes and have a longer shelf life; researchers then designed a mechanical harvester to pick it. As Jim Hightowner pointed out:

These researchers could be at work on the needs of family farmers, rather than enhancing the power of oligopolies;

they could be working to improve job conditions and developing the productive capacity of workers, rather than eliminating them; they could be considering means to improve the competitive position of small businesses, rather than servicing the giants; and they could be working directly with consumers, rather than tinkering around with nature to meet the marketing specifications of oligopolies.[24]

Through the tax system that finances government farm programs, consumers have subsidized the decline of small farmers and the rise of agribusiness; in return, they have received food of a higher price and a lower quality. Agricultural technology itself has not brought about concentration.

The outlook is for highly inflationary food prices in the future. A 1976 report by the Exploratory Project on Economic Alternatives, prepared by Joe Belden, argued that "because of the likelihood of persistent food inflation, we believe that consumer-based, ecology-oriented food politics also represent an important political force." The report quoted Representative Fred Richmond, a Brooklyn Democrat on the House Agriculture Committee:

The food policy of our nation must be geared to forging a coalition between the urban consumer and the small farmer.[25]

In Congress in 1978, a number of liberal congressmen from urban as well as rural districts sponsored a far-reaching bill, the Family Farm Development Act, which would reverse the Department of Agriculture's policy of promoting big farms and capital-intensive technology. The bill would direct the Department of Agriculture to put priority on small and moderate-sized producers. It would set up a Family Farm Development Service with responsibility to make research and demonstration grants and to coordinate other programs to help small farmers, such as reforming the extension system and aiming it at small farmers. The legislation would also establish the Commodity Credit Corporation as the agent for all U.S. farm export sales, removing the multinational grain companies as the controlling agent in marketing American grain abroad.

The bill would require the USDA to fund research on appropriate farm technologies that are inexpensive, energy conserving, and environmentally sound. Retail grocery stores would be required to display the farm value of all food items. The IRS code would be amended to discourage tax-loss farming and assist local government and community groups in acquiring land for resale or lease to younger farmers; and the Farmers Home Administration would be authorized to loan money for solar and other appropriate technological projects on farms.

The main sponsor of the Family Farm Development Act is Representative Richard Nolan, a Democrat from rural Minnesota. It was drafted by a working group of congressional aides and representatives of farm and consumer groups.

Implementation of the policy directions of the Family Farm Act need not await federal action. In the seventies, many cities and states around the country began to move toward active support for the family farm. These policy initiatives, which have been publicized and encouraged by the National Conference on Alternative State and Local Public Policy, a public interest organization in Washington, D.C., include the following.

Limiting corporate farming. Corporate farms enjoy substantial advantages over family farms. The corporation's legal structure allows it to pool capital and gives it limited liability, unlimited life, ease of estate transfer, financial flexibility, advantages under federal tax law, and market power. The large capital resources of most corporations allow them to wait longer for their investments to pay off.

Although corporate farms may be more profitable, they often have a disastrous effect on community life. Walter Goldschmidt's classic study of two California communities—one dominated by corporate farms and the other by small, family-owned farms— indicated that the family farm community had a higher educational level, higher standard of living, stronger social organization, and a more various and heterogeneous community.

Eight states in the Upper Midwest and Great Plains have enacted or strengthened anticorporate farming laws in the years since 1971: Iowa, Kansas, Minnesota, Missouri, North Dakota, Oklahoma, South Dakota, and Wisconsin. Four other states—Texas, Nebraska, West Virginia, and New York—have mild restrictions on corporate farming. In Oregon, a campaign was under way in 1978 to place an initiative on the ballot prohibiting corporations from farming or owning farmland. In the Canadian provinces of Manitoba and Saskatchewan, new laws have recently placed strict limits on the amount of land that can be owned by nonfarm corporations.

Assisting new farmers. The high price of farms and farmland is one of the biggest obstacles to the re-population of rural areas with new family farmers. Traditional commercial bank loans or the loan programs of the U.S. Department of Agriculture are too expensive. In search of a remedy for this situation, the North Dakota Farmers Union wrote and introduced into the state legislature the North Dakota Family Farm Security Act, which would provide state guarantees of 90 percent of private bank loans to farmers to purchase land; in addition, the state would pay four percentage points of the interest on mortgages. The interest rate subsidy would end when the farmer's net worth exceeded $100,000. The program would be administered by the state-owned Bank of North Dakota, which would be required to allocate

$10 million of its profits to a reserve fund to finance the program.

In Canadian provinces where the socialist New Democratic Party has been in power, programs for farm purchase/lease-back have been implemented. Under the Saskatchewan Land Bank Act of 1972, the provincial government purchases farms from willing sellers at market prices and then leases them back to new farmers on inexpensive long-term leases. Such lease-back arrangements are also offered to existing low-income farmers who need the capital they receive for their land to purchase new equipment. The leases have been restricted to farmers with incomes of less than $19,000 a year and a net worth of less than $50,000. New farmers in Saskatchewan can supplement their aid from the sale/lease-back program with help from another program, Farm Start, which provides grants and credits to new livestock ranches and farms.

Progressive legislators in a few states such as California and South Dakota have drafted bills modeled after the Saskatchewan program and introduced them into their state legislatures.

Establishing farmers' markets. A number of states have taken steps to eliminate the supermarket middleman. These direct-marketing programs are aimed at increasing farmers' income while reducing consumers' food costs. One of the most effective direct-marketing programs was begun by Jim McHale while he was Pennsylvania's secretary of agriculture. The Pennsylvania Agriculture Department set up over a dozen "tailgate" farmers' markets around the state. In addition, the department helped food-buying clubs and consumer co-ops in urban areas to buy from or contract directly with nearby farmers for Pennsylvania-grown produce. Between 1975 and 1978, nearly $115 million worth of agricultural products was sold through Pennsylvania's farmers' markets.

In West Virginia, the state Department of Agriculture operates six markets that lease space to farmers for $1 a year. In 1975, farmers sold $3 million worth of produce through the markets. In Hawaii, the city of Honolulu has sponsored a series of farmers' markets in twenty-one locations throughout the city. More than 25,000 Honoluluans shop in these "people's open markets," where farmers are required to sell their products at or below wholesale prices.

Although not yet implemented, a few cities have developed comprehensive urban food policies. A plan designed for Washington, D.C., by Frank Smith at the Institute for Policy Studies outlined a combination of city-owned greenhouses, gardens on public land, and direct contracts with nearby farmers to grow food for the city, which would then be sold through a network of cooperatives, food-buying clubs, and co-op markets using sites abandoned by supermarket chains in the Washington, D.C., ghetto. The city of Hartford commissioned a similar study for food policy by expert Catharine Lerza. The plan she drafted called for an increase in community gardens and solar greenhouses tended by CETA-funded workers; a community cannery and nutrition center; a network of food-buying clubs, food co-ops, and farmers' markets; and use of the city's institutional buying power (school lunch programs, jails, etc.) as a guaranteed market for local produce.

Two states, Vermont and Massachusetts, have established state food commissions to draft comprehensive food policies for the state that emphasize local production and distribution of nutritious, reasonably low cost food.[26]

From our examination of the cases of both solar energy and radical agriculture, we can see that the key elements in new directions of economic development are the control of capital and the creation of markets. Only government-assisted programs that include those elements will make possible the actual development of these alternative technologies.

The same is true with regard to developing technologies that are more conducive to small-scale, democratic industrial production—that is, processes which "humanize" the work place as much as possible, and which allow workers' input into decisions. An additional, key element is the willingness of workers or their unions to tackle technological issues, rather than leaving them solely to management.

The Lucas Aerospace Workers Campaign

The theme expressed in this chapter—that the *control* of technology is just as important as the state of the technology itself—has been played out in a union-management struggle in England involving the future of the Lucas Aerospace company. For the first time in the postwar period, a group of trade unionists took it upon themselves to design, analyze, and propose products they felt their company should be fabricating. Faced with the possibility of widespread layoffs, the unionists drew up a proposal called the Corporate Plan, which outlined a series of new products they hoped would both save jobs and meet social needs. These proposals, which included details of not only what would be produced, but how it would be produced as well, emerged from a lengthy, democratic process of discussion involving study groups at seventeen different plant sites around England. The drafting of the unionists' Corporate Plan was a considerable achievement in itself, and a step beyond traditional collective bargaining. What concerns us here is not the industrial democracy implications of the Corporate Plan as much as the interrelationship between technology and managerial decision-making power, although obviously the two subjects are closely related.

Lucas Aerospace is part of Lucas Industries, a British-based multinational firm that produces electrical and mechanical systems and components for the automobile, aerospace, and engineering industries. The company employs approximately 13,000 workers on seventeen sites throughout England. Lucas is essentially a specialist accessory producer, dealing in small runs of precision-engineered systems.

The work force includes a number of skilled engineers, designers, draftsmen, and technicians specializing in hydraulics, pneumatics, control engineering, and aerodynamics. The workers belong to thirteen different unions.

The impetus for the formation of a companywide unionist committee—the Lucas Aerospace Shop Stewards Committee—was the threat, beginning in 1972, of serious layoffs due both to proposed cuts in defense spending in Britain and to rationalization of company production, conditioned by Britain's entry into the Common Market as well as company plans to expand production overseas in France, Brazil, and other countries. The concerns of the workers were real. The company's rationalization policies had led to a reduction in the work force from 18,000 in 1970 to around 13,000 in 1974.

The first innovation in the workers' strategy to combat future layoffs was the formation of a cross-union combine that covered all the unions—white and blue collar—and linked all seventeen plants in the Lucas Aerospace chain. This in itself went beyond usual British practice, where companywide unions along industrial lines are uncommon.

The Lucas combine committee was made up entirely of shop stewards—union men who work on the shop floor and are elected by their union members. They are not full-time union officials and tend to be more militant than such union officers. The shop stewards representing the different union members at each of the seventeen plants selected one steward to sit on the combine committee. The combine meets regularly, four times a year, and its decisions are passed on as recommendations to each local shop stewards' committee, so that each plant retains union autonomy.

The combine is not formally recognized by the company as a negotiating body; collective bargaining is still carried out by the individual unions. What the combine provides is a unique forum for the discussion of issues and strategy relevant to the entire work force of the company.

In 1974, the combine committee set up a Science and Technology Advisory Service "to provide an early warning about the difficulties likely to be associated with the introduction of a new technology process." The committee planned to consider issues relating to "skill fragmentation, increased work tempo, job security, dangers of shift working, and possible hazards in the use of new processes and materials," and to "suggest work and wage patterns which should be negotiated." Where necessary, the committee would call upon socially responsible and sympathetic scientists and technologists at universities and elsewhere to provide help and advice. The early emphasis was on protection—on defending workers against further exploitation by management through the introduction of technological change. Each new technology would be carefully assessed by the committee and the appropriate trade union response suggested.

It became apparent to the combine committee, however, that simply a defensive strategy would not be sufficient to halt rationalization at Lucas and the layoffs that were certain to come.

The idea of preparing an overall corporate plan for Lucas arose in November 1974 at a meeting between the combine committee and the minister of industry at the time, Tony Benn. Benn suggested that aerospace business was likely to fall off under Labour government policies and advised the combine committee to develop its own corporate plan, independently of the company. The idea was to devise a complete program of alternative technological products that would be presented to the government in hopes of attracting financial support. The plan would then be negotiated with management through conventional collective bargaining.

British journalist David Elliot, an advisor to the combine, described the process that ensued:

This was a highly original idea and required a considerable amount of work by the Combine Committee. Shop Stewards Committees on each site were asked to develop ideas for alternative products based on their knowledge of the existing products, the factories' equipment, services, siting and layout, and the skills of the workforce. Project teams were established on each site and at the largest, Burnley in Lancashire, a mass meeting was held to discuss the plan concept. Detailed technical feasibility and "state of the art" reviews were produced in the energy, transport, economics and medical technology areas and sent to each site to stimulate discussion. At each stage an attempt was made to link existing skills to the needs of the community and to subject proposals to assessment on environmental grounds. Contacts were made with potential customers, local community groups and trades councils in order to try to identify specific needs.[27]

After several months, drafts of the Corporate Plan were discussed and circulated among the stewards' groups at each plant site. The final version was released at a press conference in January 1976. The complete plan consisted of five 200-page documents outlining some 150 new products and making a number of radical proposals as to how the production of these new products should be organized.

Elliot notes that "self-reliance was in fact the key-note to the whole campaign." An open letter inviting ideas or alternative products was sent to 150 organizations and individuals in the environmental and alternative technology movement, but results were minimal. The combine secretary reported,

One of the things that disappointed us most was that in spite of years of talk about alternative technology only from three sources did we get anything positive or useful. The Corporate Plan . . . is therefore largely our own work and of course there is nothing wrong in that kind of self-sufficiency.[28]

In this case, the work force itself—a fairly skilled one—had more than enough ability to devise alternative products.

A detailed reading of the Corporate Plan demonstrates the interaction of technology and political choice. The committee, of course, wanted to devise products that could actually be produced by the company's work force and existing facilities, so as to preserve the jobs of the workers; but committee members did not automatically select just "advanced technology" ideas. They concerned themselves with so-called intermediate technology that met many of the criteria laid out by Californian Sim Van der Ryn in his definition of appropriate technology.

One section of the plan dealt with alternative energy technologies and included detailed cost assessments and technical proposals. In the past, Lucas has manufactured a small wind-electric machine, and the company had the expertise for the development of windmill systems. It also had the capability to manufacture heat pumps and fuel cells, as well as solar collector systems.

The committee, however, steered away from small windmills and solar collectors suited only to individual domestic usage, on the grounds that such products could benefit only those who could afford to experiment with self-sufficiency. Instead, it was more concerned with designing medium-scale systems suitable for complete communities, housing tracts, etc., and with building marketing ties with local government authorities and community groups planning energy-conservation projects.

Also included were a variety of high-technology products such as handling gear for undersea oil rigs, "telecheric" devices for firefighting, artificial limb devices, and lightweight rubber-wheeled vehicles and a hybrid electric-gasoline vehicle, both of which had low fuel consumption and pollution.

The combine committee was also concerned that it would be foolish to produce socially useful and environmentally appropriate technologies in a way that was unsafe, polluting, exploitative, and alienating. The committee wanted to depart from the dehumanized, fragmented production common in highly skilled industries where computer systems control a great deal of the production process. As Mike Cooley, chairman of the Lucas combine, stated on British television:

The result is redundancy for some and intensified deskilled work for the remainder. Shift work is becoming common, as the companies try to make maximum use of the expensive capital-intensive computer equipment.[29]

The Corporate Plan included a number of ideas for new models of production organization and control. The combine wanted to develop arrangements

in which the skill and ability of our manual and staff workers is continuously used in closely integrated production teams, where all the experience and common sense of the shop floor workers would be directly linked to the scientific knowledge of the technical staff. This would be done on a much more equitable basis than is now the case, and would give rise to much greater job satisfaction.[30]

In addition to such project teams, the Corporate Plan discussed the need for education and retraining of less-skilled workers and for the training of women in technical jobs. The aim of these organizational and educational proposals was to enable *all* members of the work force to exert a real degree of influence not only over the production process, but over the aims and priorities of production. As such, the Corporate Plan goes directly against the logic of managerial-controlled introduction of new technologies, in which the sole criterion is the reduction of costs and expansion of profits. Workers are rarely consulted on the introduction of new equipment or new products—or, if they are, only to the extent that such measures help to improve the output of workers by reducing their control over their work and decreasing their skills.

The Corporate Plan did not ignore the need to manufacture products that made a profit. Roughly half of the proposals were for products that were profitable as projected into the marketplace and half for products that, although socially useful and necessary, were not at present profitable in strict market terms. The combine felt, however, that many of the socially useful products would be of interest to the National Health Service, housing and transport departments in many countries, and other government agencies; consequently, the Corporate Plan suggested a shift away from business with the Ministry of Defense to business with other, nonmilitary government departments.

In preparing the plan, the combine committee did not imagine that it would be accepted wholeheartedly, or even in any significant part, by the company. As the combine declared in a statement to the public, it did not believe that Lucas Aerospace

could be transformed into a trailblazer to transform this situation in isolation. . . .

The intentions are much more modest, namely to make a

start to question existing assumptions and to make a small contribution to demonstrating that workers are prepared to press for the right to work on products which actually help to solve human problems rather than create them.[31]

Of course, the combine hoped that by publishing the plan and reaping some publicity, it could help to educate workers and energize them with regard to the possibilities of their situation, and that the company might be forced, through government and public pressure, to adopt the plan. The former indeed occurred, but not the latter.

The company's response was to reject the plan and declare that the planning of new products rested with management. In addition, the company avoided ceding any collective bargaining rights whatsoever to the combine. One business magazine, *The Engineer*, even chastised Lucas's management for its harsh response, saying the company had "scuttled potentially profitable ideas as well as a peaceful future" and caused possible "damage to personnel morale."

The company's rejection of the plan and its refusal to discuss the issue with the stewards' combine served, not surprisingly, to stiffen the resolve of the combine to fight any company plans for layoffs. Interestingly enough, many local plant managers had expressed a willingness to carry out the plan; but the central management was adamant. Company attempts to lay off workers in 1977 were met with threats of industrial action, including strikes and tampering with components produced at different sites, and the company did not send out the layoff notices. A kind of stalemate resulted and continued into 1978. The concept of a worker-produced corporate plan, however, spread to other industries in Britain.

As *Industrial Management* magazine commented, "What has happened at Lucas is likely to be the forerunner of a development which will ultimately affect the whole of British industry."

A number of similar incidents have occurred

elsewhere: stewards at Chrysler called on the company to concentrate more on mass-transit vehicles and less on private pleasure cars; machine workers at textile manufacturer Ernest Scraggs, faced with layoffs, drew up a proposal for alternative products, including health and safety equipment for the textile industry; the Vickers National Shop Stewards Combine Committee produced a paper urging diversification from defense products to sea-based technologies such as wave power, submersibles, and ocean tub barge systems.

The importance of Lucas Aerospace and the combine committee's Corporate Plan is that it clearly raises the question of who decides on technology, and raises it in a concrete, not an abstract, manner. It demonstrates that decisions about what is produced and how products are produced do not have to be left to an unaccountable group of elite managers and corporate planners.

The only American union that has acted at all aggressively and positively in issues of technology and production is the United Auto Workers, and this action occurred in mid-1945. Angered by the closing of aircraft plants in Michigan as the war came to an end, UAW president Walter Reuther published a booklet titled, "Are War Plants Expendable?" The booklet outlined a program for the conversion of government-owned war plants to the mass production of modern railroad equipment and low-cost housing. Reuther suggested the establishment of a Housing Production Authority and a Railroad Equipment Authority modeled after the Tennessee Valley Authority. Reuther's plan described in some detail how government-owned aircraft and aircraft engine, magnesium, aluminum, electrical equipment, ball-bearing, and tank plants could be reorganized to produce lightweight railroad rolling stock and low-cost housing.

Business Week declared that the plan had "socialistic earmarks." "It proposes," noted the magazine in a condemning tone, "that resumption of civilian goods output should be conditioned by social needs rather than free competition."[32] The UAW plan was never given serious consideration by the government, and Reuther—after the initial publicity surrounding its release—did not mobilize his union around the plan. Instead, many wartime facilities such as steel, rubber, and aluminum plants were sold to large private firms. Arsenals and aircraft plants were kept in reserve and made available to military contractors when the military budget increased again with the onset of the cold war.

In the immediate postwar years, the UAW Research Department also produced a detailed proposal that argued for GM production of a cheaper, lightweight "compact" car. As with the peace conversion plan, the idea was never carried into collective bargaining sessions by the union nor made a key part of union political and economic strategy.

As the decade of the seventies closed, the UAW had begun to revive the idea of union participation in management decision making. In 1979, in initial negotiations with Chrysler, the union introduced the demand for greater worker participation, arguing that "the Corporation can no longer afford to overlook the talents of the workers when making the decisions that affect their livelihood." The union proposed worker participation on the board of directors and worker committees at various levels with authority equal to management on questions involving plant location, product planning, quality control, health and safety, and overtime.

A Democratic Technology

As we have seen, in at least two distinct areas—solar energy and agriculture—movements for greater public control over technology have appeared in the

1970s and are slowly gaining in strength, chiefly at the level of city and state government. Constituencies for these movements already exist and are expanding. The key strategic elements in democratic development of solar technology and in the democratization and decentralization of agriculture are greater public control of capital and public sponsorship and organization of markets. The development of a democratic technology (a term we prefer to alternative or appropriate technology) in mass production industry is a trickier and longer range matter.

In addition to the policies discussed in previous chapters, such as public support for worker-owned firms, two political approaches—operating together where possible—are required. The progressive unions representing workers in the major manufacturing industries—for example, the United Auto Workers, the Steel Workers, the Mineworkers, and the Machinists—should adopt the corporate plan approach. Through strengthened research departments reaching out to friendly technologists in universities, and mobilization of worker knowledge at the plant level, these unions should develop corporate plans similar to the Lucas Aerospace plan for the major firms in which they represent workers. As with the Lucas workers and Lucas Aerospace, these plans would become both negotiating tools for collective bargaining and educational-political devices for the union.

Government has a major role to play wherever progressive public officials have power. Existing governmental support programs for appropriate technology (for example, California's Office of Appropriate Technology or the federally funded National Center for Appropriate Technology) need to be broadened and expanded to encompass the idea of democratic technology—the redesign of entire plants around technology that is conducive to self-management and worker control rather than authoritarian, assembly-line-type organization. The most important thing such public programs could do in the immediate future would be to establish centers of democratic engineering (through the creation of new schools or the transformation of existing industrial engineering institutions) that would begin to train a new generation of engineers with more democratic values and attitudes. These schools of democratic engineering could also begin pilot programs in technological education for workers, so that as firms with more democratic work places were established, workers could be educated in line with their expanded responsibilities. As much as possible, technology would be demythologized and subjected to democratic discussion and control.

Finally, the research and development departments of publicly owned firms—the competitive public enterprises organized under our proposed government holding company—would direct their efforts toward the design of new factories and plants in which the technological processes utilized were consistent with work place democracy. Public enterprises would also attempt to design products and market them, so as to provide consumers and other enterprises with products that encourage popular understanding and control of technology. For example, a public automobile firm might design a car or a particular model of car that could be repaired by the owner with the use of simple tools and a manual included in the sale of the car, or a public computer firm would market minicomputers designed specifically to help co-ops and middle-sized worker-owned firms with their management problems.

State and federal governments have supported and subsidized technology solely to raise productivity (and profits) for private firms or, in the case of military research, to kill our enemies more efficiently. We propose a new criterion: that government support of technology be consciously aimed at promoting decentralization and democratic participation.

CHAPTER SIX

Controlling the Corporation

Even if all of the structural reforms proposed in previous chapters were initiated by a serious reform government and fully supported by the nation's major labor unions, consumer groups, civil rights organizations, women's organizations, and others, the country's largest corporations—the *Fortune* 500—would still hold captive the nation's economy. A capital strike—or refusal to invest—by the large corporations or large-scale capital flight overseas by multinational firms would plunge the economy into a recession and threaten the reform government with a national crisis.

A strategy aimed at greater democratic participation in economic affairs and a more equitable distribution of economic wealth must deal with the dominant role of the large corporation in American society.

The large corporations are the most ardent and successful planners in the United States. Early in the twentieth century, these firms became multi-units with branches spread across the United States and the world. As much as possible, the corporations became integrated by purchasing their sources of supply and their distribution outlets. The managers of the large corporations, in the words of business historian Alfred Chandler, replaced the invisible hand of competition with the visible hand of planning; they became the nation's economic planners—but in pursuit of private profit, not the public interest.

Such corporations operate under advantageous regulation and with a wide variety of government subsidies, contracts, and tax breaks. They control sizable shares of national and foreign markets, having long ago swallowed up less powerful local and regional firms. They are run not by their private owners—the stockholders—but by a managerial elite that is overwhelmingly white and male, and is unaccountable to any constituency for its action.

Galbraith, in *The New Industrial State,* and other economists and journalists have examined how corporations plan product cycles, predetermine desired rates of return, and create demand for their products through mass advertising.

These complex organizations could not be converted into worker-owned cooperatives overnight. The organizational problems would be staggering, and the expense of buying out too great, given the possible sources of funds for the task. Large-scale nationalization of entire industries or of a great number of large corporations is neither politically nor economically feasible, and would lead to chaos were it attempted by a reform government. Our policy of *selective* public enterprise using a government holding company that purchases shares (not necessarily 100 percent) in a number of leading firms is the most workable policy, at least for the next ten to twenty years. But this would involve twenty-five to thirty firms at most. The bulk of the *Fortune* 500 will remain in place—an economic and political force to be reckoned with.

To forestall a united front of corporate opposition to a program of economic democracy, the large corporations must be brought under greater democratic control at the same time that alternative sources of finance—public banks and pension funds, for example—and of production—worker cooperatives and competitive public enterprises—are being created. The elements of a more democratic economy are thus constructed *alongside* and *within* the existing system; simultaneously, the power and prerogatives of the corporations' managerial elite are steadily reduced by opening up the corporation to workers, consumers, and community representatives, as well as to public representatives.

What are sensible approaches for controlling corporate behavior and reining in the now unaccountable managerial elite?

There is a large body of experience that can be examined in search of an answer. In the United States, there has always been a tradition of antimonopoly sentiment that, from time to time, has supported attempts to reduce corporate concentration and corporate power. In Western Europe, both trade unions and the government have tried a number of strategies designed to bring corporations under greater public control.

In the United States, policies for controlling or influencing the behavior of corporations in a desired direction (i.e., that of a public- or labor-oriented policy rather than simply the priorities or imperatives of strictly private decision making) fall generally into four categories: antitrust, regulation, collective bargaining, and subsidies and incentives. While all of these policy thrusts have been tried during this century, even their *combined* effect has not greatly altered corporate dominance of the American economy. Each policy alone has suffered from numerous defects in practice.

Antitrust

The Sherman Antitrust Act was passed almost ninety years ago. Yet recent Federal Trade Commission (FTC) statistics show that the top 200 manufacturing corporations control more than 60 percent of U.S. manufacturing assets.

Antitrust is a criminologist's approach to economics. It seeks to punish or deter unwanted conduct (i.e., monopolistic practices); yet it supplies no model of desired behavior. As in other lines of police work, the prosecution of misconduct is subject to many personal whims and political interventions. ITT is only the latest of many corporate giants that have been dealt with gently for political reasons; a number of others—General Motors, for example, have never been even gently attacked. Definitions of illegal antitrust behavior are so vague, and the burdens of proof so demanding, that cases are tied up in court for years, at great public expense and usually with sparse results. Only rarely does a corporate executive go to jail; fines are minimal and tax deductible; the few divestitures that have been ordered have not changed conditions notably in any industry nor brought lower prices. Nor is it readily apparent how, even if stiffer penalties were applied and more lawsuits filed, any substantial economic benefits to the public would be achieved.

In 1970, to take one example, the late Senator Philip Hart (D-Mich.) asked the Federal Trade Commission to investigate anticompetitive practices by the nation's eight largest oil companies. Three years after Hart's request, the FTC staff finally prepared the legal briefs and filed what is called the Exxon suit because Exxon was listed first on the complaint—it is the largest. By 1978, after five years, the FTC suit had gone nowhere. It was still in the discovery stage and had not yet received one substantive document from any of the oil companies. At every point in the legal process, a battery of highly paid and highly skilled lawyers representing the oil companies has challenged the FTC, appealing every request for information to the whole commission.

Even Senator Hart recognized the futility of the efforts he had initiated. "The sad part is that we won't get a verdict—and relief—for eight to ten years," Hart told the *Washington Post*. "The FTC has to prove not just monopoly power, but anticompetitive behavior. This will mean a search of millions of documents to confuse everyone."[1]

Similarly, a suit filed against IBM in 1969 still continues with no end in sight.

Testifying in the summer of 1978 before the House Small Business Antitrust Subcommittee, Alfred Dougherty, head of the FTC's Bureau of Competition, said, "I am not very hopeful that we can stop the large conglomerate acquisitions that are occurring today without additional legislation."

In the same hearing, Assistant Attorney General John Shenefield observed, "Under the present state of the law, as to pure conglomerate mergers . . . the antitrust laws apparently don't apply."

FTC Chairman Michael Pertschuk told Congress, "The trend line is for increasing concentration and increasing elimination of small business."[2]

Thurman Arnold, who headed the Antitrust Division of the Justice Department from 1938 to 1943 (the period of its most active pursuit of monopoly), believed that the antitrust laws actually aided monopoly by satisfying the popular taste for anticorporate rituals without actually changing anything. "By virtue of the very crusade against them," Arnold wrote, "the great corporations grew bigger and bigger, and more and more respectable."[3]

The lack of positive results with the antitrust approach does not mean we should abandon antitrust altogether and disband existing antitrust units. The present threat of antitrust action has probably made economic concentration occur somewhat more slowly than otherwise. It is possible that antitrust can serve as a positive weapon in a policy aimed at decentralizing and democratizing economic power, albeit a minor one.*

A recent (1977) report by the National Center for Economic Alternatives, "Extending Divestiture," prepared by lawyer Judy Kincaid, argued that:

> Divestiture could accomplish the transfer of economic enterprises to more socially responsible ownership. . . . Preference would be given to broadly representative community groups wishing to purchase the divested firm, including, for instance, employees of the divested subsidiary, cooperatives, neighborhood development corporations, and public community trusts. Supplementary legislation making special government loan guarantees or subsidies available for community ownership could assist such local groups for purchasing divested assets.[4]

In some instances, through antitrust action, a particular division of a conglomerate might be detached and converted into a worker-owned or worker/community-owned enterprise. But we cannot rely on antitrust alone as our major structural reform for controlling corporations.

Regulation

In recent years, numerous studies by Ralph Nader and others have demonstrated that most, if not all, regulatory agencies have been captured by the very industries they were created to regulate. There is a constant flow of personnel between the regulatory agencies and the regulated industries, guaranteeing a single vision of the so-called public interest.

---

*In March 1979, Senator Ted Kennedy introduced a bill that would prohibit mergers between companies with assets or sales exceeding $2 billion; it would also prohibit mergers between large firms accounting for over 20 percent of an industry's sales. These provisions would affect the nation's top 500 companies. The bill is useful, but limited preventative medicine; it is not a positive structural reform.

Revisionist historians such as Gabriel Kolko who have studied the establishment of regulatory agencies contend that the "first generation" of regulatory agencies was created at the behest of the most forward-thinking corporate leaders and that they were designed to control and modulate competition in the interests of the largest, most powerful corporations in the industry. Whatever the historical reasons for the establishment of regulatory agencies (at the state as well as the federal level), in practice the operations of the agencies have served mainly to raise the cost of products to the consumer and assure a return on investment to the regulated industry.* Thomas E. Kauper, assistant attorney general of the Antitrust Division during the Nixon administration, explained in a 1972 speech:

> There have been instances in our history in which the industry to be regulated may at first view the regulation as inhibiting, but over the years learns to control such regulation to its own purposes either by reason of its expertise in dealing with the intricacies of the regulatory scheme or due to the fact that it eventually becomes the primary "constituent" of those who regulate.[5]

Prices may actually decline for a time when regulations are lifted, as happened in 1978 when the Civil Aeronautics Board began a program of deregulation: prices to consumers dropped while business volume increased; however, safety standards may also have decreased and, for some small and middle-sized cities, service declined as airlines cut back traffic on less profitable routes.

In the area of social cost regulation—pollution, industrial health and safety, and product safety—the establishment of federal minimum standards has, to

---

*"First generation" regulatory agencies include the Interstate Commerce Commission (1887), the Federal Trade Commission (1914), the Federal Power Commission (1920), the Federal Communications Commission (1934), the Civil Aeronautics Board (1938), and similar bodies at the state and city levels.

some degree, improved the products produced or made industrial work somewhat safer. In none of these areas, however, have the standards been pursued aggressively. At the federal level car manufacturers have been able to win delays and postponements in auto emission and auto safety standards; OHSA (Occupational Safety and Health Administration), the federal health and safety agency, is understaffed and faces the impossible task of surveying thousands of plant sites around the country; unsafe, unhealthy, or otherwise dangerous products are created faster than federal agencies can keep up with them, and most such products are discovered only after some harm has been done.

The problem with regulation is that it does not intrude into the corporate decision-making process in any significant way. Decision making is left up to unaccountable managers, and the penalties for making decisions that run blatantly against the public interest are mild. The occasional and infrequent tough regulator—such as former Pennsylvania insurance commissioner, Herbert Denenberg—who cannot be seduced by the promise of a future job in the industry, can be subverted by its resources. A sociological study of Denenberg's tenure in office showed that the insurance industry blocked Denenberg by plying favors to the agency's bureaucracy, fought him in legal proceedings, and generally took the position that it could stall his reform efforts for four years, after which his term in office would end and a more malleable commissioner would be appointed.[6]

Some national minimum standards in all spheres of economic life are necessary, regardless of who owns and controls the means of production, so that the imperatives of a single enterprise do not trample the overall interests of the public at large. As much as possible, however, these considerations of social cost should be factored into the decision-making process *within* the enterprise.

In the case of "natural" monopolies such as electric power, gas, or telephone service, in which competing enterprises make no economic sense, public ownership and democratic control of utilities by a publicly elected board of directors is preferrable to the attempt to control private utilities from the outside. At the state level, a long-range planning board or commission should function to coordinate the overall activities of the various local utilities. In Sacramento, California, for example, the board of the publicly owned Sacramento Municipal Utility District (SMUD) is elected by voters; this has made it possible for candidates to run and win on a program of energy conservation and development of nonpolluting, renewable nonfossil fuels such as solar and wind power. A state energy commission in California engages in long-range analysis and planning of the state's overall energy needs and has the power to approve the location of all new power plants in the state. This combination of a local public utility with a democratically selected board and a public planning agency at the state level functions to serve the public interest of the state.

In industries that are not natural monopolies, most "first generation" regulation is inherently contradictory and unsatisfactory. These industries should be subject to other policies discussed in this chapter. While we would retain "social cost" regulation in such areas as pollution and health and safety, we believe that through worker control measures the role of the government can, over time, be greatly reduced.

Subsidies and Incentives

Another policy direction has been the government's paying corporations, in one form or another, to do certain things. In 1972, the congressional Joint

241

Economic Committee undertook an extensive study of federal subsidy programs. The results of the inquiry revealed that "federal subsidies constitute an incredibly diversified and pervasive system of economic assistance to the private economy."[7] The JEC found that, in 1970 dollars, federal subsidy programs cost $63 billion a year, including $12 billion in direct cash payments, $38 billion in tax subsidies, $4 billion in credits, and $9 billion in benefit-in-kind subsidies. The committee found that the majority of subsidies went to producers rather than consumers, though many were justified in terms of their alleged benefits to consumers.

Until the 1972 study was undertaken by the JEC, no attempt had ever been made by the federal government to consider comprehensively the magnitude and impact of government subsidy programs. From the JEC's study as well as a number of microeconomic studies on the effects of subsidies and incentives on business decisions, it is clear that these programs do not entice business enterprises to do anything that they do not wish to do. They are not an effective means of controlling the behavior of corporations. Instead, subsidies are a system of benefits that different enterprises and industries enjoy because of their political power to win these benefits from the government, and because of the blackmail power they have over people's lives by virtue of their control of capital. The greatest weapon of private enterprise is its ability to threaten to relocate and/or to refuse to produce products and, consequently, jobs. To insure "business confidence" or a "good business climate," government at all levels provides business with the range of subsidies detailed in the JEC and other studies.

In cases where the public interest requires the operation of social or business enterprises that are unprofitable on strict business terms (i.e., costs are greater than income generated at the publicly desirable price), public agencies or enterprises should be funded directly from tax dollars to carry out the activity, as in the case of schools, road maintenance, police and fire services, and so on. If a large enterprise such as Chrysler, whose closing would affect thousands of working class families, seeks tax breaks or government funds, then in return the government, through the public holding company, should take an equity position in the firm, place public representatives on its board, and restructure the firm.

Tax dollars should be used in the public interest, not to enrich owners of private enterprises; and the benefits to the public should be as specific and direct as possible, rather than "trickle down" through a corporate filter.

Collective Bargaining

In the United States, trade unions have relied mainly on collective bargaining to influence corporate policy. As Milton Derber described in his study, *The American Idea of Industrial Democracy,* industrial democracy has been viewed by American unions as essentially collective bargaining.[8]

The great gains in collective bargaining—the right of union members to negotiate legally over wages, hours, and to some extent working conditions, as well as benefits such as pensions and health care insurance—were won through militant direct action in the 1930s under the leadership of the CIO and with the support of the Roosevelt administration. From the postwar period to the present, these gains have been consolidated, but not expanded.

There is no doubt that the victories of industrial unions led to real improvement in the lives of union members in the mass-production industries. One result, however, has been the creation of what economists call a dual labor market, with a cleavage between better-paying, career-oriented, generally unionized jobs and lower-paying, nonunion, less secure jobs. The costs of unionization have generally been passed on to the public at large, as consumers, in the form of higher prices. Collective bargaining has achieved no discernible shift in income or wealth from capital to labor, nor have management prerogatives been yielded to workers to any great degree. American managers still make all major decisions on what is produced, where it is produced, how it is produced, and at what cost it will be sold (within the bounds, of course, of technologies and markets, both nationwide and international).

Prevailing union attitudes on challenging management's decision-making powers are typified by the remarks of Thomas Donahue, executive assistant to George Meany, at a 1976 international conference in Montreal:

> We do not seek to be a partner in management—to be most likely the junior partner in success and the senior partner in failure.
> We do not want to blur in any way the distinctions between the respective roles of management and labor in the plant. . . .[9]

This attitude is common even among more liberal union leaders. William Winpisinger, president of the International Association of Machinists and Aerospace Workers and an openly declared democratic socialist, rejected the notion of worker representation on the boards of corporations. In a 1976 statement on the subject, Winpisinger declared:

> Although American workers might gain some short-term advantage by having representation on corporate boards of directors, they would also risk having such representatives co-opted by management interests. As worker-

directors become more concerned with management's problems, they might become less responsive to the needs of the work force. Anyone who has read George Orwell's *Animal Farm* will recall what happened to the pigs when they took over management after driving out the former human owners. They began to walk and talk and think like men until, finally, when they sat down to meet with men, "The creatures looked from pig to man, and from man to pig, and from pig to man again; but already it was impossible to say which was which."

Through unions, American workers have negotiated—co-determined—contract provisions limiting management's once unlimited arbitrary power to lay off, recall, promote, or discharge.

Through collective bargaining, grievance procedures have been established to protect the worker's right to be heard and represented in disciplinary actions. Through collective bargaining, Americans not only have gained higher wages, shorter hours, and better working conditions, but they have also pioneered a host of benefits that were once considered beyond the reach of working people. These include cost-of-living adjustments, paid sick leave and holidays, vacations, health insurance, supplemental unemployment benefits, dental care, and pension plans.[10]

The gains made through collective bargaining have been real—but they have not expanded in recent years, and the percentage of the working population enjoying the fruits of collective bargaining is declining.

Critics of contemporary American unionism (such as sociologist Stanley Arnonowitz in *False Promises,* or journalist William Serrin in *The Company and the Union*) argue that American unions have *already* been co-opted by the collective bargaining process itself and by the limits to this process accepted by the unions. Examples such as lobbying by union representatives in the halls of Congress to promote management's case (as with the B-1 bomber, the SST, pollution controls, etc.) are numerous. Serrin concluded his study of General Motors and the United

Auto Workers with a quote from a black worker: "The Company and the Union, they are more or less business partners."

From this critical perspective, unions can be viewed as organizations that discipline the work force and allow corporations to engage in long-term planning without the disruption of wildcat strikes, excessive grievances, or demands for new infringements on management power. As a number of sociological studies have demonstrated, most unions are not run by their rank-and-file members in a participatory fashion. The majority are bureaucratic, hierarchical, and not very democratic. A union member does derive some tangible benefits from union membership, but it is difficult to consider these as falling under the category of democracy. To take one example, under present union grievance procedures workers accused of wrongdoing are considered guilty until they prove themselves innocent—the exact opposite of rights enjoyed outside the work place. Employees' rights of free speech and assembly are greatly circumscribed at work, and in many firms scarcely exist at all.

Employee participation in decision making about what is produced, how it is produced, and where it is produced, is almost nonexistent except in a few isolated, management-initiated experiments. In addition, in most cases the employee is not even represented in these decisions by the union; they are outside the scope of collective bargaining as practiced in the United States.

In some instances—for example, the agreement between the United Steelworkers and the steel industry involving productivity gains, wages, and a no-strike promise—the workers' right to strike has been bargained away by the union leadership through acceptance of *industry's* plans for the rationalization of plant and equipment.

There are a few cases in which union leaders have raised planning issues in negotiations. In 1948, in the midst of wage negotiations with General Motors,

UAW president Walter Reuther argued that GM could afford to increase workers' wages *and* hold the line on new car prices. Reuther offered to prove his case, if GM would open its books to the union so that the union could see the firm's cost figures. The company refused, and the union was ultimately forced to settle the strike on relatively unfavorable terms. Reuther never raised the issue again.

In England, unions have begun to take a broader view of collective bargaining. In a 1977 report on industrial democracy, the Trades Union Congress argued that traditional collective bargaining had failed to cover a range of important decision areas:

> It is clear that this leaves a wide range of fundamental managerial decisions affecting workpeople that are beyond the control—and very largely beyond the influence—of workpeople and trade unions. . . . Major decisions on investment, location, closures, and take-overs and mergers, and product specialization of the organization are generally taken at levels where collective bargaining does not take place and indeed are subject matter not readily covered by collective bargaining. New forms of control are needed.[11]

These "new forms of control" will be examined later in this chapter when we review new labor legislation in Western Europe. While in the past American unions have been reluctant to broaden the range of issues raised in collective bargaining, adverse economic circumstances (coupled with democratic stirrings from rank-and-file movements within the unions) could change this situation.

New Approaches

The activism of the 1960s and 1970s—particularly Ralph Nader and the consumer movement—focused critical attention on the large corporation and its effect on people's lives. A number of reform proposals have been put forward by the movement. Legal reforms regarding the corporation such as federal chartering and/or a federal minimum standards act for corporations have been proposed by Ralph Nader and other public interest lawyers.[12]

The approach of Nader, Christopher Stone, and other lawyers is, not surprisingly, legalistic rather than political. A legal remedy—i.e., tougher or more prescriptive or punitive laws—is proposed for the problem of corporate power with little regard for institutional relationships within and outside business enterprises, and little consideration of the constituencies that might be affected by or involved in the new arrangements.

It is easy, for example, to talk of consumers or the consumer movement in the abstract; but, in reality, it is not a mass movement and certainly not a democratic movement. Instead, a handful of well-minded activists, usually lawyers, speak for "the public interest." The reforms proposed by the movement reflect the lack of a political base for the movement itself. Who would enforce the legal reforms proposed by Nader and others? Presumably the courts, in which corporations have tremendous advantage, or the government, which is not a neutral force but one currently dominated by corporate influence. This situation, not the inherent unworkability in theory of a reform such as federal chartering or public representation (which "public"?) reduces such reforms to mere "schemes" that are unlikely to be enacted due to lack of political support or, if they were, would fail because of their violation of the realities of political power.

Rather than discuss abstract proposals for reducing the power of corporate managers or in some way curbing or guiding the behavior of corporations through laws or administrative directives, it is more useful to examine the practical experience of countries similar to the United States—the democratic, mixed economies of Western Europe—in which some far-reaching steps have been taken toward controlling corporate power and democratizing the operation of large business enterprises, and in which the debate over economic democracy, as opposed to simply industrial democracy, is a real public debate with significant reform measures on the political agenda of major political parties.

Workers on the Boards of Directors

The issue of increased democratic control over the corporation and increased worker participation within the corporation arose in Western Europe in the context of the economic downturn of the 1970s. Simultaneous inflation and unemployment, coupled with the development of a more highly educated work force and the call of the New Left for "participatory democracy," which challenged old attitudes about work, produced a heavy strain on the industrial relations systems of all Western European countries. Old accommodations between corporate leaders, union officials, and government politicians and planners were challenged by wildcat strikes, plant takeovers, and increasing absenteeism, as well as the rise of small but militant parties of the Left and Right.

The 1970s brought an increasing concern with the "quality of life." Economic growth as an end in itself was challenged. A Green Paper prepared for the European Economic Community recognized these social changes:

The current economic situation, with its reduced possibilities for growth, has emphasized the need for mechanisms which will adequately ensure the pursuit of goals other than economic growth, such as the improvement of the quality of life and working conditions, the protection of the environment and the interests of the consumer. The pursuit of such goals can probably be secured only by the existence of decision-making processes in enterprises which have a broader, more democratic base than such processes often have at present.[13]

One of the major reforms of this period, which has been proposed in almost every Western European country and implemented in some, is the placement of workers' representatives on the boards of directors of the major corporations of the country. The theory behind the reform, at least to the extent any clear theory exists, is that corporations ultimately are governed by their boards and that the employees of the firm are a constituency that must be recognized and represented on the governing body of the firm through their own elected representatives. In this way, diverse views other than those of the managerial and financial elite are introduced into corporate decision making.

A variety of claims have been made for this reform. On the Left, it is sometimes viewed as what André Gorz terms a "reformist reform"—one which does not change power relationships in a society. On the Right, it is considered a move that will destroy the capitalist system by hopelessly crippling the corporation—the engine of economic growth that produces the goods people want.

While the reform itself has been in effect for only a short while in some countries (as little as a year or two), some tentative conclusions can be drawn based on the numerous recent studies and investigations conducted in Europe on the subject.

The most thorough study of worker representation on company boards of directors has been made in England by the Committee of Inquiry on Industrial Democracy—known as the Bullock Commission after its chairman, historian Alan Bullock. The commission requested research papers from Eric Batsone of the Industrial Relations Unit of the University of Warwick and author of *The Worker Directors: A Sociology of*

Participation, and from P. D. Davies, fellow and tutor in law at Balliol College, Oxford.

In a review of the European experience prepared for the commission, Batsone concluded:

> Worker Directors have generally had little effect on anything, and, second and consequently, they have certainly had no catastrophic effect on anything or anybody.[14]

The final Bullock Commission report, which recommended equality of representation for workers on corporate boards, took a slightly more sanguine view. The report cited a study of the National Swedish Industrial Board which, on the basis of three years of minority representation for workers on boards, concluded:

> Although one may question whether the reform *per se* has so far meant any significant increase on the influence wielded by employees, it has undoubtedly improved the opportunities of insight. In the long run it should serve to increase their influence as well. . . .[15]

P. L. Davies, in his report to the commission on the European experience, observed:

> The picture appears to be that minority employee representation on the board may increase somewhat employees' access to information and improve management communication channels, and may somewhat encourage current trends towards the breakdown of autocratic management and a recognition of the need to take social and personnel matters into account in the setting of corporate objectives, but that such representation does not provide the opportunity to change the nature of board decision-making. The reasons for this are various but the major one would seem to be that with minority representation there is no effective transfer of power from shareholders and management towards workers, and worker representatives are thus in a relatively powerless situation dependent completely on the goodwill of management and other board members.[16]

Large corporations are run by their managers; corporate boards serve largely as a device for "validating" decisions management has already taken. There are a number of reasons for this, as has been shown in numerous studies. Sociologists who observed a number of corporate board meetings concluded:

> To be sure, the final yea or nea at a board meeting may be seen as the decision point, and may so appear in corporate histories. . . . But the board actions we have observed are better interpreted, we feel, merely as ratifications of decisions made earlier and elsewhere, sometimes by much more junior men, about which the board had no practical alternative. The distinction between "making" and "taking" decisions is relevant. Boards of directors, we feel, are best conceived as decision-taking institutions, that is, as legitimating institutions, rather than as decision-making ones.[17]

Corporate boards—indeed, boards of directors as presently operated *no matter who sits on them*—are problematical in terms of enterprise decision making for fairly obvious reasons:

1) any group that meets so rarely and is so dependent upon others (i.e., management) for information and advice cannot hope to control in any real sense;

2) managers have authority within the firm, detailed knowledge and information, and large resources in terms of personnel; the exact opposite is the case with outside directors (and inside directors are, of course, management);

3) to the extent that the board does make any real decisions, these are usually arrived at *in advance* through informal communication between like-minded directors; troublemakers—worker-directors, for example—are simply excluded from the process. Sometimes, committees of the board are formed and control can be maintained by excluding worker-directors from the key committees.

The failure of corporate boards to play a strong role in enterprise decision making, however, is not absolutely inherent in the concept of a governing board. It results more from the fact that, until the advent of worker-directors (and, in the United States, a handful of corporate-selected "public" directors representing in a vague way women, minorities, or consumers), boards have been composed of like-minded men of the same class and race who found it unnecessary and unthinkable to meddle in a detailed way in the affairs of their friends and social equals who run the companies on which they serve as board members. Members of boards traditionally have been heads of other companies or representatives of financial institutions who agree with the overall objectives of the firm (to make a healthy profit or to expand market share), so it is not surprising that boards have not adopted a more aggressive role. Indeed, it would have been exceptional had they done so.

Entering the corporate boards as outsiders, the worker-directors find themselves joining a "club" of their social betters, with its own mystique and peculiar atmosphere. As Batsone described it:

> Thus the new worker director enters a strange situation in which, given the formalities of board activity and the norms of board conduct, he is dependent upon other directors to "show him the ropes" and to instruct him on how to act as a "proper director." Although the worker director is not seen by his board colleagues to qualify as a "proper" director in terms of managerial talent or property rights, a process of "negotiation" implicitly occurs in which he is treated as such on condition that he acts accordingly, accepting the assumptions and priorities of the board and conforming to the norms of "gentlemanly" conduct.[18]

Worker-directors consequently have tended to raise questions mainly on matters of plant closure and security of employment. They have accepted management's arguments for rationalization of the company (i.e., closures, layoffs, new plants in other locations) and concentrated their efforts on winning adequate social policies to help the affected workers.

Much of the interest and anxiety regarding worker representation on company boards has focused on the German co-determination industries (iron and steel beginning in 1950, and all major companies from 1976 on) in which parity representation gives worker-directors the ability to "sabotage" policies favored by management or shareholder representatives. In practice, these fears have proved groundless, at least in Germany. The German government, through its Biedenkopf Commission, found that worker-directors showed little desire to influence the general business policy of the firm and confined their interest to social and personnel aspects of board discussions. Consequently, worker-directors have had little impact on investment decisions, dividends, takeovers, and so on.

The Biedenkopf Commission observed that "while participation of workers on the supervisory board did indeed lead to a stronger emphasis on the social aspects . . . nevertheless the validity of the principle of profitability as the keynote of entrepreneurial initiative and planning was in no case called into question."[19]

Workers appear to understand the limited role that worker-directors can play. A study of worker-directors in the British Steel Corporation found that workers believed their representatives on the boards rarely had any significant degree of influence.[20]

Of course, it is difficult to separate universals from the political and social context in which reforms come about. In West Germany, co-determination was introduced in the immediate postwar period, when the social consensus held that co-determination in the iron and steel industry would help prevent the reoccurrence of Nazi-style fascism. As Winpisinger of the

International Machinists and others have suggested, German co-determination has been largely a replacement for aggressive collective bargaining at the plant and industry levels, *not* a conscious step on the road to a socialist worker-controlled economy. As Alfred Diamant concluded in his study, "The Myth and Reality of Mitbestimmung [co-determination] in the Federal Republic of Germany":

The German version of industrial democracy clearly bears the stamp of the peculiar national experience of that particular labor movement. But the achievements on the road to industrial democracy so far are more nearly *system maintaining rather than system transforming in character*. This has been so not only, or perhaps not even chiefly, because of the political and economic constraints imposed on the labor movement, but because the labor movement—at least since 1949—has moved almost entirely within a moderate, evolutionary ambience.[21]

Diamant and others who have investigated German industrial relations have found that even full co-determination—an equal number of worker and shareholder-management directors with a neutral, tie-breaking director—is not at odds with a corporate-dominated, profit-maximizing economy, as long as the labor movement accepts management's goals as its own and views the success and prosperity of the labor movement as linked to the success and prosperity of the major corporations.

In his report, Eric Batsone suggested conditions under which worker-directors can be *somewhat* effective in influencing company operations. These include the following:

1) Workers should be given parity representation on the board of directors and full participation in all company committees on which board members sit.

2) Resources should be available to help worker-directors analyze the information they acquire. These

include staff help and backup research facilities, which Batsone recommends be provided by the unions.

3) Worker-directors should be based firmly on in-plant organizations with direct ties and accountability to plant-level organizations. What this means in American terms is putting on boards not just international vice-presidents of unions, but local presidents and local union officials as well. A concern expressed by other authors is that compensation for worker-directors not accrue to the individual, but go into a union fund, to minimize the gap between the worker-directors and other union members. (Board compensation in the United States and Europe often equals a full-time worker's salary for an entire year.)

4) More information must be made available to the worker-directors. In effect, company books must be opened to union scrutiny. Current worker-directors suffer from legal and informal restrictions on what topics covered at board meetings they are free to discuss with their constituents.

The Bullock Commission, which recommended parity representation for workers, also recommended that government funds be allotted for the training and education of new directors. In Sweden, since the introduction of worker-directors in 1973, the Swedish Trade Union Confederation has operated a training school for worker-directors, briefing them on the fundamentals of finance, accounting, and planning. Any move to establish worker representation on boards of directors in the United States would require similar training facilities.

The danger of worker-directors, as is clear from the European experience, is not that they constitute a subversive force, but that they may be simply irrelevant and a sham. Such an outcome can be avoided only if worker-directors are seen as just one part of an overall strategy to democratize the economy. Democratic theory requires that the boardroom be opened to worker directors and to "special" directors representing components of the overall public interest—consumers, environmentalists, minorities, and women. "Special" directors will be effective only under the conditions outlined by Batsone for worker-directors: they must come from a recognizable constituency—i.e., a consumer group, women's group, environmentalist group, or minority organization with a constituency to which they are accountable in some way; they must be provided with resources, including a staff and research help; and they must, by law, have access to company information.

Over a period of time, the opening of boardrooms to such interests will affect to some degree the decision-making priorities of managers. Opening the boardrooms will not necessarily make the work place itself more democratic, however, nor will it insure that parties other than managers participate in business decisions. This is more likely, as the European experience shows, to come through aggressive collective bargaining and innovative labor legislation that introduces democratic participation into all levels of the firm, particularly inside the plant.

Collective Bargaining and Plant-Level Democracy

The same crisis in industrial relations and economic downturn that stimulated interest in worker representation on boards of directors also pushed collective bargaining and labor legislation in Western Europe beyond the well-established boundaries of the 1950s and 1960s, when management's decision-making power went unchallenged.

After World War II, works councils were created in many Western European countries. Works councils were plant-level committees with elected worker members who consulted with management on a variety of work issues; actual collective bargaining was conducted by large national unions and national employer associations.

A survey of the works councils experience by an official of the International Labor Organization concluded:

A rapid survey of the role played by works councils around the world shows that there is often disenchantment with their functioning. There is a broad consensus in many countries that works councils have not lived up to the expectations that were placed in them when they were first initiated. Many examples could be given from various parts of the world to show that the works council is not, perhaps, an ideal means of handling employer-employee relations at the enterprise level. One of the reasons for this seems to be the lack of real decision-making power possessed by most councils. Experience has shown that a purely advisory arrangement under which workers are given information and may express an opinion, but have no influence on whether this opinion is taken into account or not is not likely to create much enthusiasm or even interest.[22]

In place of moribund works councils, new workers' organizations appeared in many Western European countries in the late 1960s and early 1970s, fueled by a new worker militancy and backed up by new labor legislation. In Italy, for example, where there is little interest in co-determination of the German variety, strikes throughout the country in the fall of 1969 resulted in the creation of new structures for worker participation: shop floor and factory assemblies, elected work place delegates, and factory councils. Workers directly off the shop floor controlled plant-level negotiations. The older consultative works council commissions faded away, supplanted by these more active and militant-based worker organizations.

As Martin Slater noted in his study of Italian industrial relations, "The [new] workers' councils were unusual in extending the area of bargaining while bringing permanent confrontation into the workplace. The councils accepted no limitation on which topics could be brought up in negotiations."[23]

The Italian workers' councils challenged management over the organization of work in the factory: job classification, working conditions, and job enrichment. At the same time, they challenged the power of the employers in the area of planned investments. Fiat workers agreed to spread a reduction in working hours over a longer period of time in return for a commitment on the part of the company to invest in underdeveloped southern Italy. The agreements laid out specific plans for this investment, including detailed provisions for social infrastructure spending by Fiat in the south. Workers at Alfa-Romeo, the state-owned automobile firm, challenged the company's investment plans and won significant victories. Chemical workers called for tighter pollution control measures by the firms where they worked.

"The significance of the councils has not been just in the fact that they now confront the employer on an unlimited range of issues," noted Slater, "but in that they now *define the issues.*"[24]

In France, where worker representation on the boards of directors has also not been a key issue, worker militancy erupted during the events of May 1968. Many plants were occupied, and the old, atrophied works councils were revived. A symbol of the new mood of French workers was the occupation of the watch plant at Lip (see chapter 4 for a detailed discussion). Lip inspired hundreds of other factory occupations. The most interesting and politically creative response to the events of May 1968 and their immediate aftermath came from the country's second largest union organization, the Confédération Française Démocratique du Travail (CFDT), the socialist but noncommunist union. At the CFDT's national congress in May 1970, it adopted *autogestion* (self-management) as its primary objective, and *socialism autogestionaire* (self-managed socialism) became the official union platform; it was adopted soon after by the revived United Socialist Party headed by François Mitterand. The concept and slogan of self-management played a crucial role in the revival of the noncommunist Left in France. It has also pushed the discussion of economic reforms beyond such limited notions as worker representation on the boards of directors to encompass the entire nature of industrialized society. Because self-management is also a critique of socialism as practiced in the Soviet Union and Eastern Europe, the Communist Party of France and its trade union arm, the CGT, were slow to adopt the phrase. Only in 1978, after the defeat of the leftist coalition, did the French Communist Party even begin to use the term "self-management" in public, and the sincerity of its interest in self-management as both a strategy and a goal remains doubtful.

The CFDT vision is similar to participatory democracy as first proposed by the American Students for a Democratic Society in the 1960s, but with a clear anticapitalist cast. For the CFDT, self-managed socialism is distinguished from both capitalism and centralized socialism in the role played by ordinary citizens. Real power must come from the bottom up, not the top down. A massive restructuring of education and information systems, a radical reduction in salary differentials, a regular rotation of tasks, and a reorientation of the way knowledge and competence are acquired and socially rewarded are necessary components of a culture compatible with self-management.

The French Communist Party and the CGT criticized Lip as "setting up an island of socialism in a sea of capitalism," and denounced the strikes that followed as undisciplined actions which jeopardized the possibility for a united leftist front. Because of the defeat of the leftist coalition in 1978, many of these matters are under discussion and debate. Interestingly, one of the criticisms to appear has been the lack of democratic participation within the French Communist Party itself.

Of all the countries in Western Europe, Sweden has made the greatest progress in legislation to increase workers' control, both at the work place and in broader corporate decision making. The structure of authority within Swedish companies has been substantially altered by a series of laws enacted since 1971. The legislation curtailed managerial prerogatives by bringing into the collective-bargaining process a whole new range of managerial decisions. Olaf Palme, prime minister of the Social Democratic government during the period these reforms were enacted, called them "the greatest diffusion of power and influence that has taken place in our land since the introduction of universal suffrage." How true this assessment is remains to be seen. Most of the laws are too recent to judge how they will work in practice; but it is clear that Sweden has begun to make a break with its past system of industrial relations.

The new Swedish laws include the following:

The 1973 revision of the 1949 Work Safety Law. Among other things, this law gives the in-plant health and safety steward the right to halt any process he or she regards as dangerous, pending a judgment from a government health inspector. The law guarantees the steward's job security, training, and time off with pay to perform duties. If challenged by the company, the steward's decision to halt a process remains in effect until the matter is adjudicated in a labor court. The law shifts from the union to the employer the burden of initiating a legal challenge and submitting proof. The safety steward thus has the right by law to stop a hazardous process without first having to summon a safety inspector.

The safety stewards' authority and an obligatory plant safety committee must be provided with information about anticipated changes in plant layout, equipment, and new construction in advance of the changes. Union representatives may hold up the plans on health and safety grounds. In addition, the law widens the concept of health and safety to include not only physical well-being but also psychological well-being.

Job security. The Security of Employment Act requires employers to give notice of termination from one to six months in advance, depending on length of service and age. All "unreasonable" dismissals are illegal, and the term is defined legally with special reference to older workers. In a dispute, the affected individual retains his or her job at full pay until the matter is heard by the labor court. Again, the burden of proof is on the employer.

Job promotion. The Law on Employment Promoting Measures increases opportunities for older and otherwise disadvantaged workers by requiring employers to notify both the local union and the local employment office of impending layoffs up to six months in advance. Tripartite committees comprised of union, company, and government employment office representatives are created to modify personnel policy and redesign jobs so as to adapt local demand for labor to the available local supply.

Status of union officials. This law extends to union officials all the protection provided to safety stewards under the Work Safety Law. It spells out the rights of officials, including the right to information and to time and training for union work at the employer's expense. In disputes over these rights, the union's position prevails unless challenged in labor court by the employer.

Worker representation on corporate boards. After a four-year trial period of two worker representatives on the boards of large corporations (100 or more employees), a law was passed in 1976 requiring that all firms with twenty-five employees or more—including banks and insurance companies, and, in modified form, institutions of state and local government—have two worker representatives on the board of directors or directing body. This is not considered as a first, tentative step toward parity representation; rather, it is viewed as a way to provide unions with more information, so that they will be in a better position to exercise their new rights in collective bargaining.

Co-determination at work. This bill, passed in 1976, represents the linchpin of the move toward increased democratic decision making within enterprises in Sweden. It specifies that unions can negotiate agreements for co-determination rights *in all matters* concerning hiring and firing, work organization, and management of the enterprise. The law sets certain minimal standards. Management is required to initiate negotiations in advance of important changes in operations, such as expansion, mergers, and reorganization of the enterprise. It is also obliged to negotiate on *all other changes,* if the union so demands. In most cases, the company must postpone decisions until negotiations are completed. Management is also required to supply information from company accounts and other data to the unions and to conduct whatever studies may be needed to supply additional information requested by unions.

As in the rest of Western Europe, these laws were enacted by the governing Social Democrats and their union allies, the Confederation of Swedish Trade Unions, in response to the increasing number of wildcat strikes, growing absenteeism, and rising educational level of the work force.

There is no doubt that the new legislation represents a major transformation of the structure of authority in Swedish enterprise; and it is the most far-reaching labor legislation reform in any Western mixed economy. Obviously, the significance of the legislation depends on how the opportunities for democratic participation that have been opened for the unions and their members are utilized in practice.

A spokesman for the trade union confederation told journalist David Jenkins:

It will take many years to get real industrial democracy. We must educate people. You can't tell people that everything is going to change overnight just because of one law. It may take five or six years to see the first real effects.

Jenkins commented that

one almost certain effect of the law will be to help push union power down to local levels. In recent years, plant agreement on wages above the national accord have become increasingly common, and this practice irritates both union officials and employers' representatives at the national level. But this trend, though very gradual, appears very strong. . . .[25]

American unions will face tough decisions on political strategy in the coming decade which might lead them down the path chosen by the Swedish labor movement. In 1978, after some of the heaviest business lobbying in the post–World War II period, labor's key bill—the Labor Law Reform Act—was defeated in Congress. Some union leaders such as William Winpisinger of the Machinists and Douglas Fraser of the Auto Workers, viewed the concerted action of business as a clear violation of the consensus that had governed American industrial relations and national politics for thirty years. Fraser, in a highly publicized speech, announced that big business had declared "class war" on the unions, and that the labor movement had to fight back by building a coalition for change with allies in the consumer, women's, minority, and environmental movements, and by going on the political offensive with new policy positions.

The Swedish laws offer models for such new policies. In place of greater government regulation, which has been under attack from the Right in the United

States, the Swedish approach offers democratic participation by workers at the work place, backed up by the resources of their unions.

If the existing leadership of major unions does not challenge management prerogatives along the lines of the Swedish model, then it is possible that new, younger leaders will raise these issues and win high-level union positions by mobilizing rank-and-file sentiment.

Planning and Planning Agreements

A final avenue of control over management decision making is government planning, in which the government, representing the public interest, exercises control over some management decisions. Often, this control can take the form of negotiated agreements between the government and the company; frequently, unions are included in the process, making it a tripartite planning arrangement.

Plant location and plant closures are one area in which governments in Western Europe exercise considerable control. In England, a corporation that wishes to close, relocate, or build a new facility must first secure an industrial development certificate from the Department of Trade and Industry. The application is considered on the basis of whether or not the proposed action will be consistent with an appropriate distribution of job opportunities throughout the country. Not only have corporations been prevented from closing plants in high-unemployment areas, but they have also been required to locate new facilities in job-scarce regions. When shutdowns are permitted, workers must be offered suitable alternative employment by the company at another location and, if such transfer does not occur, the employee is entitled to a tax-free severance allowance in addition to unemployment benefits.

In France, the country's federal labor code provides that no employee can be laid off or dismissed unless the corporation receives approval from the local government employment agency. That agency is empowered to reject shutdowns after considering the employment situation in the area and the economic rationale for the proposed closure. French law makes it illegal to dismiss employees in a closure or relocation to avoid collective-bargaining agreement increases or to escape the consequences of governmental restrictions on closings, and requires consultation with factory committees representing the workers. Failure to do so can result not only in reversal of the closure but in cash damages for employees.

In West Germany, any relocation or transfer of work must be approved by the government and submitted to a works council elected by employees. If they do not agree to the proposed shifts, binding mediation occurs. No plant may close without a permit from the state labor exchange, which can reject the proposed action when substantial unemployment exists in the area affected.

These sorts of planning requirements have been demanded by unions to mitigate the effect of industrial rationalization, though they do not eliminate it.

In 1978, Congressman William Ford (D-Mich.) introduced the National Employment Priorities Act, a moderate version of the plant location laws found in Western Europe. The act would require employers to give two years' warning when a plant shutdown or relocation is planned. It would also provide financial and job-training assistance to displaced workers (paid for in part by the company) and, at the same time, reduce certain incentives to locate plants out of the country, such as tax breaks on foreign income. The UAW announced that passage of the legislation is one of its major political priorities.

Planning as an abstract concept can be both confusing and almost meaningless. All families, government agencies, enterprises, and so on, plan their activities. What we are discussing here is a type of planning in which a number of different units—in most cases, business enterprises—are encouraged and/or required to coordinate their activities with one another and with an overall set of publicly articulated goals, or to take into account nonmarket factors outside the enterprise itself.

Michael Watson, in his essay, "Planning in the Liberal Democratic State," points out:

Planning, it seems, can have a dual nature, either reforming or rationalizing, according to who is effectively wielding power or major influence, within government, over the planning process.[26]

The aim of industrial policy planning in Western Europe has been essentially to improve the market position of national industry, especially internationally. The government's major role has been to provide technical and financial assistance. Its contact with industry has involved direct, symbiotic relationships with particular firms, from which are expected to flow greater efficiency, technical development, and the creation of national "pacemaker" firms.

An example of such a planning policy is the National Enterprise Board (NEB) in Great Britain. Viewed by its original designers as a state holding company that would take equity positions in leading, dynamic firms in Britain and guide economic development along a "socially responsible" path, in practice the NEB has followed a sophisticated form of state capitalist planning in which the government provides the necessary infusion of funds and technical assistance to firms it considers to possess a potential for technical growth and competitiveness in the world market. The equity position taken by the government is viewed not as permanent public ownership, but as a short-term form of capital assistance. One instance of NEB activity is the transfer of Rolls-Royce into public ownership under a Conservative government because the firm was undergoing a short-run cash flow problem in the development of sophisticated, high-technology engines.

Britain's NEB is almost exactly the kind of new Reconstruction Finance Corporation that liberal investment bankers in New York have advocated to help smooth out problems in the American economy. As Felix Rohatyn of Lazard Freres told *Forbes* magazine:

We're talking about temporary equity investments by the government. Two, three years might be sufficient for Lockheed or a major airline that may have a temporary problem.[27]

In France, national planners have worked closely with the country's managerial elite. Many were educated at the same schools, and together they form a select club. Their goals, as in England, have been to rationalize and modernize French industry and improve its competitiveness on the world market.

Professor John Sheahan, an economist at Williams College, pointed out that the greatest beneficiaries of French planning have been the largest corporations. Sheahan commented:

A method which requires the (Planning) Commission to grant favors to corporations in return for cooperation is tantamount to making the commission a spokesman for business within the government. In particular, the Commission acts as a representative for the firms which it finds easiest to deal with: these are the largest companies with professional managements best able to understand and influence the plans. The Commission has almost automatically favored greater industrial concentration. This attitude has led to increased concentration both where it may mean greater efficiency and where it may entail disfunctional size. It has weakened any chance of significant domestic competition. *If ITT were a French corporation, the Planning Commission would be its natural ally.*[28] [Emphasis added.]

In land-use planning, regional and national government planners have aided mainly in overcoming the resistance of local interests to industrial and commercial development. Planners have sought to promote an orderly physical organization of economic expansion, including the necessary infrastructural support, that goes beyond traditional town boundaries. So-called new towns have, in most cases, become support systems for industry or middle-class suburbs serving urban needs.

Regional policy has tried half-heartedly to spread the benefits of economic growth, but with little success. In fact, regional policy has become a form of subsidization for industrial location.

Not unexpectedly, the experience with planning in Western Europe reflects the sociopolitical forces in each country. Indeed, it would have been surprising had liberal governments used their planning powers to redistribute wealth or control over the economy rather than to assist in the rationalization and development of industry.

In 1975, a group of liberal American businessmen and academics proposed a rationalizing planning system for the United States. The late Senator Hubert Humphrey and Senator Jacob Javits were persuaded to introduce the Balanced Growth and Economic Planning Act, which would create a small office of national economic planning. Its major function, according to the sponsors, would be informational. The office would accumulate, collate, and analyze economic data from numerous sources, then provide the president and the Congress with alternative economic programs for both the long and short term. The backers of the bill noted:

> It should be clear that the planning office would not set specific goals for General Motors, General Electric, General Foods, or any other individual firm. But it would indicate the number of cars, the number of generators and the quantity of frozen foods we are likely to require in, say,

five years, and it would try to induce the relevant industries to act accordingly.[29]

Large corporations already engage in such analysis of future demand for their own planning purposes. Having a government planning unit engage in similar studies, or perhaps more sophisticated ones, seems to offer little, particularly if the government is to remain without the means (public banks or competitive public enterprises) to carry out whatever goals are set by the planning office. Under current political and economic power arrangements, the result of such efforts would be simply another form of subsidy to large corporations.

If such informational planning by the government has little merit as a structural reform, is there *any* form of government economic planning that might make sense in the American context?

The Soviet and Eastern European model of central planning, which is neither terribly efficient nor very democratic, is not an attractive alternative, and we need not investigate it here. However, a few younger European economists have proposed a *democratic* form of socialist planning for Western Europe that merits attention. The economist who synthesizes these views best is Stuart Holland of Sussex University, former economic advisor to Prime Minister Harold Wilson under his Labour government. Holland, in a number of works (most notably *The Socialist Challenge*) has put forward the concept of planning agreements.

Holland believes that a socialist government concerned not simply with managing corporate capitalism, but with gradually transforming it in a more egalitarian direction, can conclude planning agreements with the major firms in each industry. These planning agreements would be a form of negotiation between government planners and senior management of the firms; union representatives

would be included in the planning process and represented on the board of the firms. In order for the
process, which would be more indicative than coer-
cive, to work well in practice, Holland believes that
the number of publicly owned firms in Britain would
have to be increased to include at least one major firm
in each of twelve or more major industrial sectors.
These would be dynamic, profit-making firms—not
losers. By negotiating planning agreements with
leading firms, the government would set overall
priorities for the economy that would be followed by
secondary firms. (His notion is similar to that of
competitive public enterprise as spelled out in chapter
2.)

These planning agreements would require firms to
provide detailed information on their corporate plans
for up to five and ten years ahead—information on
investment plans, plant locations, managerial salaries,
exports, and so on. Based on the information in the
planning agreement, the government would conduct
a social audit of the firm that would stress the consumer implications of the enterprise's activity, including advertising expenditures, misleading or de-
ceptive ads, deterioration or improvement in the
quality of service, and so forth. In drafting the social
audits, the government would request written sub-
missions from national consumer organizations.

The government would be empowered by law to
receive detailed material. In fact, the U.S. government currently obtains a great deal of information on
the performance of major firms, but not on future
corporate plans.

Analogous to the kind of planning agreements
Holland proposes is the bargaining and contractual
process that goes on in the defense sector of the
American economy. There, private firms respond to
Department of Defense (DOD) requests for proposals
on new weapon systems and then provide the DOD
with detailed information on the system they propose

to build. Once a contract is granted, the DOD is empowerd by law to work closely with the firm on the production process itself. DOD cost-control personnel are often stationed within the plant or firm itself to monitor progress on the contract.

This is an indicative planning process, based on government-enterprise cooperation to achieve overall social goals. Unfortunately, in the United States it has been applied chiefly to produce weapons; there is no reason, however, why such planning could not be used to produce a wide range of goods, to locate new plants in underdeveloped sections of the country such as Appalachia, to experiment with new plants designed to facilitate the establishment of new working arrangements that are more democratic and humane—and, of course, there is no reason why major unions could not be involved in the planning process. In effect, this is what Holland is proposing with his planning agreements.

Obviously, there is the danger that such planning will be nothing more than government-planned capitalism. The only way to avoid this problem is with a political solution, not a technical one. The government must be committed to social goals that include a fairer distribution of wealth and income, democratization of the work place, and more balanced and environmentally oriented economic development. The government must have the means at hand to carry out economic development in the event that private enterprise refuses to enter into planning agreements—in other words, there must be a core of publicly owned firms more responsive to government requests than private ones—and real sanctions must be levied against private firms that choose not to bargain. These could include denial of tax advantages and other subsidies, denial of export licenses, threat of antitrust suits, and so on.

Such a process of planning agreements would be facilitated by placing worker and special interest (such as consumer advocate) directors on the boards of all major corporations, and by requiring that corporations open their books in collective bargaining with unions and meetings with government officials. These policies, of course, can be expected to be carried out only by a reform government committed to economic democracy as its long-range goal.

Not just the federal government, but state governments, through stronger state economic development commissions and planning agencies, can also conclude planning agreements with firms. But this will be possible *only* if states have their own public sources of investment—banks and insurance companies, and pension funds—to give them the resources and leverage to act as equal partners in the planning process.

Planning and Democracy

Outside of their immediate work place, citizens can have the most impact on planning at the state and local levels. It is more likely that a concerned citizen will go to city hall or to the state capitol than to Washington, D.C. As at the national level, effective public planning would require new public enterprises at the state and local levels. The experience of certain Canadian provinces is worth noting in this regard. British Columbia has a publicly owned development company, Dunhill Developments, that buys land and constructs houses and industrial facilities. The provincial government also owns an economic development corporation that makes loans, provides equity, and engages in long-range economic planning. In the city of Saskatoon in Saskatchewan, extensive city ownership of land is used to guide the area's economic development. Public enterprises and public ownership of land are not simple panaceas; provisions for citizen access and participation in the planning process are necessary too.

Freedom of information acts, sunshine laws, and

expense reimbursement for citizen groups appearing before state agencies should enable and encourage participation by citizens in planning decisions that concern them. City-owned enterprises should have democratically elected governing boards.

Individuals have the greatest opportunity to participate directly in planning at the neighborhood and community level. In Vancouver, the city operates neighborhood planning offices. Each is established for a four-year period on a rotating basis. The planning office, in conjunction with a planning council composed of local residents who are either elected or appointed, depending on the specific neighborhood, develops a comprehensive plan for the neighborhood.

In the United States, interest in planning at the community level has fostered a movement for neighborhood government—an effort to decentralize government and economic decision making. In Washington, D.C., twenty elected neighborhood planning councils disburse an annual average of $1 million for youth services and employment projects. In Dayton, Ohio, neighborhood priority boards have allocated money for a community health center, a senior citizen center, community schools, a citywide development corporation, and minority small businesses. Such efforts are encouraged by a nationwide Alliance of Neighborhood Governments and serviced by research centers such as the Institute for Local Self-Reliance in Washington, D.C. To date, however, these neighborhood government mechanisms have mainly disbursed service money and have not created new economic enterprises such as cooperatives or worker-owned firms.

In the late 1960s, the Office of Economic Opportunity (OEO), funded a number of community development corporations (CDCs)—enterprises owned by residents of a geographic area—which have succeeded in establishing many community-based small businesses. Among the strongest of these development corporations are the Bedford-Stuyvesant Restoration Corporation, the Harlem Commonwealth Council, the East Los Angeles Community Union, and the Watts Labor Action Council. Unfortunately, while these CDCs and others have provided much-needed jobs, they have been less successful in encouraging citizen participation. As part of the federal poverty program, these CDCs were thrust upon the community from the outside; and frequently a single, charismatic leader has guided them from their birth. Development corporations need not be limited to poverty areas, however. They can serve as an economic vehicle for neighborhood government units to take more direct control over economic planning in their communities.

In a democratic economy, planning would not replace market relationships in *all* aspects of society. Currently, the United States is a mixed economy—a combination of planning and market relationships—but the planning is carried out either by large corporations in their own interests or by government in the service of corporate interests. Democratic planning would produce an overall public framework within which market exchanges between enterprises and between consumers and enterprises would take place. Consumers, through tougher laws, would be provided with more product information and would be better equipped to make purchases.

Under economic democracy, the rules of the market game would be changed: there would be more players (cooperatives, worker-owned firms, community development corporations, public enterprises), and the relationships between the players would be more balanced. This kind of market actually resembles Adam Smith's laissez-faire vision of the "invisible hand" more than does the existing corporate-dominated U.S. economy. The invisible hand works only when producers and consumers are relatively equal in terms of knowledge and power.

As for the visible hand of planning *outside the work place*, it would be most prevalent in the *physical* organization of communities—in land use, transportation and energy, housing, and recreation. Here, the public interest would take precedence over corporate interest —and the public interest would be defined through a process of *democratic* participation that begins at the level of the neighborhood and works its way upward.

PART THREE

Inflation, Unemployment, and Welfare

CHAPTER SEVEN

Inflation and Employment

Current Policy

In an economy based on competitive markets for goods and production inputs, such as labor and capital, mainstream economics—what Galbraith calls "the conventional wisdom"—views the wages workers earn as "just." The distribution of income, as dictated by the market's evaluation of individuals' worth, reflects this "marginal product justice." The poor are poor because they produce "less," while the rich receive their due reward. The unemployed are either lazy or ineffective—or both; or they simply may possess no skills the market wishes to purchase.

A number of problems arise in a system justified by such an ideology. Enormous fluctuations take place in the overall value the economy assigns to work. So, in times of economic expansion, work is highly valued and people can find jobs—many at decent pay. But, in times of contraction and depression, income and wages fall sharply and many workers cannot find work at all.

. The very high incomes earned by some in the economy and the very low incomes earned by others are also hard to justify in terms of social contribution. Is a corporate executive really "worth" ten times a worker on the assembly line? Is a male factory worker "worth" more than a female one?

As pointed out by economist Arthur Okun, former member of the president's Council of Economic Advisors, "society" demands a greater equality and stability of income than the market delivers. The degree of government intervention in the production process is such an important point of conflict among wage earners—the unemployed, blacks, women, all those who feel that the reward system is unjust—that it is somehow necessary to offset interests in the private sector that would like unfettered free enterprise. This struggle has resulted in government recognition of labor unions as bargaining representatives for groups of workers, minimum wage laws, Social Security, progressive income taxes, pension funds, welfare payments, unemployment compensation, and a commitment to steady growth through an interventionist monetary and fiscal policy.

In the Keynesian view of public policy, forms of government intervention such as taxation and public expenditures for steady growth and income distribution are meant to correct the injustices and inefficiencies of market capitalism. Large fluctuations in the growth rate under the market system are unacceptable to the mass of American workers, and even to most corporations (because of the potential political threat to the system itself). So government monetary and fiscal power is used in an attempt to stabilize business cycles. Until recently, Keynesian economists believed that, with a combination of varying tax rates and public expenditures (generating government surpluses and deficits) plus monetary policy, the American economy could grow steadily with stable prices and low unemployment. Okun wrote of the "nine years of prosperity" between 1961 and 1970:

More vigorous and more consistent applications of the tools of economic policy contributed to the obsolescence of the business cycle pattern and refutation of the stagnation myths. The reformed strategy of economic policy did not rest on any new theory: Ever since Keynes, economists had recognized that the federal government could stimulate economic activity by increasing the injection of federal expenditures into the income stream or by reducing the withdrawal of federal tax receipts.[1]

Taxes and public expenditures still are considered by Keynesians to be the foundation of efforts to "correct" the market's inequitable distribution of jobs and income. Most economists admit that the decision to tax the rich at progressive rates is a political one, not a decision based on some economically defensible logic. The Keynesian approach, operating primarily through public expenditures, attempts both to solve capitalism's economic growth–price stability–unemployment problem and to achieve a more socially and politically tolerable distribution of income.

Most economists, except the Friedman monetarist school and its more recent version, the "rational expectations" school, are now heavily influenced by this approach. Although Keynes was concerned especially with unemployment and less with inflation (inflation was not a very important problem during the Great Depression), and while today U.S. economists are concerned more with inflation than with unemployment, the concept of using monetary and fiscal policy to attain steady growth with stable prices —or at least a stable (and fairly low) inflation and a controlled level of unemployment—is part of the repertoire of even "conservative" economics. So, for example, Herbert Stein, head of Nixon's Council of Economic Advisors, declared:

Although the relative roles of fiscal policy and monetary policy in affecting aggregate demand remain a subject of debate among economists, it is probably prudent in analysis as well as in policy to assume that both have significant influence.[2]

Whether Keynesian policy ever was successful in achieving its objectives in America is questionable, however. Although the United States had the longest recovery in its history between 1961 and 1970, this was also a period of massive defense buildup and a war that cost 50,000 American lives and millions of Vietnamese. The seeds of relatively high inflation rates with high unemployment were sown in those years. Economists can claim that after 1965 they no longer controlled economic policy, but even before that date, federal tax and expenditure policy was based on increasing defense and space programs rather than expanding labor-intensive services. How long such a pattern could have been maintained without the war mobilization is a key issue. The longest recovery might have been just another thirty-six-month expansion followed by a mid-sixties recession. Many would argue that this would have been healthier in the long run, since we would not have been faced by the "institutionalized" inflation of the early and mid-seventies and would thus be able to deal more effectively with unemployment.

But this misses the point. If a mid-sixties recession would have been healthier for the economy than the relatively high rates of growth that accompanied the war, where is the steady growth within a "free market" economy promised by Keynesian theory? We have never witnessed it under peacetime conditions. And where is the income redistribution also promised by this policy? Between 1950 and 1970, family income after taxes did become more equally distributed, but only slightly (as judged from official government figures, which actually understate inequality). In 1950, after taxes, transfers, and government expenditures, the bottom 20 percent of income earners had 7.2 percent of national income; in 1970, they had 7.9 percent. The comparable figures for the highest 20 percent of income earners were 38.0 percent and 36.6 percent. More interesting, the principal equalization occurred between 1950 and 1961. In the nine "prosperity years," after-tax/expenditure income became more *unequally* distributed. MIT economist Paul Samuelson put the matter in graphic perspective when he commented in his famous textbook *Economics* that, if a pyramid of personal incomes in the United States were constructed from children's blocks, each representing $1,000, it would soar higher than the Eiffel Tower—but most of the American population would be within a yard of the ground.*

This does not mean that Keynesian policies cannot serve to achieve full employment, more equal income distribution, and low rates of inflation in a capitalist economy. But apparently the economy must be much more "managed" than it has been in the United States. Political conditions also must be quite different. Such policies seem to have worked over a long period of time in Sweden, but with a much different type and degree of intervention by the government in the economy than in the United States. The economic dilemma in America must be viewed in terms of the failure of Keynesian antidotes in a corporate capitalist economy relatively unmanaged by the government. Although Keynesians may argue that conservative monetarists and President Johnson's war policies are to blame for the inability of "fine tuning" to set the economy on a price-stable, full-employment growth path, it is much more likely that the prosperity of the early sixties represented an event in U.S. economic development unlikely to be repeated soon.

The cheap energy that fueled the post–World War II expansion has disappeared. Energy policy has become a crucial factor in U.S. capitalist development, and the energy price rise has contributed significantly to increases in consumer prices, both directly and indirectly through its influence on other products, even food (fertilizer). Yet the Carter administration,

---

*The distribution of wealth is even more unequal. The richest 1 percent of American families owns nearly one-fourth of all personally held assets.

like the Ford administration before it, has tried through traditional fiscal and monetary measures to attain both a sustained, gradual recovery to "balanced labor market" full employment (now defined as a 5 percent rate of unemployment) and a gradual slowdown of inflation. No serious attempt has been made to redistribute income except through whatever effects fuller employment might bring for the poor and the doubtful redistributional impact of a tax cut and a mild tax reform. But such a strategy cannot succeed. Recovery from the deep 1975-76 recession was not complete, and double-digit inflation continued.

All indications are that since 1970, and particularly since 1973, income distribution has become more *unequal.* The average real wages of production workers fell rapidly from 1973 to 1975, from $109 per week (in 1967 dollars before taxes) to $103—back to the average wages of 1970. By 1978, real wages had risen, but barely back to 1973 levels. More telling is the fact that, according to the Bureau of the Census, the money income of the top 5 percent of family income earners increased 48 percent between 1969 and 1975, while the twentieth through fortieth percentiles of family income showed only a 38 percent increase during the same period. Stagflation has hurt lower incomes much more than higher incomes.

The Carter economic focus has emphasized the stimulation of overall growth. This is completely consistent with previous policies of Democratic and Republican administrations, which have seen the solution to all economic problems to lie in increasing the amount of output per capita. Even the Keynesian critics of Carter's policies stress macroeconomic alternatives for achieving growth rather than raising any fundamental disagreement with the concept of overall growth as the route to full employment and "prosperity." But, if this growth policy does not produce more equal income distribution, where is such increased equality supposed to come from under the

Keynesian plan? Most economists are now so concerned with inflation that income distribution and unemployment questions are ignored. Apparently neither can be solved unless the problem of growth with stable prices is resolved first. The focus is on aggregate "demand management"—keeping inflation at an acceptable and constant level while trying to maintain growth. Unemployment is overcome by defining it away, as Arthur Okun did:

After thirty months of economic expansion, we have moved only about half the distance from the depths of recession to a *reasonable and feasible* level of prosperity of full employment. Serious statistical studies designed to estimate the unemployment rate associated with reasonably balanced—neither slack nor tight—labor markets converge on a range between 5 and 5.5 percent. They demonstrate that with today's structure of labor markets, full employment certainly cannot be defined as a 4 percent unemployment rate.[3] [Emphasis added.]

Or by deciding that low unemployment is unattainable—the tack chosen by Herbert Stein:

We should avoid commitment to any unemployment rate as a guide to fiscal and monetary policy. Political pressures will almost certainly force the unemployment goal down to a point that is unattainable, or unattainable without unsustainably escalating inflation. The unemployment goal of fiscal and monetary policy should be a steady moderate growth of aggregate demand so that the effort of workers to find jobs *by moderating their wage demands* is not frustrated by a parallel decline in the growth of nominal GNP.[4] [Emphasis added.]

Economists—both liberal and conservative—are preparing the public to accept a degree of slackness in labor markets that is much higher than in the past. Downward pressure on wages would be increased in such a situation—or, to put it another way, many groups of workers who previously enjoyed favorable bargaining power to increase wages as much or more than the rate of growth, will lose that power. Other groups with slightly higher rates of unemployment, such as young people—particularly minority youth—and women, will never gain increased bargaining power. All this pressure on wages is designed to raise economic output and keep down inflation. In a period of actually and potentially rising energy and capital costs, industry is going to try to save on labor costs to maintain profits. It is already realizing such savings by hiring more women, producing goods in low-wage Asian and Latin American countries, and pressuring the immigration authorities to turn their heads to undocumented workers. But the overall macroeconomic policy of high unemployment will have its greatest single effect in keeping down wages.

While such a policy might promote growth, it will also prevent equalization in the distribution of income. For it is the poor who suffer most from high rates of unemployment; a "soft" labor market will keep wages low relative to the returns to capital, which are concentrated in higher income brackets. An anti-inflationary policy which begins with the acceptance of high unemployment rates implies a growth policy during inflation that favors capital owners and employers. This type of policy relies on economic growth stimulated by a buyer's market in labor and high profits. Yet it leaves untouched the contradiction of high unemployment and unchanging income distribution.

Neither is the public tax expenditure system sufficient to correct the inequities of the present Keynesian growth policy. We noted how small has been the effect over the last three decades in improving the relative position of the poorest 20 percent of Americans. This weak performance can be explained by the *structure* of the tax system. In the prestagflation days (1973), Galbraith argued that the heart of a policy to guarantee a "reasonable flow of income and product at reasonably stable prices" was large public-sector expenditures at the expense of other sectors and groups of individuals. A high-salaried techno-structure would manage the economy. In practice, however, public monetary and fiscal policies have favored greater corporate concentration and an unchanging income distribution. The technostructure itself avoids paying its fair share of taxes.

Ultimately, Keynesian anticyclical policy as practiced in the United States (tax-cut stimulation) depends on private-sector decisions to expand production in response to increased consumer spending and decreased corporate taxes. But the private sector is now controlled by large corporate planning units that make their investment decisions according to a variety of criteria besides consumer spending and corporate taxes in a given short-term period. These stimuli are designed for a competitive market economy that no longer predominates. Its importance in the overall employment-price picture is greatly reduced.

Galbraith calls for tax reform, the abandonment of reliance on monetary policy, and tax cuts (which, he agrees, favor the wealthy), as well as for wage and price controls in the "planning (monopoly) sector." These changes would recognize the fact that the private sector is an economic system dominated by units which "plan prices and wages through price setting and collective bargaining" (Okun and many other Keynesians agree with Galbraith on this point). These reforms, according to Galbraith, would also go far toward controlling inflation and redistributing income. The stability of growth and employment would be assured by the *level* of taxes and expenditures. Wage and price controls would face the greatest resistance, partly for ideological reasons— that is, the notion that such controls represent the relinquishment, once and for all, of the now mythical free enterprise system—and partly because of recent experience with Republican controls under which labor paid a heavy price. It is perfectly natural that workers should be wary of controls in the hands of a pro-corporate-enterprise government.

Unlike the Carter administration and many of its Keynesian critics (such as Okun), Galbraith is willing to deal directly with the root cause of the problems in stabilizing today's capitalist economy in an equitable way: corporate power over macroeconomic policy. Since the economy is already planned, he says, let's plan it for the mass of Americans instead of the few. Macroeconomic policy should serve that end. What would happen if the United States were to adopt a policy similar to that advocated by Galbraith? What effect would such a policy have on employment, income distribution, and inflation, as well as on individual freedom?

Galbraith is not the only proponent of such a full-employment strategy. In 1978, another left-liberal economist, Robert Lekachman, proposed a similar policy in *Nation* magazine, and socialist author Michael Harrington published a pamphlet which argued that full employment should be a top priority for the American labor movement and its allies.

Most significant is the fact that a number of liberal congressmen sponsored the Humphrey-Hawkins Full Employment bill which, in a weakened version, passed the Congress in 1978. George Meany and the AFL-CIO gave strong support to the Humphrey-Hawkins bill, and a coalition of minority and liberal groups headed by Coretta Scott King lobbied for its passage.

Full employment or something close to it (2 to 4 percent unemployment) will not follow passage of the bill because, for reasons already discussed, sufficiently strong policies will not be implemented to achieve the goal. Should a successful policy of full employment in a basically capitalist economy be realized, however, it will not be unique—the United States to a large extent will have followed the Swedish economic path.

Although Sweden is very different from America, the Swedish government has attempted to achieve full employment with price stability and income redistribution for almost forty years. This has been carried out in the context of a corporate capitalist economy. In what ways is the Swedish experience relevant to the present situation in the United States?

Swedish Macroeconomic Policy

Sweden's management of macroeconomic fluctuations has been followed with intense interest by other capitalist countries. Appearing to pull itself out of the Depression through deficit-financed fiscal policy to stimulate demand at a time when Keynes was still working on his *General Theory,* Sweden seemed to offer an example of how to handle the inflation-unemployment dilemma while preserving the essential components of a capitalist economy, that is, the role of the profit motive and private ownership of the means of production. But, as Andrew Martin of Harvard has pointed out, Sweden's approach was somewhat atypical in that it involved dependence on what was essentially a labor movement strategy. The Swedish labor movement was rooted not in opposition to the position of capital, but rather in a program to reform capitalism, while preserving its major features. This strategy has been based on the appropriation of *income,* not investment, by the government, and on the use of public funds to equalize consumption distribution through the transfer of cash benefits and public services. Government programs have buoyed up aggregate demand and also have retrained workers made obsolete by declining industries.

Sweden differs widely in some fundamental historical, political, and social aspects from most other capitalist "democracies." The main differences identified by observers are its neutrality in the two world wars, its insularity, its natural resources, its virtually homogeneous racial composition, its alleged pervasive commitment to the Protestant work ethic—and a good measure of luck. From the Depression until 1977, Sweden's governing political party was the labor-dominated Social Democrats.*

Over 90 percent of Swedish industry is privately owned. Large power blocks—labor and capital—bargain over the division of national product, with the government serving as intermediary. Sweden's economy is distinct from contemporary Keynesian-type systems in that it goes beyond demand management and countercyclical intervention to nearly complete control of all major economic activities and detailed government direction of resources, but in a way that preserves private ownership. In return for the cession of such control, large private concerns receive protection from the government.

In this sense, the Swedish economy is not "socialist." Investment is still mostly in private hands. But the government has intervened massively in the economy and has intervened on behalf of the organized labor movement it represents. It has entered directly into the bargaining process between capital and labor, tilting the process in favor of labor to a much greater extent than in other industrialized countries, on the one hand, and guaranteeing profits to capital, on the other.

For example, the Swedish parliament passed laws in 1974-75 to increase government control in favor of labor. The most significant of these was the requirement that any sale of majority stock in a Swedish firm with more than $1 million in capitalization must be approved in advance by the government. Yet virtually

---

*British political scientist Francis G. Castles has argued that the key factor in Sweden has been the relative weakness of conservative forces compared with the rest of Europe or the United States.

no securities regulations exist to protect the public. The Social Democratic government was also somewhat embarrassed by the enormous corporate profits in 1974 (several times those of 1973), since Sweden has the highest personal income tax rates, the second highest sales tax (nearly 18 percent and food is included), and among the lowest corporate and capital gains tax rates in Europe.

In 1975-76, the unions received wage increases of almost 20 percent per year, while productivity remained essentially unchanged. This may have been due to overoptimism by Swedish planners in Sweden's ability to handle the energy crisis, but it probably also grew out of the high 1974 corporate profits and labor's political claim to them. In 1977-78, the pendulum swung back again, with a serious recession and a real-wage roll-back for 1978-79.

In 1976, the Social Democrats passed a law that gave unions a good deal of control over the hiring and firing procedure. This was added to worker representation on boards of directors (granted in 1972); both these union gains continue to be implemented.

This process of political bargaining over surplus between unions and capital under government arbitration can be viewed as a reformist response by the government of an advanced capitalist country to the accelerating intensity of capitalist crises. This process continues despite the loss of a parliamentary majority by the Social Democrats.

The attempt to control political action through welfare and other benefits for workers not only generates real gains for labor, but also creates contradictions for capitalist development that must be dealt with by the government. Workers are continually demanding high wage increases, better working conditions, and more control over the work place. Increasingly, the Swedish government (now in the hands of the "bourgeois" parties) has had to take over industry (shipbuilding and steel, for all intents and purposes, have become government corporations in the last three years) to preserve jobs.

Labor Market Policy

Economist Daniel Mills has written:

The single most important element in the success of a wage stabilization policy is that there be some understanding between management, labor and the government regarding the form, content, and environment in which the program will operate. No particular type of arrangement is required. Rather, the understanding may be made to fit the circumstances of the moment.[5]

This understanding has taken a peculiarly institutionalized form in Sweden. The relationship between the government, dominated until 1976 by the Social Democratic Party, and the labor unions, dominated by the blue collar Confederation of Swedish Trade Unions [Landsorganisationen i Sverige, or LO], has been a key determinant in the success of Sweden's economic policy. It is rooted historically in the basic strategy of the Social Democrats, initiated in the thirties, which centers on controlling the level, composition, and distribution of output by a combination of government and labor union policies, while leaving production itself to capitalist firms. The government's first task was the kind of Keynesian demand management carried out successfully during the Depression.

The development and implementation of a new demand-management/labor-market policy in Sweden after World War II was principally a response to an increasingly serious problem—inflation. The authorities recognized that inflation, not unemployment, was the critical destabilizing factor in the economy. The economic policy of the early postwar years, when fears of recession prevailed in the capitalist world, created strong excess demand in the economy as a whole. The government tried to limit this excess demand through a broad set of restrictive regulations, such as price controls, foreign trade controls, investment controls, and so on, as well as repeated requests to the trade unions to abstain from wage increases in exchange for price subsidies and other guarantees against the risk of reductions in real wages or in the share of wages in GNP. The labor unions were too powerful and their bargaining position too strong (given the prevailing high level of demand) for such a policy to succeed. Ultimately the efforts of the government were sure to be undermined by some form of wage explosion. This indeed occurred after the contractual wage freeze of 1949-50. It appeared that *voluntary* agreements between labor and employers' organizations would not constitute a successful "incomes policy"—a lesson President Carter and his advisors, with their program of voluntary restraints, had not learned, at least by mid-1979.

Recognizing that any given level of aggregate demand would affect employment, wages, and prices in different parts of the economy, economist Gosta Rehn proposed a policy to deal with these aspects selectively.

The high degree of labor unionization and the LO's unitary wage policy, which set wages nationally regardless of industry conditions, squeezed the profits of small, competitive firms while large corporations could pass on wage increases to consumers in the form of higher prices. To make smaller, competitive industries profitable—and thus to increase employment in these industries—it was necessary to maintain a level of aggregate demand that was excessive as far as the more profitable firms were concerned. Combined with a tight labor market, this situation generated inflationary pressure from the oligopolistic sector. Some form of wage restraint was needed.

The labor confederation objected to wage restraint, however, because to espouse such a policy would necessarily compromise its role as the workers' advocate. The Rehn model provided a way out of this dilemma. It proposed a system of measures that included: job information, training, and financial support for worker mobility; inducements to firms to move into labor surplus areas (regional policy); the timing and location of public works expenditures to coincide with labor surpluses; and temporary subsidies to enable declining firms to maintain employment until alternative jobs became available. This labor market policy was to offset the employment effects of restrictive fiscal policy, thus keeping unemployment down while controlling inflation.

Profits would be squeezed between rising wages and restrictive demand for commodities. The result, however, would be a tendency to reduce business savings at the very time that acceleration in the rate of structural change increased the need for capital. This problem could be solved through public savings, which Rehn anticipated might take the form of budget surpluses (resulting from the more restrictive fiscal policy). Furthermore, this process would supposedly contribute to a reduction of economic inequality in the long run.

Thus, the role of the government in this strategy was twofold. On the one hand, it would carry out a restrictive fiscal policy through indirect taxation on goods in proportion to the inflationary increase in demand resulting from wage increases, thereby inhibiting a wage-price spiral while increasing public savings. On the other hand, it would implement a labor market policy along the lines described above. The cooperative response of the labor unions would be to carry out a coordinated wage policy, in accordance with the "solidaristic" principle of equal pay for equal work in all parts of the country, to inhibit the development of an inflationary wage spiral, to provide additional impetus for structural change, and to reduce economic inequality.

The implementation of this economic strategy required considerable boldness on the part of the government and a huge expansion of government intervention in the economy. Political conditions were not right for this in the immediate postwar period. As a result, the strategy was not seriously attempted until a decade or so later, by which time inflationary forces had come to dominate Sweden's economic development. It was a decline in exports that forced the implementation of selective labor market measures in the late fifties and not a deliberate program to carry out Rehn's recommendations. Once the recession had passed, the government chose to develop measures facilitating labor mobility and adjustment, such as retraining, grants to cover workers' relocation costs, labor exchange programs, incentives for job creation through more intensive regional development policies and reduction of seasonal variations in demand, and the direct provision of new jobs by the government—for example, through new types of relief work focused especially on the relatively underdeveloped regions.

Over the years, labor market policy in Sweden has been separated from fiscal and monetary policy and raised to independent status. Besides satisfying the labor movement's desire to increase income equality (or, at the very least, to prevent inequality from increasing) and the government's desire to control inflation, active manpower policy addresses an important dimension of welfare in industrial society: the issue of freedom of choice. The goal is not merely full employment, but a situation in which workers are employed in jobs they select through personal choice. This concept, moreover, is extended to *all* groups in the population who wish to participate in the labor force.

In the 1960s and 1970s the Swedish labor market

has been characterized by an increase in the proportion of workers in nonmanufacturing sectors. Since 1970, over half of the total labor force of 4 million persons has been employed in commerce, transport, administration, medical and social care, and other services. Less than 7 percent are employed in agriculture and forestry, 29 percent in mining and manufacturing, and 7 percent in building and construction. Despite the decline of employment in manufacturing, total employment has been rising rapidly. During the sixties, an additional 300,000 people were employed. Much of this increase came about through a fairly high level of net immigration, particularly in the latter years of the decade, as well as an increased rate of labor force participation by women. The proportion of women employed rose from 37 to more than 60 percent of the female adult population between 1965 and 1975.

According to a Swedish government report, most of this additional employment was provided by the central government, local authorities, and county councils—for example, through the creation of jobs in nursing, social services, teaching, and other school and child-care areas that contribute to an increase in social welfare. Tax reforms, the rapid expansion of educational services, active regional and labor market policies, government stimulants to investment (through a public investment bank and other initiatives), and reforms in family policy also helped to increase the employment rate despite a large rise in the number of students aged 16 to 24 and early retirees aged 60 to 67.[6]

Regional development policy is an important example of the efforts to permit more freedom of choice in employment. The basic principle is to make work available at the individual's place of residence. Thus, since 1965, the government has been providing financial support for plant location, with priority given to a designated developmental area reaching from upper-middle to northern Sweden and representing two-thirds of the national land area and 15 percent of total population. Grants and loans may cover up to two-thirds of total costs for building investments, while loans but not grants may be advanced toward equipment costs. Loans may be interest-free for a maximum of three years and without amortization for a maximum of five years.

Employment subsidies for net increases in employment are granted to manufacturing firms in the most underdeveloped areas (so-called inner-aid areas). Special training subsidies cover a wider area. Relief work is provided in high-unemployment areas as a short-term measure. Mobility grants are awarded to facilitate migration from high-unemployment areas to areas with more employment opportunities. About 5 percent of all intracountry migrants receive such grants each year.

For the handicapped and otherwise disadvantaged, various forms of "sheltered employment" have been provided. About 35,000 handicapped persons are employed in sheltered workshops run by local governments with central government support, in special subsidized positions in the private sector, and in public agencies.

Countercyclical employment measures include a stand-by program for initiating relief work projects and for placing public orders with industry to compensate for employment reductions in times of recession or seasonal shutdowns. Subsidies are provided to local government bodies covering 75 percent of the costs for programs to predict and compensate better for unemployment.

As a result of labor market policy, however, no success was achieved in reducing the excess demand for labor that plagued certain sectors and had an inflationary impact on the economy as a whole. Furthermore, the solidaristic wage policy at most prevented income differentials from widening among groups of workers and had little success in narrowing these differentials. Structural change progressed at an especially rapid rate, with about three times as many firms closing down as in earlier periods. The share of wages in national income rose somewhat during the sixties, to the disadvantage of profits, but the increase flowed directly to the public sector rather than to the working class itself.

An ironic aspect of the joint government–labor union strategy is the effect of solidaristic wage policy on the incentives for labor mobility. The evening out of wage levels among sectors and among firms runs counter to the fundamental market mechanism by which labor is attracted from labor surplus areas to areas of labor shortage. Such a policy aids structural change with one hand by squeezing out marginal firms, but holds it back with the other hand by reducing the attractiveness to workers of changing jobs.

Unemployment has been lower in postwar Sweden than in other countries, fluctuating around 1 or 2 percent. In 1977, the rate was 1.7 percent, down from 2.5 percent in 1973—and this in a period when unemployment rates rose substantially elsewhere in Europe and, of course, quite dramatically in the United States.

The Political Impact of Labor Market Policy

By the end of the 1960s, it had become evident that Swedish labor market policy, predicated on the special relationship between the trade unions and the government, was not equal to the task of controlling inflation without exacerbating tensions between capital and labor. Complicating the issue was the government's commitment to a stabilization and welfare policy that involved a high level of taxation. Thus, while the highly progressive tax system operated as a built-in stabilizer for demand, it may also have served as a built-in destabilizer for costs through its effects on the formation of wages.

Economist Assar Lindbeck claimed that "the comparatively high progressivity of the Swedish tax system has led to violent wage increases; it is a powerful mechanism that reinforces inflation once it has started." For example, for the average worker to realize a 4 percent increase in real disposable income given a 10 percent rate of inflation would require, according to Lindbeck, an income increase of around 25 percent in nominal terms, before taxes. With such wage increases, inflation would be far greater than 10 percent. This dilemma could not possibly be resolved by the sort of macroeconomic policy that has been pursued up to now.

In Lindbeck's view, the government has two options: (1) to decrease the progressivity of the tax system; (2) to enter directly into the collective bargaining process on each bargaining occasion and offer the trade unions the alternative of receiving a significant portion of their increases in real disposable income via tax reductions rather than by way of wage rises. To follow the latter course, however, would preempt the trade unions' traditional role of negotiating this issue directly with employers and would imply a significant change in the form of the existing alliance between labor and government. The unions would shift their focus to the relative wages of various groups as well as to nonwage conditions of employment. Lindbeck suggested that, the more successful labor market organizations are in eliminating income differentials before taxes, the less need there will be for a highly progressive tax system. Thus the government and the trade unions could exchange or sacrifice their historical roles as necessary, according to the vicissitudes of political-economic "management."[7]

In 1971, the government set the pattern of wage

negotiations through its offer to public employees and introduced cooling-off legislation for the first time in Swedish history to terminate its intense dispute with professional employees. This strongly influenced collective bargaining in the private sector. In 1974, negotiations were less tense, but the government had to assume an even larger role. Taxation and price rises had reached such a high level that real disposable income could not be increased significantly by negotiated wage hikes of reasonable dimensions. Faced with this dilemma, the government transferred the burden of pension contributions from workers to employers, on the understanding that in the next round of negotiations wage demands would be reduced accordingly. Joint regulation by management and labor also declined in the area of plant relations. As dissatisfaction grew at the plant level, the process of central negotiation of shop floor issues was abandoned, and the labor confederation sought and obtained legislative intervention. Discussing these events, a Swedish government document concluded that "the experiences gained have impelled a forward push to the now-ongoing task of legislation aimed at increased industrial democracy."[8]

Labor market policy failed to check inflation. As originally conceived, the policy was to be a means of fighting inflation without bringing the Swedish government into direct conflict with the labor unions, thus avoiding counterinflationary government intervention in wage bargaining. The high wage drift that has persisted under this policy betrays its inability to control spiraling wage costs (wages rose at an annual rate of 10.7 percent between 1965 and 1977). Among other things, labor market policy failed to counteract the inflationary effect of a high-productivity sector—the export industries—existing side by side with a low-productivity sector geared to the internal market. The rapidly increasing productivity of the competitive sector sets the norm for wage levels in both sectors. Under these conditions, high inflation has resulted overall, at the same time that the fast pace of structural change, rationalization, and concentration which has facilitated high competitive-sector productivity has also caused greater insecurity and stress among workers. These have been important factors in the decision to promote increased industrial democracy.

The impossibility of coping with inflationary crises by conventional methods therefore required a fundamental change in Social Democratic strategy. With the labor movement tied so closely to the government, the transition of the trade unions from a role predicated on the struggle for wages to one more concerned with nonwage issues has probably proved easier in Sweden than in other mixed capitalist economies.

Not only did labor market strategy fail to satisfy labor, in 1978 a serious downturn hit the Swedish economy. Export industries (more than one-half of Sweden's industrial output is sold abroad) were pricing themselves out of their traditional markets. GNP fell by 2.4 percent and industrial investments by 6.2 percent as basic industries such as shipbuilding, steel, paper and pulp, and iron ore showed extensive losses. The *New York Times* reported on March 24, 1978:

In iron ore mining, for example, Swedish deposits are just too deep to hold a price line against more accessible Australian and Brazilian ore. No revival is foreseen in shipbuilding and Japanese and Korean steelmakers have been able to master the sophisticated techniques that once distinguished the Swedish product.

Although these losses were principally the result of factors that would have affected Swedish exports of these goods even if Swedish labor costs had been much lower, increasing wages contributed to difficulties in the export trade. To help solve the problem, the Swedish krona was devalued three times in 1977. The Swedish Employers' Federation pushed for higher unemployment, lower taxes (for more pecuniary incentives), and lower wages. Swedish workers are paid an average of $8.91 per hour of work—the highest figure in the industrialized world. The 1978 wage negotiations moved to "correct" the high wage increases of 1975-77. The LO agreed to a 1.9 percent wage increase in 1978 and a 3.1 percent increase in 1979. Given the prevailing 12 percent inflation rate, this amounted to almost a 20 percent decline in real wages over two years. Although inflation has only slowed slightly as a result of these wage restraints, the economy began to recover by early 1979.

Thus inflation has contributed to the contradictions of Swedish development both at the plant level and in terms of Sweden's overall growth possibilities. The struggle over wages—inherent in the relation between capital and labor—necessarily remained part of the Swedish economic landscape.

Andrew Martin of Harvard maintained that the crux of political economic crisis in Sweden in the late 1970s was the changing character of the international economic environment. Since the mid-sixties, in particular, the scope for domestic economic policy has grown increasingly narrow with the expansion of multinational enterprise, the breakdown of the monetary arrangements on which most postwar international transactions had been based, and the energy crisis. Similar problems have beset the U.S. economy, of course. Therefore, Martin concluded, "it may be that the democratic control of capitalism has become impossible elsewhere because it remains impossible in the United States."[9]

Lessons of the Swedish Experience

The Swedes face rather unusual conditions in their labor market. With almost 90 percent of the labor force unionized and a unified wage policy adopted in bargaining, the situation is completely different from that in the U.S. labor market, even its unionized segment. The issue, however, remains the same: how does the government provide a full-employment policy with stable prices? Wage drift could not be prevented in Sweden because of particular structural conditions, but full employment *was* achieved and maintained over a long period of time (without war or a huge defense buildup). Income distribution after taxes and expenditures apparently *was* equalized somewhat.

The Swedes accomplished this with the aid of a fiscal policy totally opposite from that in America. Rather than cut taxes to expand aggregate demand, they increased public expenditures and *raised* taxes. This increased aggregate demand but shifted resources from high-income individuals to the government, which then spent the appropriated resources on public services. The income-distribution effects of this type of fiscal expansion tended to equalize post-tax incomes while maintaining full employment. Of course, the government was controlled by a labor party and was committed to full employment and income equalization. The whole concept of trusting the government to collect *more* taxes and use them in a socially productive way is ideological anathema to most Americans.

The Swedes did *not* manage to stabilize prices, especially in the late 1970s, even though the government had considerable political leverage over unionized workers. The very structure of union bargaining in Sweden was largely responsible for continued inflation: the unions' national wage policy across industries made it necessary to increase aggregate demand to inflationary proportions in order to reach full employment. In this regard, the U.S. labor market is more amenable to the Swedish policy, since wages in the competitive sector generally are not subject to union collective bargaining; where it exists, bargaining in all sectors is carried out on an industry-by-industry basis.

This also leaves open some possibility of avoiding the increased industrial concentration that resulted from the Swedish combination of government fiscal and monetary policy and labor's unified wage policy. A full-employment policy will put pressure on profits, particularly in the competitive sector where labor market slackness has the greatest effect on wages; hence, it will probably contribute to increased concentration in the long run.

But, if wages are tied to productivity increases, and these are allowed to vary from industry to industry, less dynamic industries need not be driven out of business (at least in the short run) because of equalized wage increases based on the productivity rises in the most advanced sectors, as occurred in Sweden. This still leaves the issue of what to do about the incomes of workers in "low-productivity" jobs. In part, progressive taxation and the transfer of income and public services could offset productivity (wage) differences. But, for the longer run, the Swedish policy of retraining workers for other, higher-wage jobs as their industry declines is a measure easily transferable to the American scene. Also, the public sector employs a significant part of the labor force in Sweden, as it does in the United States. It is public-sector employment that absorbs many who have difficulty finding work in the private sector.

There is another aspect of Swedish problems with inflation that would not be as important in the United States. Sweden maintained a fairly low rate of inflation in the late sixties and early seventies, lower than most of its Western European neighbors, but it could not hold the line in the late seventies. As a small country, heavily dependent on foreign trade, Sweden is sensitive to the effects of rising world prices on its domestic cost of living. This is less true in the United States. Rapid inflation in the United States and other

European countries has a much greater effect on Sweden than European inflation has on the United States. The United States has more autonomy in controlling domestic inflation than do European countries.

The most important difference between Sweden and the United States, however, is the ability and willingness of organized labor to win government power in Sweden, and the labor-corporate cooperation that was maintained in that country during the years of labor rule. In practice this meant that, under the labor-party-led governments which lasted virtually uninterrupted for the forty-four years from 1932 to 1976, class struggle was suppressed in favor of a "cooperative" resolution of conflict. The inherent contradictions in such a strategy led workers and the labor leadership in the direction of industrial democracy (as discussed in an earlier chapter).

American unions are neither as able nor as willing to win government power as the Swedish labor movement; hence, the resolution of class conflict in America is carried out with much more ideological mysticism and leans much more in favor of the large corporations. Why should American big business and a highly paid American managerial elite agree to tax reforms, fiscal policy that favors lower income groups, wage-price guidelines that place labor and management in a controlled bargaining position possibly favorable to labor, and a full-employment policy that tightens the labor market (even though it may also favor increased concentration of capital)? In the absence of a strong, organized labor political presence in the United States, the pressure for such changes will have to come from a coalition of groups that must attack corporate power directly; at the same time, such a coalition will have to fight for an alternative government macroeconomic policy.

In the United States, it is imperative to change the nature of the power relationships in capitalism at the same time that reforms are undertaken to achieve a more just and humane society. The result will be a different order and set of reforms than occurred in Sweden or elsewhere in Europe. In Sweden, organized labor could agree to preserve capitalism in the workers' own interests because it was largely the unions who determined macroeconomic decisions. In the United States, this is not the case at all: unions are not in a position to dictate policy. The power relationship must be changed to improve the political position of workers and consumers as macroeconomic policy is changed. The structure of capitalism must be transformed while macroeconomic tactics are altered to meet the goals of full employment, income distribution, and price stability.

Such a policy in Sweden restricted unlimited freedom of choice for capital owners investing in Sweden and for managers in Swedish corporations, while increasing opportunities and options for employees. The government's policy lowered unemployment rates, provided retraining, and made it more difficult to lay off workers without offering them alternatives; thus, freedom of choice for workers was greater than in a situation where they do not enjoy such guarantees. Not only are individuals protected from the vagaries of capitalist development, but they can change jobs and even careers under government-sponsored training programs. But, under the traditional nineteenth-century view of "freedom"—that is, the freedom to become an individual capitalist—choice may be reduced in a society where increased advantages go to the employed rather than the employers. The freedom to earn *very* high incomes is also severely curtailed in a Swedish-type welfare state, although the posttax income distribution figures indicate that the highest 20 percent of income earners receive about the same percentage of income as in the United States and that average income in Sweden is somewhat higher. So, higher income earners in Sweden are not as badly off as is sometimes claimed.

American ideology continues to stress the harm government intervention can cause to individual rights, particularly the right to make economic choices. Americans are still imbued with the idea that the ultimate freedom is to be self-employed and to make one's "fortune." Yet only a small and declining percentage of Americans are self-employed (about 7 percent) or ever will be. The percentage has been decreasing steadily since the last century. The United States, like most advanced industrial countries, is an economy consisting of a few managers and capital owners centered around large corporations (with a periphery of small production units) and a mass of employees and production and service workers who are receiving wages and salaries. The American concept of freedom is anachronistic in this context; moreover, the anachronism serves the interests of those who would lose out if the concept were changed to focus on workers' choices and the meaning of "freedom" in a wage-earning society. In Sweden, these are real issues. But the discussion is on a different plane than in the United States: most Swedes have discarded the nineteenth-century notion of economic choice and individual freedom. Rather, the issue has become the rights of workers and capital owners or managers in a capitalist society and the function the government should play as intermediary in their bargaining. The "debate" is not conceived in these terms in the United States, in fact may *never* be framed this way, given the nature of American institutions and history.

It is unlikely that American unions will grow dramatically in strength over the next decade or two and employ their political strength to bring about a Swedish-style manpower policy that results in full employment. Making a political demand for "full employment" the *central* part of a strategy for reform is doomed to failure. Relatively too few people are unemployed; and well over half the unemployed are young, black, or female. As Governor Brown of California so neatly put it, "When I see unemployed rioting in the streets, I'll worry about full employment." Unemployment insurance effectively reduces the pain of the jobless, numbing them to political action. The sympathy of the employed for the unemployed is meager.

It is more likely that the issue of full employment will be included in the political debate of the 1980s as part of the questioning of the corporate economy, and that it will be cast as a matter of democratic rights and participation, as an extension of American democratic principles into the economy, perhaps as part of an "economic bill of rights."

What *is* useful about the Swedish experience in manpower policy is the careful use of public works spending for socially beneficial projects (unlike many of the haphazard CETA projects thrown together in a crisis atmosphere by local and state governments); this, of course, requires a *permanent* public employment service with the capital resources to create jobs and with plans already drawn up, ready to be implemented when needed, as well as a comprehensive program of relocation grants and retraining programs for workers—again, publicly run, not contracted to a potpourri of private contractors as was the case with the Job Corps or other current U.S. training programs.

Experience in working with the California Department of Employment Development convinced us that a state government, without waiting for the federal government to act, could engage in an active manpower policy along Swedish lines. Such a reform policy could at least reduce the unemployment rate by a percentage point or so and serve as a model for reform at the federal level. However, full employment in one state alone is an impossibility.

An Alternative Inflation Policy

While we can certainly learn some technical tricks from the Swedish experience in reducing unemployment, recent events on the world energy front and widespread inflation in the industrial countries raise serious questions about the relevance of Sweden's anti-inflation measures for U.S. policy. It is true that both countries now face a cost/profit push inflation—a supply-side phenomenon—rather than price increases resulting primarily from too much money in the hands of consumers. On this, economists such as Gottfried Haberler and Robert Lekachman, approaching the problem from very different philosophical perspectives, agree: the present inflation in the United States may have begun as demand-pull in the late 1960s, but it is not that now. Monetary policy therefore cannot be effective in solving the problem without bringing on substantial recession. The nature of the cost or profit push is complicated further by the particular political relationship between corporations and labor unions in the United States. Of course, Haberler and Lekachman do not agree as to what should be done about this problem: the former holds that greater competition must be introduced into the economy, among other ways, by reducing the power of unions; the latter believes that corporate power over prices must be reduced through radical public controls.

Inflation is a domestic political problem, distorting people's economic choices, shifting resources to the public sector (because of progressive taxation), and hitting particularly hard at the ever-growing number (in both absolute and relative terms) of fixed-income earners, as the average age of Americans increases. Higher unemployment in the United States is currently favored over continued inflation, even if the inflation is moderate. To some degree, this toleration of unemployment is justifiable on the grounds that an important part of the inflation is the psychological acceptance of steady wage and price increases (as argued by Okun and others, including Lekachman). This is not an acceptable intellectual argument, however, if the structure of the economy is the cause of continued inflation in the face of already high unemployment. In such a case, wage-price guidelines, incomes policies, or public control of corporations must be undertaken within the context of a move toward full employment.

Howard Wachtel and Peter Adelsheim, in a 1976 report for the Joint Economic Committee of Congress, carried this line of reasoning further: they argued that, in post–World War II recessions, firms tried to recoup profits on reduced sales volume by increasing the price markup for the remaining sales in order to come closer to their target profit rates. When markets became concentrated as they are now, firms were able during a short recession to take an active role in setting the prices charged for their products. In this way, Wachtel and Adelsheim noted,

the simultaneous occurrence of unemployment and inflation becomes a logical and systematic outcome of the pricing practice of firms with economic power in the market rather than a paradox.

They concluded that in short recessions unemployment feeds inflationary pressures instead of mitigating them. As they put it:

Consequently, as the concentration of economic power increases in the economy, we need longer and deeper recessions before the conventional policy of creating unemployment to reduce inflation becomes anti-inflationary.[10]

The policy implications of this analysis are that the use of unemployment to cure inflation under the current structure of the market may be self-destructive, or at least may require a degree of recession and unemployment that is unacceptable politically. Wachtel and Adelsheim suggest the use of price-markup monitoring once a recession begins (for whatever reasons), since

failing to do so might easily trigger a period of inflation making it all the more difficult to turn the recession around. . . .

Rather than trying to influence prices on a universal basis, we should make anti-inflation policies selective and rooted in some objective criteria . . . those price markups monitored in industries and firms which manifested perverse flexibility in recent recessions.[11]

They argue, therefore, for *selective* price controls during recessions.

Economist Mordecai Kurz also shows in a recent paper for the Institute of Mathematical Studies at Stanford that less than "normal" profit rates contributed significantly to inflationary pressure over the period 1909-74. According to Kurz's results, demand pull is still important, but the fact that lower profits trigger increased inflation is significant and supports Wachtel's and Adelsheim's findings.

Economist Leslie Nulty, in her study, *Understanding the New Inflation,* took a different approach.[12] She contended that the post-1973 phase of the present U.S. inflation has particular characteristics related much more to structural shortage of certain kinds of goods than to demand pull or cost/profit push. Nulty's argument centered around the basic necessities (energy, food, medical care, and shelter) that constitute 70 percent of the consumption expenditures of 80 percent of U.S. income earners. The annual rate of inflation for these four necessities between 1970 and 1976 was one and one-half times the rate for nonnecessities (7.5 percent vs. 5.2 percent). This higher inflation was not caused by economywide excess demand nor by wage increases for workers employed in the production of food, energy, housing, and health care.

Therefore, any solution to U.S. (and world) inflation must concentrate on long-run solutions to the structural problems of producing each of these products. In energy, this means developing means to conserve energy (public transit, home weatherization, etc.) and producing additional energy in ways that fit in with an overall plan for full employment and capital use. In food production, Nulty declared, farmers' production costs have to be controlled, the energy intensity of food production reduced, and food distribution reformed to increase the direct links between farmers and consumers. It is in food distribution that inflation has been most sustained. (See chapter 5 for new policy initiatives.)

In health care, a long-term plan for the education of more medical personnel and a movement away from the present emphasis on high-cost, capital-intensive treatment toward less hospitalization and more care through outpatient clinics is crucial if rising medical costs are to be contained. The problem of health care is particularly relevant to the inflation question because of the increasing age of the U.S. population and the rising percentage of income spent on health care as income increases. Present insurance schemes have also contributed to rapid price increases, so that the way in which health care is paid for must be resolved as part of an overall anti-inflation package. (See chapter 8 on the welfare state for a more detailed discussion.)

Finally, Nulty suggested that the inflation in housing prices (lowest among the necessities) be attacked by focusing on local situations and dealing with particular local housing needs. She did recognize, however, that the housing problems of one area (such as inner cities) can strongly influence the problems of another (the suburbs). Further, any housing policy is involved intimately with environmental concerns; the use of available space even affects agricultural costs through rising land prices. Tax policy also affects housing costs (particularly rentals) and thus inflation. The use of monetary policy rather than tax reform and fiscal measures to restrict inflation influences housing prices as well through the direct effect on mortgage rates. Solution of the problem of housing provision and housing prices therefore requires a type of planning that extends beyond local areas and must form part of a national strategy to meet overall employment and environmental goals.

Both Wachtel and Adelsheim, and Nulty advocate an anti-inflationary policy that moves away from the traditional concept of aggregate "demand management" and corporate stimulation, and shifts toward measures which deal directly with the structure of the American economy and its influence on prices. Each of their approaches has its shortcomings: Wachtel and Adelsheim attempt to develop policies that deal with a particular facet of the present inflation—price rises in recessions, recessions generated at least in part to correct an "overheated" economy with rising prices. But they do not discuss the issue of price increases that occur throughout the cycle—again, not because of excessive *aggregate* demand, but because of conditions in certain industries, conditions that cannot be corrected through demand management. Nulty's analysis identifies these sectors, but does not deal with the issue of price rises in other (concentrated) industries, nor with the entire issue of inflation during recessions. Neither analysis treats the highly concentrated banking sector and its ties with monetary policy and interest rates, interest rates that both rise with inflation and contribute to it.

A new long-term anti-inflation policy would combine both selective price controls and structural reforms in basic areas like food, housing, energy, and health. But such a combined policy, we believe, will be successful only within the context of greater economic democracy. "Inflation flourishes in a culture of inequality, for it feeds upon envy," economist Robert Lekachman has noted. In part, inflation is rooted in the psychological outlook inherent in our corporate capitalist economy, whereby individuals define themselves in terms of money and the consumption of goods. It is also rooted in the power arrangements of the American economy, which allow corporations to pass along wage increases or other costs to consumers in the form of higher prices.

We favor selective price controls for the major corporations, although we do not expect such a policy to be adopted by a national administration in the near future. If, however, a serious reform president committed to economic democracy were elected in the late 1980s or early 1990s, selective price controls would *have* to be employed to stabilize the economy, given the large amount of uncertainty that would be generated by the electoral victory itself. Such a policy move would be analogous to the imposition of rent controls as a short-run measure to stabilize housing costs in a city, while longer-term policies such as conversion to cooperative ownership or the construction of new public or cooperative housing were put into effect.

If unions are asked to moderate wage claims as part of an overall wage-price control policy by a reform government, then they must be offered (and should demand) nonmonetary trade-offs, including worker representation on corporate boards, greater control over investment of their pension funds, and increased worker control over in-plant conditions such as health and safety. In this way, the work place reforms we discussed earlier would become part of an anti-inflation policy predicated on greater economic democracy.

Inflation in specific sectors such as food can be attacked at the state and local levels as well as at the national level, as part of a strategy for democratizing the economy. Many of the pertinent reforms, such as consumer co-ops, direct marketing, and promotion of the family farm, were discussed in an earlier chapter. In the final section on political strategy, we will expand on the concept of an anti-inflation program as part of the effort to build a political base in cities and states.

Elements of a Macro Anti-Inflation Policy

Were we appointed to the Council of Economic Advisors in a national government (even by a liberal Democrat), we would recommend adherence to the following basic principles:

1. Stimulatory fiscal policy should not be based on tax cuts. Tax cuts rely on increased aggregate demand from individual consumers (resulting from income tax reductions) and increased investment by private corporations (responding to increases in aggregate demand and decreases in corporate taxes). In the past thirty years, unemployment has been reduced below the 5 percent level only during the massive defense buildups associated with the Korean and Vietnam wars. But the idea that the "market" can be brought into full-employment equilibrium without direct public intervention dies hard. If we abandon our reliance on the large private corporation to use its tax-cut-stimulated investment "correctly" for full employment, the alternative becomes very clear: maintain tax rates and levels (or even raise taxes for the rich) while increasing public expenditures and investments. This gives more power to the public sector, but allows for public directed employment programs as well as public stimulus of the production of specific goods and services.

2. Large public investment programs could re-

orient production. For example, in the 1960s, public expenditures created massive defense production and space technology industries. This move put the United States in the forefront of world electronics technology. Government expenditures on mass transport, solar and wind energy, housing, food production, and health care could make the United States a leader in the development of these goods and services. No one would argue that the defense industry produces goods that must be marketed profitably to consumers. Why must these other necessities be produced profitably under some market criteria? At this point, the private sector cannot or will not do the job in producing these goods; with public investment, they could be produced in much greater quantities and probably in new ways. Their increased production would also greatly ease inflationary pressures, since it is in precisely these goods and services that prices have risen the most.

3. Income redistribution requires more than tax reform, although a reform that seriously attempts to increase taxes for the rich and lower those for the poor would contribute to some redistribution (as it did in Sweden). Income redistribution means an adjustment of the salary structure and a change in the share of national product going to capital relative to the share going to wages. This second change in capital and wage shares, however, can have dangerous consequences if carried out too rapidly. A sharply rising wage bill (with correspondingly lower profits) leads to decreases in production in the face of increases in aggregate demand and, ultimately, to a rapid increase in prices. Only massive public intervention in production and distribution can avoid these consequences. Given the U.S. situation, it seems much more fruitful to concentrate first on readjusting salary differentials without increasing the share of national product going to wages. Such a readjustment should begin with a decision—on the part of the

society—as to what a reasonable and just upper allowable income should be. If we as a society determine that no one should earn more than $100,000 annually, we can devise a tax schedule (with all loopholes closed) that would implement that determination. The rest of the tax schedule could be set accordingly to meet the total taxation needs of the public sector. It might be decided, under such a tax schedule, to eliminate sales taxes because of their regressiveness and to coordinate state income taxes more adequately with federal taxes. But the main point would be to establish new *actual* posttax earnings structures. The total wage bill might be the same, but the distribution of wages and salaries would be altered. If a worker earns one-third or one-half the salary of a corporate representative rather than one-sixth, his relationship to that individual may change in some way. Further, if the worker is sure of his or her employment (at a relatively high salary), the relationship between the worker and his or her superiors is also likely to be qualitatively different. Nevertheless, it will take much more than our suggested macroeconomic policy to change relations in production significantly.

Redistribution and Inflation

If the government employs large numbers of the presently unemployed or if the incomes of the lowest-paid workers are raised substantially (or both) while production is not increased at the same time, prices will surely rise, particularly on those goods that low-income workers consume.

Extreme forms of such a phenomenon occurred in Chile and Portugal in the 1970s. In these countries, revolutionary socialist regimes redistributed incomes rapidly by raising minimum wages and fixing prices of consumer goods. Profits fell sharply, from 45 to 38 percent of national product in Chile between 1970 and 1971, and from 50 to 0 percent of national product in Portugal between 1974 and 1975. Real salaries rose in these periods, especially for low-income workers and peasants. But, in both cases, the salary increases were short-lived because of subsequent inflation. In Chile, the inflation rate was 163 percent in 1972 and 508 percent in 1973, decreasing real income to its 1970 level. In Portugal, inflation in 1975 eroded two-thirds of the previous year's salary increase. The redistribution of income in Chile and Portugal had an additional effect: imports increased significantly as workers had more to spend, while higher wages at home generally decreased exports. Foreign currency reserves were reduced rapidly. Since national and international banking interests generally are not friendly to revolutionary socialist regimes, the loss of reserves made these governments particularly susceptible to boycott by international capitalism. Falling real wages and loss of foreign currency reserves contributed to the overthrow of both movements.

In his analysis of these two revolutionary failures, French author Serge Kolm drew the following lessons.

The redistribution of income—more specifically, wage increases for low-income workers—requires simultaneous government intervention in the marketplace. The market cannot be relied upon to produce an adequate volume of goods and services under conditions of falling profits. The government must formulate an appropriate investment and production strategy before redistributing income. At the same time, the market performs important functions that make it useful for the distribution of goods and allocation of resources. This is the dilemma that must be resolved to avoid rapid inflation and failure of the redistribution policy.[13]

To remedy these problems, Kolm argued, the government can substitute nonmarket allocation and distribution mechanisms to various degrees: rationing, quotas, and planned distribution are "strong" nonmarket measures, while price control, exchange-rate devaluations (and revaluations), and taxation are "weak" measures. In both cases, however, the measures serve as adjustments to the economy when political needs require inflationary redistribution.

Alternatively, income can be redistributed in noninflationary, or at least less inflationary, ways. Change in relative salary levels, with redistribution from high incomes to lower—does not necessarily increase the share of wages in national product relative to profits. But it does raise low wages relative to high salaries and equalizes income distribution. Profits are not reduced overall, and so investment coming out of profits should not be reduced. Production levels should be maintained or even increased for most products. Savings may be reduced as income is shifted to those levels where people consume a higher percentage of their incomes. If production is already at full capacity, some inflation may result, but, in general, the inflationary effect of such a redistribution is small compared with that resulting from a rise in the overall wage bill. This makes it much more feasible to maintain higher real wages for low-income groups and to raise these wages even more over time with a planned employment and investment policy that favors those groups.

Yet, such a policy fails to change the wage-profit relation in the short run. If profits remain a high percentage of national product—as they are in most low-income countries—the question becomes one of increased government intervention in the market *after* the redistribution of intrasalary incomes to shift national product from private profits either to wages or, more likely, to government investment.

In the United States, the major problem in income distribution is among different salary levels, although the control of profits raises other important power issues. Shifting income from the high-salaried to the low would have a definite influence on the kinds of products demanded and would put inflationary pressure on food and low-cost housing prices, possibly on energy and, to a lesser extent, on health-care prices. But there would be little danger of increased demand for imports, since the kinds of products demanded by the lowest-income families in America are almost all produced domestically (almost 100 percent of low incomes are spent on food, shelter, medical care, and energy). A reduction of exports, especially food exports, might ensue, and this might cause some balance-of-payments difficulties. These would be small, however, compared to the balance-of-payments problems resulting from the present inflation, capital outflows, and increased oil imports.

The lessons of Chile and Portugal, though only marginally applicable to an economy like that of the United States, are clear: raising low incomes drastically through either a full-employment policy or rapid minimum-wage increases or both would have consequent inflationary effects which could be prevented only by immediate government intervention in production and investment. Even then, the intervention might not be able to prevent a reduction in the real wages of the very groups that were supposed to gain by the new wage policy. To achieve an income redistribution without generating inflationary consequences, an intrasalary adjustment is required. *If low wages are to be increased, they must be raised at the expense of high wages.* High wages could even be lowered with only a small increment in low wages and increased employment.

This is a lesson that liberal advocates of the Humphrey-Hawkins Full Employment bill either failed to understand or chose to ignore. Full employment *without* rampant inflation is a politically difficult maneuver. Similarly, the American labor movement's position favoring a higher minimum wage while sidestepping or ignoring the issue of a *maximum* wage, is self-defeating and economically wrong.

There is also a lesson here for radical advocates of greater equality in American society. Attempts to drastically equalize wealth and income over the period of a few years would lead almost inevitably to economic chaos. The process must, of necessity, be a long-term one, occurring over at least a generation or more—after a national government dedicated to economic democracy comes into office. Over the long run, a combination of stricter inheritance laws and the democratization of sources of economic wealth— the large corporations—would reduce inequality substantially to a more reasonable level. We have seen, for example, that the ratio of highest to lowest wage is significantly lower in worker-owned firms than in capitalist-owned firms. As more of the economy becomes worker owned over time, wage differentials will shrink. And as control of capital investment passes into the hands of more and more public institutions, the opportunities for making personal fortunes through financial dealings will decrease.

CHAPTER EIGHT

What Kind of Welfare State?

To most Americans, the welfare state means big government providing for its citizens with guaranteed income, health care, and old-age pensions, but, at the same time, controlling people's lives and inundating them with a sea of red tape and bureaucracy. Since the 1930s, in fact, the government has passed legislation providing many of these services to Americans—if not guaranteeing them income, at least making available unemployment insurance, Social Security, welfare payments, food stamps, Medicaid, and Medicare. While such benefits are less comprehensive in the United States than in some other industrialized countries, they do represent a similar movement by the U.S. government: the appropriation of private income through taxation to provide public welfare for (generally) lower-income families.

What effect does welfare have on the distribution of income, unemployment, and the organization of work? In our analysis of macroeconomic policy, we argued that the distribution of rewards (jobs and income) under the market system was unacceptable to most Americans. The injustice of this distribution is most apparent among those groups in the population with high levels of structural unemployment, and during periods when the market system slumps, pushing large numbers of people willing to work into the ranks of the unemployed. So, in part, unemployment insurance and Social Security are attempts to correct for unacceptable facets of the market system. In part, they are also an attempt, along with welfare payments and food stamps, to redistribute posttax income toward the poorest population segments.

Social insurance and welfare have apparently had at least some success in this direction. The principal shift of posttax, postexpenditure income in the American economy occurs between the top 5 percent of income earners and the bottom 20 percent. The legislative actions of the mid-1930s represented victories primarily for the poorest 20 percent of the population.

In testimony before the House of Representatives' Task Force on Distributive Impacts of Budget and Economic Policies in October 1977, Robert Reischauer of the Congressional Budget Office showed that, as judged on the basis of income before taxes and excluding transfer payments, 26.5 percent of all families in the United States were designated as "poor" in 1975; 58 percent of elderly families were poor, 43 percent of single-parent families, and 61 percent of families with disabled heads (all before transfers).

Government transfer programs are designed to do something about these extremely high levels of poverty by directing resources to those who cannot or are not expected to work.

The government transfer system can be conveniently broken down into two components. The first of these is the social insurance system, which distributes roughly three-quarters of all Government transfer benefits. The system includes such programs as social security, unemployment insurance and Government retirement. By and large the benefits distributed through this system are not means tested. Therefore, some of them go to the nonpoor as well as to the poor.[1]

The effect of the social insurance system is to reduce the share of "poor" families from 26.5 percent to 14.5 percent (before taxes, including social insurance income). The program has the greatest impact on aged and unemployed families; it does little to reduce poverty among working or female-headed families.

The second component of government transfers is welfare. These are the programs that are means tested. They distribute about one-quarter of all Government transfers. Included in the welfare system are such cash assistance programs as AFDC, SSI, general assistance, which is given out by the states, and a number of in-kind programs, including the food stamp program and housing assistance programs.[2]

Welfare programs overall reduce the incidence of poverty, according to Reischauer, from 14.5 percent to 10.6 percent, before taxes. When measured after taxes the total reduction of poverty through *both* social insurance and welfare is from 26.5 percent to 11.2 percent. Thus the incidence of taxation actually works to *reverse* some of the impact of transfers on poverty. Under pre-Carter welfare reform proposals, two-thirds of the means-tested welfare recipients are from families with incomes of less than $5,000; this group received about 75 percent of the benefits paid out by welfare programs in 1975.

Employment Programs

Welfare policy includes more than income transfers. Since a large part of such transfers may go to the temporarily or permanently unemployed, any discussion of the welfare state is tied intimately to employment policy. Part of that issue was covered in our analysis of macroeconomic alternatives. U.S. monetary and fiscal policy—except during the mid-sixties (and then as part of a war economy)—has not been oriented toward full employment as a primary policy target. Stable prices have been and are the *principal* goal of postwar countercyclical government action. Welfare policy is the complement to fiscal and monetary policies concerned more with inflation than with full employment. Welfare and social insurance, rather than a tight job market, are to offer relief to those who are out of work. This is directly opposite to the Swedish welfare system, which is organized around a full-employment macroeconomic policy. Unemployment insurance and direct welfare assistance represent a very small part of the Swedish program compared with their role in the U.S. system. Direct government employment programs are also very different in Sweden.

Instead of a full-employment macroeconomic policy, the government has devised a work strategy for the poor in the United States based on the same principles that support the welfare system. In the 1950s it was assumed that the poor did not work because they were lazy and had to be forced into jobs through either coercion or "inducements." In the 1960s, the concept changed. Policymakers decided that what the poor lacked was education and training. This argument also was consistent with the concept of "structural" unemployment: the idea that the poor could not be incorporated into the labor force by economic expansion because their low educational level formed a barrier to employment. The post–New Deal employment strategy of the Democrats has therefore been based on assumptions of labor market homogeneity (entry barred because of workers' *personal* characteristics rather than because of barriers in the job market itself) and human capital theory, which argues that increasing the education and training of workers will remove the obstacles to their employment.

If the barriers to entry are in the labor market, however; if poor people cannot obtain higher-paying, permanent, career jobs because there are not enough such jobs in the economy for everyone, then higher-paying jobs will be rationed, and the poor will not get better access to these jobs unless their level of education rises *relative to the mean.* They must obtain more schooling and training than the labor force already employed. Furthermore, they may have to change other behavioral characteristics or overcome racial differences. They will probably also have to grow older, since youth are experiencing increasing difficulty in finding career jobs. The evidence shows that blacks who start out in what are termed "secondary" jobs—those jobs that are menial, that require workers only to follow direct orders, and that are generally low-paying—have a very high likelihood of remaining in such jobs as they grow older, while young whites are likely to move up into "primary" higher-paying, career-type jobs.

The assumption that barriers to job entry reside in the personal characteristics of the poor—the presumption of the architects of the War on Poverty—is incorrect. The labor market is divided into rather distinct segments. One of these segments—comprised of the menial, low-paying jobs generally available to the poor—may not reward higher education or training with much of an increase in pay. MIT economist Bennett Harrison presents evidence that, in fact, education and training of urban ghetto residents in the 1960s did not carry the trainees into regular employment or higher-income jobs. The effect of the training programs was essentially negligible for both of these variables.[3]

Yet the Carter administration—ten years later—proposed to train unemployed potential workers and to provide short-term employment through CETA, Job Corps, and other programs. At the same time, welfare recipients were to work part time, accepting jobs offered at the minimum wage.

Under Carter's program the Government will create 1,400,000 public service jobs. These jobs will pay minimum wage, hopefully. . . . The jobs are not intended or designed to train us to work in private jobs. The administration says that the jobs will be so bad that nobody but recipients, who will have no choice, will take them. They are dead-end jobs, paying the minimum wage and with no fringe benefits such as medical care or retirement plans. They have no career ladder.[4]

Given the evidence from similar programs in the 1960s, why should they be introduced again? One reason is ideological: the concept that people cannot get good jobs because the production system is structured so as to make finding such work difficult is antithetical to the capitalist ideal that success is tied to hard work and motivation. But, perhaps, more important, the present program may be designed to match one achievement of the War on Poverty programs: the young unemployed are taken off the streets *temporarily* in order to diffuse potential political problems. Further, forcing welfare recipients to work not only puts downward pressure on wages, but it offsets some of the growing reaction by the working class (especially the near poor) to welfare programs. For it is these low-middle- and middle-income groups which are now at the forefront of the taxpayer revolt, and welfare payments to "non-workers" are high on their list of complaints.

U.S. capitalist development has been characterized by business cycles and an apparent inability or unwillingness to achieve full employment even at the crest of most expansionary phases. With the Great Depression, the government began to intervene to calm the political unrest resulting from high unemployment and poverty by transferring income to the poor and unemployed. When large numbers of blacks immigrated to northern cities after World War II—a migration that ultimately created the urban disturbances of the 1960s—the response of the government was again to provide income payments directly to these groups to forestall any further political instability.

Sociologists Frances Fox Piven and Richard Cloward wrote of the mid-1930s:

> Still, many of the poor had at least gotten relief. What needs to be understood, however, is that relief was not easily conceded to them. The spread of destitution itself was no great force; for a considerable period of time elites remained aloof from the suffering in their midst. But then the destitute became volatile, and unrest spread throughout the country. It was only when these conditions, in turn, produced a massive electoral convulsion that government responded.[5]

The welfare explosion of the sixties had similar causes:

> In the 1960s, the growing mass of black poor in the cities emerged as a political force for the first time, both in the voting booths and in the streets. And the relief system was, we believe, one of the main local institutions to respond to that force, even though the reaction was greatly delayed.[6]

But in the quiet years between the 1930s and the 1960s, argued these sociologists, relief systems were designed to *reinforce work norms*—to bring the poor into the labor force at low wages. The welfare system excludes many poor from the welfare rolls and tries to keep welfare payments low enough so that the poor must work in order to subsist.

> . . . the structure of the American public welfare system meshes with and reinforces the work system, not least by excluding potential workers from aid. The "fit" of the welfare system in a stable but diverse economy is assured by varying the pattern of exclusion in accord with regional differences in labor requirements. Furthermore, harsh relief practices also maintain work norms by evoking the

image of the shamed pauper for all, especially the able bodied poor, to see and shun.[7]

As the relief rolls rise, so does the concern with work. And the government attempts through various means—either by restricting the relief available or requiring those who receive welfare to work at least part of the time—to put the poor to work, in any kind of job. Most of the jobs taken by the poor are temporary, low-paying, and dead-end (no prospects for promotion). More important, under conditions of steady, high unemployment, it is difficult for many welfare recipients to find any job at all.

Health Insurance

The other major component of the present U.S. welfare system is Medicare and Medicaid. Enacted in July 1965, these two programs represent three legislative schemes designed to cover the costs of medical care for special groups. Medicare Part A is a compulsory federal program providing hospital insurance benefits to individuals of all income levels who are 65 years or older; it is financed by payroll taxes. Medicare Part B is a program of insurance covering doctors' bills for those 65 or over but available only to individuals who enroll and pay a monthly premium, which is matched by the federal government out of general revenues. Medicaid is an extension of the federal-state public assistance program; entitlement to its benefits is limited by a means test. The program is administered by the states, which may have differing benefit schedules and eligibility requirements within federal guidelines, and is financed by open-ended matching grants from federal general revenues. Medicare thus comprises part of the social insurance portion of government income transfers, while Medicaid is part of the welfare portion.

These programs have been plagued with many

problems, although they have also greatly benefited the groups they were designed to serve.

They are better for the aged and the poor than no health-care plan at all. It is clear, however, that, aside from these two groups, the principal beneficiaries have been hospitals, doctors, and fiscal intermediaries such as Blue Cross and some other insurance companies. It is these latter groups which have had the most influence in shaping the plans to their advantage: they are reimbursed on the basis of "reasonable costs" for hospital expenses and of "reasonable charges" for physicians' services.

Such a health-care scheme, in which the taxpayer has no control over health-care costs—and the government chooses not to control them—has led to rapid increases in the cost of medical services to all Americans, as well as in the taxes paid to finance Medicare and Medicaid. Since neither of these programs is run directly by federal or state governments, which would allow some regulation of costs, and neither rewards lower-cost hospitals or doctors with increased numbers of patients under the program, there is no cost control and no incentive for private hospitals and doctors to keep expenses down. Community hospital expenses per adjusted patient day rose from $49 in 1967 to $111 in 1974. Hospital net income, which increased at an annual rate of 11.8 percent during the four years preceding Medicare and Medicaid, rose at an annual rate of 18.9 percent in the first two years of the programs' operation. Physicians' fees also rose more quickly after the legislation than before—from an annual increase of 2.8 percent to an increase of 7 percent annually.[8]

These cost increases have had two effects: first, they have made health care and health insurance more expensive for Americans not covered by Medicare and Medicaid; and, second, they have made Medicaid particularly susceptible to criticism by non–welfare recipients and have generated pressure for cutbacks in the program as well as in other welfare payments.

The increased cost of health care for nonrecipients takes the form of rising Social Security taxes to finance Medicare Part B, increased diversion of state and local tax revenues to fund Medicaid, as well as the direct costs of health insurance and medical services paid by individuals. The lower-paid working class has suffered most because of the regressive nature of the taxes levied and because of the high percentage of consumption expenditures which goes for health services at that income level.

A Medicaid cutback at the state level has been supported by the Congress, which in 1967, 1969, and 1972 passed a series of amendments to the Medicaid statutes that have hurt the poor. These amendments: (a) set ceilings on income levels of the indigent for whose coverage the states could receive federal matching funds; (b) permitted states to impose deductibles and coinsurance on the medically needy for hospital care; and (c) pushed back the target date by which the states must provide comprehensive Medicaid programs.

Given this experience, it would seem that proposed legislation for national health insurance should move to correct these severe problems. For the most part, however, this is not the case. Even the most comprehensive of the proposed bills—the Kennedy-Griffiths Bill (now Kennedy-Corman), originally proposed in 1971—provides for government *financing* of health services rather than for direct government supply of such services, though it does introduce much more cost control than under the present system of Medicare and Medicaid financing. Even this bill, then, does not deal with the serious limitations of health care in the United States, such as differential treatment for rich and poor, the great variation in the quantity and quality of health care from region to region and locality to locality, the exorbitant fees charged by hospitals and physicians, and the shortage of medical personnel in many areas. In 1979, as a presidential candidate, Kennedy retreated from his own relatively strong bill; in its place, he released a general set of "principles" that included continued involvement of private firms in the health insurance field.

Work Relations

Our brief description of the American welfare system indicates that the appropriation of income by the government for transfer to the poor, the unemployed, and the elderly provides a real gain in income for these groups and is the outcome of political action, if not by the working class as a whole, at least on the part of labor-oriented interests. But is welfare legislation in America (or indeed, in Sweden or other European countries) therefore anticapitalist? Has it changed the ownership of productive property or the organization of production or relations between workers and management? Not significantly, if at all. Although government benefits for the unemployed, the elderly, and the poor have been opposed by business, and unemployment insurance and welfare were legislated only when the stability of the capitalist system was threatened by the poor, the nature and application of the welfare program has worked to maintain the continuity of corporate capitalist development under politically difficult conditions.

Yet, the welfare system *has* redistributed income. In the previous chapter, we suggested that a more equal income distribution may have some *indirect* effect on work relations: if workers with lower incomes increase their economic position relative to those with higher incomes, relative power positions may change as well. But welfare, while it does improve the relative income position of the poor, does so in a way that confirms the low status of the poor and makes them continue to feel vulnerable to the vagaries of the economic system. Public assistance linked to work incentives is more discouraging than income maintenance alone. The welfare system, tied as it is to a policy of less than full employment, guarantees that a significant portion of the potential work force will feel "in excess" or "marginal" to economic production. At the same time, another part of the labor force correctly assesses that it is bearing the brunt of support for the public assistance programs.

Differences between workers are increased and emphasized. Workers in lower-level jobs feel particularly threatened by the availability of an unemployed, unskilled labor force. Again, for lower-skilled workers, the welfare system reinforces the hierarchy even while redistributing income. There are alternatives to this way of providing income and human services. Sweden is often cited as the "model" welfare state. In the previous chapter, we discussed how Sweden attempted to achieve full employment without inflation. Although this policy has finally run into difficulty—in part because of Sweden's dependence on exports and imports—we found that important lessons could be learned from the differences between Swedish and U.S. macroeconomic policy. The Swedish government has traditionally been a *labor* government; it has supported the capitalist mode of production—the ownership of capital by the private sector and the control of most investment decisions by private business firms—but it has appropriated income through heavy taxation in ways that equalize posttax income more than in the United States. Full-employment policy has been a central element in the economic program of the Swedish government. Swedish welfare policy—including both social insurance and welfare payments—is much more comprehensive than in the United States, and welfare assistance is not tied to work incentives. Much more than in America, welfare and social insurance are viewed as the *right* of every Swedish citizen, just as is access to employment. The

Swedish system has had a greater equalizing effect on incomes and is more comprehensive in reducing unemployment.

The Swedish Welfare System

In Sweden, there is relatively less public ownership of the means of production than in most other Western European countries, and the concentration of economic power in the hands of private capitalists is greater. For example, an estimated average of 9.6 percent of total gross investment was generated in the public sector from 1961 to 1975. On the other hand, 44 percent of GNP flowed into the public sector through all forms of taxation, and total public-sector revenues from all sources represented 52 percent of GNP. Thus socialization of *income*, not production, has been the aim of the continuously expanding welfare apparatus of the Swedish state since the Great Depression, and particularly since World War II. As in the United States, social welfare policy has represented an important instrument of reform in the attempt to resolve the social conflicts growing out of the pronounced income inequalities characteristic of capitalist development.

In most official accounts, the history of welfare policy in Sweden is divided into three stages: (1) the provision of poor relief, beginning with the Local Government Reform of 1862; (2) from 1932 to the 1960s, the commitment to full employment as an integral component of government stabilization policy; this involved expanded and more permanent public works projects, vastly increased public service expenditures, increased levels of public assistance ("welfare" benefits to the poor), and government contributions to the unemployment insurance societies run by the trade unions; means-testing was the basic approach to the provision of public assistance; (3) from 1960 to the present, the establishment of a universal system of social insurance, based on an intensified commitment to the so-called principle of normalization, which holds that, regardless of any physical, psychological, or social handicaps, all persons should be enabled to live, work, and develop in a "normal" environment; the social insurance system has focused on the provision of "equal opportunities" to all income groups—for example, in the areas of housing, health, education, and special training and services for older and other disadvantaged workers, including women and immigrants.

From 1870 to 1930, drastic structural changes occurred in Swedish social, economic, and political relations as a result of rapid industrialization. The proportion of the labor force in agriculture dropped from 72 to 32 percent, while the share in industry grew from 15 to 36 percent. At the same time, over a million Swedes left the country from 1850 to 1920—most emigrating to the United States.

During this early period, assistance in kind was the predominant form of relief in the rural sector. At rural iron foundries, for example, retired workers or their widows were often allowed to keep their houses and received a supply of food and basic goods until they died. Such provisions did not exist for urban workers or for those in the growing forest industry. Basic safety conditions were lacking for workers in all sectors until 1889, when the first work safety law was passed. An 1891 law channeled government contributions into the trade-union health insurance funds, and in 1901 a workmen's compensation law was passed covering industrial injuries. The eight-hour work day was mandated by law in 1918.

The Basic Pension Act of 1913 created a national pension system which, though providing only small benefits, nevertheless covered the entire population. Other measures enacted prior to the Great Depression included limited manpower programs during the period of high unemployment following World War I; the 1918 Poor Relief Act requiring local governments to establish poor relief institutions and according relief recipients the right to appeal local government decisions in relief cases; and the Child Welfare Act of 1924, which formally separated the child welfare system from the poor relief system.

Vastly expanded manpower projects were a key element in the response of the Social Democrats to the Depression. Deficit financing was used for the first time to pay for social welfare expenditures, signaling perhaps the most profound change in Swedish economic policy thinking in this century. The outlines of social welfare policy as a means of achieving some degree of income equalization began to form in this period, but it was not until after World War II, when the trade unions became increasingly aware of the detrimental consequences to workers of the rapid structural changes in the capitalist economy, that the commitment to income equality began to be expressly articulated by the Social Democratic Party.

Housing policy became closely tied to manpower policy in the 1930s as a powerful means of generating employment in the public as well as the private sector. Municipal nonprofit housing corporations were created, leading to the predominance of the public sector in the housing industry. Medical care was also expanded significantly, and a type of "family policy" emerged in the late thirties. In 1937, a law was passed authorizing the creation of family planning, maternity, and pediatric centers, and hospital care and medication related to childbirth were made free of charge. A law was passed forbidding employers to fire female workers who became pregnant or took maternity leave. Means-tested vacation trips for housewives, discounts in food prices, and free school lunches were also provided. A major step away from the provision of such benefits in kind was the introduction in 1948 of universal children's allowances, an income-transfer mechanism that was estimated to reduce the inequality of income distribution by about one percentage point.[9]

The ratio of total social welfare expenditures to GNP had risen to 23.5 percent by 1974. The largest expenditure was in the area of health insurance (amounting to 41.29 percent of total expenditures); the second largest was old-age and disability insurance (34.5 percent). General public assistance, in contrast, comprised a mere 1.03 percent of total expenditures.

Thus, social insurance in various forms accounted for approximately 97 percent of total social welfare expenditure, while general public assistance accounted for only 1.03 percent.

Labor Market Policy

In the previous chapter, we discussed the general Swedish use of labor market policy as part of an overall fiscal and monetary program for full employment. But specific measures have also been used as a welfare mechanism during recessions. In the 1975-76 recession, the government attempted to maintain the employment of those who still had jobs by granting investment subsidies to firms, making extra national and local government purchases, beginning additional government construction earlier than scheduled, and working to delay or prevent layoffs and dismissals at firms where output had to be cut. Government grants were paid to firms that trained personnel instead of laying them off or firing them. During the spring of 1977, the government introduced similar assistance for firms in declining sectors—those particularly susceptible to competition from imports or those losing export markets. Thus, the government supported elderly employees in the textile and clothing industries, and promoted the employment of redundant personnel in activities apart from their regular production work.

A second type of measure has been the support of those who are put out of work and experience difficulty finding new jobs, and of young workers who are having trouble finding a first job. Included are training schemes and relief work projects over a rather wide range of occupations; for example, supplementary government grants for labor-intensive municipal relief work projects in the conservation sector and in the nursing care and service sectors were raised to 75 percent of the total costs of such local programs in 1976. Grants were made to firms that hired workers under 20 years of age on a relief work basis.

These measures helped to keep unemployment rates low despite continuation of the recession into 1977-78.

Housing

Government assistance in the area of housing was limited between the wars to the provision of means-tested loans and rent subsidies. During the Second World War, an entirely new and comprehensive national housing policy was adopted that sought to improve housing standards for all citizens regardless of income. Specifically, the policy aimed at eliminating the overcrowding of residences (in 1941, 47 percent of all new dwelling units consisted of one room or a room and a kitchen); raising housing standards, especially in rural areas; making available decent and spacious housing at rents equaling no more than 20 percent of average family income; and encouraging the construction of nonprofit housing. Prior to World War II, rents were so high in relation to income, and the marginal cost of extra space was so steep, that many people were forced into one-room flats. Swedish housing policy therefore had to assure that larger flats were built and rented at rates people could afford in order to alleviate overcrowding.

About half of all families with two or more children are eligible for rent allowances, which are funded by the central government but administered by local authorities. The allowances are paid directly to landlords, who pass them on to tenants in the form of lower rents.

Three agencies dominate the housing industry: so-called public utility companies, cooperatives, and private contractors. Public utility companies have built around 30 percent of all new Swedish housing. These corporations are sponsored and controlled by municipal authorities, which appoint over 50 percent of the directors. The cooperatives, which have produced about one-third of total housing output, are nonprofit companies that build blocks of flats or apartment buildings for occupancy by their members, who own and manage the buildings on a joint basis. The remaining third of housing output is generated by the private sector. In addition to the considerable subsidy in the form of low-interest loans granted to each of these sectors, the government attempts to prevent temporary fluctuations of interest rates by covering any interest payments in excess of certain limits (3.5 percent in the early sixties). By shielding the housing industry from the pressures of tight credit periods, Swedish housing policy has maintained one of the highest rates of overall housing construction in the world.[10]

Comparison of the U.S. and Swedish Systems

An important difference between the U.S. and Swedish social insurance/welfare programs is their relative size. In Sweden these programs represented almost 24 percent of gross national product in 1974—an expenditure of about $1,625 per capita. In the proposed U.S. federal budget for 1979, Social Security, federal retirement, disability benefits, unemployment compensation, and public assistance were expected to cost $160 billion; Medicare and Medicaid, $50 billion; veterans benefits, $19 billion; and for public service jobs and training, $18 billion. The total—$247 billion—represents 10.6 percent of 1979 projected gross national product and equals $1,120 per capita. Even if state and local welfare expenditures, including Medicaid, are added, total public expenditures on social insurance and assistance do not exceed 14 percent of GNP, or about $1,460 per capita. Both figures are considerably less than in Sweden (in 1974 prices, $1,460 equals about $1,100). Much of the difference is represented by the higher Swedish payments of social security and welfare benefits to individuals, although unemployment compensation is much smaller per capita than in the United States. The largest single item in Sweden's social welfare budget is national health care, which comprised only about 20 percent of federal expenditures on welfare in the United States.

There are other differences as well. Because social insurance and social welfare programs in Sweden are far more comprehensive, many individuals who would require public assistance in the United States do not need this type of assistance in Sweden. Sweden's two-tiered social security system makes coverage universal. All the aged and disabled and all widows and children are covered under at least one tier of the social insurance system regardless of prior income. In the United States, in contrast, the aged and disabled who are ineligible for Social Security must seek means-tested benefits under the Supplemental Security Income program, and the family of a deceased worker without Social Security coverage must resort to Aid to Families with Dependent Children (AFDC).

Divorced, separated, deserted, and unmarried women in Sweden are eligible for children's allowances, as are all families with children under the age of 16. The absent parent is ordinarily required by law to make support payments, but if he or she cannot be located or is unable to provide support, a child-support advance is paid by the Child Welfare Board.[11]

In Sweden, far more than in the United States, public assistance tends to be a *temporary* solution to personal economic difficulties. In the city of Malmö, for example, the average length of stay on public aid in 1972 was just under five months. On the other hand, individuals with permanent problems, such as those resulting from illness or injury, are granted permanent solutions. For example, an older worker who is unemployed may receive an early pension if the employment service fails to find the individual a suitable job. By 1974, the number of workers who had abandoned the labor market by opting for early retirement totaled 278,000, compared to 1,038,000 old-age pensioners. Early retirement pensions have thus served as a mechanism for lowering the unemployment rate.

Families and individuals who are in need but are ineligible for the various social insurance benefits or for whom the latter do not provide an adequate income, may obtain Swedish public assistance without regard to marital status, employment status, or the presence or absence of children. In the United States, on the other hand, only twenty-three states provide AFDC benefits to families in need because of the unemployment of the male head of the household, and benefits to workers earning an income below the poverty line are virtually nonexistent. Welfare assistance is ruled out for single persons or childless couples in the United States unless they are blind, aged, or disabled. Many U.S. policymakers appear convinced that poverty is the only adequate work incentive among the lower classes, and that more generous or extensive welfare benefits would thus lead to a reduction in total economic output or growth. In Sweden, where policymakers typically hold a different view, there is no evidence to suggest that this is the case.

Thus, the welfare populations of the United States and Sweden bear little resemblance to each other. In the United States 16 percent of those receiving federal public assistance are aged, blind, or disabled; 11 percent are families with dependent children in which both parents are present; and 73 percent are families with a female head of household. In Sweden, taking Malmö as a representative city, we find that a full 62 percent of public assistance cases are single men and women without children (41 percent single men, 21 percent single women). Single women with children represent only 11 percent; couples with children, 15 percent; and couples without children, 12 percent. Thirty percent of divorced men, mainly those who have trouble keeping up with child-support payments, receive assistance. The relatively small proportion of single mothers receiving public assistance in Sweden may be explained in part by the existence of a number of state programs allowing such women to remain in school or on the job; such programs are not restricted to unwed mothers but rather are intended for all women. They include a parental insurance scheme that currently provides benefits for seven months in connection with childbirth. An expectant mother may receive a parenthood benefit and leave her job one month before the baby is due, and she is entitled to an additional seven months of benefits once the child is born. (In the case of married couples, the parents together decide how to divide the seven months between them; either the father or the mother may opt to remain at home with the child, but not both at once.)

A parent who must remain at home to care for a sick child under 10 years of age is entitled to sickness benefits for a total of 10 days each year per family. Child-support advances are available from the Child Welfare Board for a single mother, if the father is unknown or unable to provide support, as mentioned above. Educational loans and grants are available if the single mother wants to further her studies; alternatively, if she wishes to return to work she must, by law, be reinstated in her former job. Single parents are given priority at day-care centers. Also, a state-employed babysitter may be obtained when a child is ill.

The level of public assistance in Sweden compares very favorably with wages in manufacturing. In 1973 in the city of Malmö, for example, average annual earnings for workers in manufacturing after taxes were 25,500 kronor, while public assistance for the average family of four totaled approximately 23,700 kronor, or 93 percent of the expected manufacturing wage. Public assistance in the United States in the same year, including food stamps, averaged around 49 percent of after-tax manufacturing wages. In terms of median incomes, public assistance in Sweden ranged from 111.9 percent at the highest levels of benefit to 68.3 percent at the lowest, while in the U.S. public assistance represented 53.9 percent of median income in the highest-paying states and only 22.7 percent in the lowest-paying states. Therefore, unlike the United States, work incentives play no part in the Swedish welfare scheme. Tax on marginal earnings is virtually 100 percent and, as we have shown, grant levels are nearly as high as wage levels.

A New American Welfare State?

The growth of welfare in Western Europe and the United States represents an important change in the lives of workers and the poor in these countries. As two American economists have noted:

To be able to go to the hospital and not be treated as an indigent, to have money enough to live in retirement without too much fear, and to know that in case of unemployment or the wage earner's disability that at least some income will be available is a far cry from the Social Darwinian world of the 1860s and 1870s.[12]

In the same way, increased coverage by social insurance and public assistance to the poor are direct benefits for lower-income groups and for those who have only their labor to sell. Much of the political action of organized labor in Western industrial societies has focused on just such income transfers from high- to low-income earners, with the government serving as intermediary.* Even in the United States, where levels of social welfare are much lower than in countries like Sweden and Germany, social insurance gradually is coming to be regarded as a legal right.

While this gain for working people in industrial society is important, the concept of government-provided social welfare has little to do with democratization of the economy. The appropriation of income by the government and its redistribution to the lowest-income groups has taken place within the context of increased concentration of private capital and the continued control of investment by large private corporations. Although income appropriation has been much greater in Sweden than in the United States, in neither country have social insurance and public assistance altered the fundamental power of the private corporate sector over the economy, nor have they changed the basic capital-labor relationship. The welfare state is an attempt by the govern-

---

*In 1977 Jerald Hage and Robert Manneman attempted to test various theories of welfare expansion in Britain, France, Germany, and Italy. Despite their rather poor measure of the true extent of leftist political power, they found that in all of these countries but Germany, this variable is a significant correlate of welfare expansion.

ment to ameliorate the most blatant injustices of capitalist development—unemployment, old-age insecurity, and great disparities in the rewards to work—so that corporate capitalism can continue to function with no significant shift in economic control and power.

But what, then, is the meaning of this gain in income for the poor? The government redistributes income over the objections of higher-income earners and of corporations, whose taxes pay part of social insurance and public assistance. At the same time, the poor are placed in a position of constant defensiveness with regard to assistance and insurance: first, not all low-income earners are eligible for assistance; second, assistance and social insurance in the United States are low relative to mean income; and third, assistance is used in the context of work incentives, and applied so as to avoid disrupting the low-wage labor market. There is a marked difference between social insurance welfare in Sweden and in the United States, largely because of the much greater political power of the Swedish labor movement. In the United States, the government appropriates income and gives it to the poor; but at the same time, it controls social insurance and welfare so that the poor are never sure when benefits will be cut back or expanded, and uses these programs to move people in and out of the labor force. In both the United States and Sweden, income transfers operate to make capitalism more palatable. So the growth of the welfare state is, at one and the same time, a political victory for the aged and the poor, and a means of preventing more profound changes in the economy—perhaps even serving as a *substitute* for the kind of changes necessary to achieve full employment, much greater and more fundamental equalization of income, and economic democracy in production.

This presents us with a basic dilemma: if we are to move toward a more democratic society, what do we do about the welfare system? Should we support welfare expansion? national health care? welfare reform? increased Social Security? Piven and Cloward argued that:

In the absence of fundamental economic reforms, therefore, *we take the position that the explosion of the rolls is the true relief reform,* that it should be defended, and expanded.[13]

Even if social insurance and welfare are an attempt to ameliorate market inequities, they also represent real gains for the poor, aged, and disabled. The greater and more comprehensive the insurance and welfare schemes, the greater the gain for these groups. Furthermore, even in an economic democracy, where workers and consumers—rather than a handful of corporate board members and their managers—make the investment, allocation, and employment decisions, social insurance will be necessary. A more democratic economy still must provide in some form for retired workers, for the disabled, for single-parent families, and for everyone's health care. We expect that the cost and form of social insurance and public assistance in such an economy will resemble the Swedish system: with a commitment to full employment and child-care centers, welfare payments will be a small percentage of total social welfare expenditures, while national health insurance and pensions (Social Security) will comprise the bulk of the social services package. So, while we recognize that the Swedish model of the welfare state speaks to public control of investment rather than to economic democracy, it is at least a partial model of the social insurance side of a more democratic American society. Increases in social services in a corporate economy such as the United States are qualitatively different from what they would be in a full-employment, worker/consumer-controlled economy, relying much more on work-incentive public assistance rather than the guaranteed *right* of everyone to work; even in a full-employment economy, however, some form of national health care, retirement pensions, and disability pay would have to exist.

Increased welfare payments in today's America are not only a response to the contradictions of corporate growth and concentration—they create contradictions themselves. Economist James O'Connor has characterized these as the "fiscal crisis of the state." According to O'Connor, the origins of this crisis lie both in the financing of expenditures and in the rising expenditures themselves. The corporations, he argues, require more government services in the form of defense expenditures as they expand abroad and more services at home to pacify unemployed and unemployable workers as the relative expansion of domestic jobs declines. At the same time, rising interest rates increase the cost of government borrowing. So heavier taxes become the main source of income transfers, social insurance, and defense spending. As the taxes needed to finance such transfers increase, the low- and middle-income wage earners who bear the brunt of these tax hikes begin to revolt, making it more and more difficult to appropriate income in order to soften the inequities of the market or protect U.S. investments abroad.[14]

While we favor expanded social insurance, important reforms are also required. Any future Social Security system and national health care would have to be structured differently than these programs are today, and some of these structural changes can take place even within a corporate economy.

Social Security taxes are currently paid in part by employers (who supposedly are willing to hire less labor because of this payroll tax) and in part by a very regressive tax on workers' wages. More progressive ways must be sought to finance old-age pensions.

Furthermore, under the present system employers pay a high fraction of wages for lower-paid workers, which probably biases their hiring policies.

An expansion of Social Security benefits thus should include changes in financing. All the more so since the age structure of the society has changed so that a higher and higher proportion of the population is over 65. Younger workers are being called upon to pay an increasing share of their wages toward the pensions of previous generations; therefore, it is even more crucial to collect these taxes progressively, either through income taxes or through a very progressive wage tax.

In addition to paying Social Security taxes, many workers contribute to pension funds. Under present law, pension funds are invested "for the worker" in a diverse portfolio, which may include the stock of companies that have transferred some of their production operations abroad. The size of these pension funds and their coverage are one issue, and their investment another. Both affect employment and income distribution and ultimately could be manipulated to finance greater worker control of production and investment (as discussed earlier).

In the present context, however, the pension fund issue is of interest because such funds give some workers the option of increasing their old-age security far beyond that provided through the public system. Yet, pension funds are now restricted to certain classes of workers; usually the secondary labor market of low-income, nonunionized, or temporarily employed workers (45 percent of the labor force in the United States is part-time or part-year and only 23 percent of all workers are unionized) is excluded. Thus, the very workers who are in greatest need of additional protection after age 65 (because their Social Security payments are the lowest) do not receive it.

In Sweden, national pension reform became a

major political issue and was finally approved by special election in 1958. Debate centered around the best means for providing a much-needed supplement to the existing national pension scheme. The conservative parties and the national employers' association proposed an expansion of private pension plans, but the labor union federation and the Social Democratic Party successfully enacted a universal, compulsory scheme to supplement the existing transfers with earnings-based benefits; together these pension benefits amount to about two-thirds of the average earnings in a worker's fifteen best years, up to a limit of more than twice the median income. A payroll tax finances the entire system of supplementary pensions; the funds have accumulated during an extended period (1958-80), building up a large surplus while the number of recipients has grown. In 1974, the funds in the Swedish national pension system were invested as follows: 45 percent in housing, 12 percent in national government bonds, 9.5 percent in municipal bonds, and approximately 33 percent in industry (bonds, not stock purchases).

A similar national pension system should be established to offer pensions to those in the American work force not covered by existing pension arrangements. Such a system would benefit lower-paid workers in the nonunionized sectors of the economy, and the funds could be invested in sectors such as housing—an area of social need as well as a secure investment.

National health care is a different issue from Social Security. The way Medicare and Medicaid are now functioning is probably the single worst way to provide publicly funded health delivery. The government is subsidizing higher profits for hospitals, doctors, and private intermediaries such as Blue Cross and the insurance companies. Billions of tax dollars are flowing to these private institutions and individuals with no semblance of public control. Any national health-care plan that builds upon this system can only compound inflation and corruption. Nor do Medicare and Medicaid provide particularly good medical care or preventive medicine. The system creates tremendous bureaucracy. It has increased the number of medical operations Americans undergo, but has not improved their health. A new concept for national health insurance must be developed—a concept based on a decentralized, community system of health care. In 1971, the Medical Committee on Human Rights and Congressman Ronald Dellums presented a plan that would establish a network of service areas and a corresponding governance structure of service-area health boards comprised of health workers and consumers. The system would be financed by corporate and progressive income and wealth taxes. National health care under the Dellums bill directly confronts the concept of health-care delivery adopted by the American Medical Association and American Hospital Association. It also shifts the most onerous costs of such a program off the shoulders of low- and middle-income earners. The plan was drafted into legislative form and introduced into Congress in 1976 as the National Health Rights and Community Service Act.

The provision of increased and restructured social insurance and public assistance in a democratic economy still leaves unanswered the question of what will motivate people to work. The general assumption behind work-incentive welfare programs is that poor people stay on welfare because they do not like to work—because they are lazy. If this assumption is true, a comprehensive public assistance program without work incentives could cause considerable trouble in the labor market: even if offered the possibility of productive and adequately paid employment, poor people would choose to stay on welfare rather than work. Not only would this be demoralizing for those who did work, it would also be very expensive.

But there is an increasing body of evidence which indicates that this assumption is not true. Leonard Goodwin's careful 1972 study for the Brookings Insitution showed that

poor people—males and females, blacks and whites, youths and adults—identify their self-esteem with work as strongly as do the nonpoor.[15]

Goodwin concluded that work enforcement programs (tied to welfare) for the poor have an effect exactly the opposite of that intended: they negatively influence work orientation because they reinforce the pattern of failure in work that is characteristic of welfare recipients. The program studied by Goodwin was successful in getting jobs for only about 2 percent of the total eligible welfare population—this, during a period when welfare rolls were rising by about 40 percent. He argued that work requirements for welfare mothers mean pushing them through training programs that place only a small percentage of them in regular jobs. Moreover, the jobs that such women do obtain are low-paying and temporary, contributing to their sense of failure and willingness to stay on welfare without trying to find work. "If the jobs are ill paid and regarded by employers and employees as 'make-work,' they may prove even more discouraging to the poor than no jobs at all," commented Goodwin.

Welfare is not a substitute for permanent, decent-paying jobs—which brings us back to employment policy. The traditional human capital model has infused work and welfare programs with a training component designed to bring the poor into "good" jobs. The evidence, however, indicates that these attempts do not function to help people escape unemployment or welfare dependence. What, then, are the implications for employment programs in a democratically run full-employment economy?

The only way to enable low-income workers to escape the poverty and unemployment trap is to make career-type jobs available to them. Full-employment macroeconomic policy will be an important element in making such jobs available, but direct public employment will still be necessary to get the poor into meaningful, permanent jobs during the transition to greater public control of industry and investment, largely because the private sector will not be able to absorb everyone who wants to be employed. Such public employment will have to allow for job rotation and other forms of work organization that will enable the poor to move up into more skilled and higher-paying jobs while still getting the less desirable jobs done. In such a context, training and education would have to have a much greater effect than now: less-educated workers would have the opportunity to apply their training in jobs with greater "productivity." In the long run, this is the only way to break the poverty cycle; a true antipoverty program is a program that places the presently poor into permanent, career-opportunity jobs and trains them for those jobs.

Such a program will be implemented in the United States only when there is a national government willing to exercise greater public control over investment, and when workers and consumers have greater influence in economic decision making, so that planning for local economic development is based on overall community needs, not simply the imperatives of large corporations.

A poor people's movement, by itself, cannot bring about a government committed to community-based full employment. The only political route with any chance of success is the formation of a progressive alliance that includes not only poor people's organizations but trade unions, women's groups, environmentalists, consumer organizations, and progressive public officials.

Can such a progressive alliance become a genuine political force in the United States in the coming decade?

In the final section of this book, we examine the questions of political organization and strategy— matters that must be considered by policy planners such as ourselves. All of the structural reforms discussed in previous chapters will be little more than wishful thinking if there is no political movement that adopts these reforms as part of its program for change.

PART FOUR

Can It Happen Here?

CHAPTER NINE

A Different View of the 1970s

The conventional wisdom is that the 1970s, especially the last half of the decade, were a bad time politically for progressive forces in the United States. Writer Tom Wolfe labeled the 1970s the "Me Decade" and described it as a period of rampant narcissism. Mystical eastern religions from the Reverend Sun Myung Moon to various gurus gained a multitude of followers. Thousands of former activists gave up politics for personal discovery through EST, rolfing, Buddhism, body massage, and Inner Tennis. *Time* and *Newsweek* pronounced the New Left dead, playing up Eldridge Cleaver's religious conversion and Rennie Davis's new job at John Hancock Life Insurance Company. The protest movements of the sixties were packaged and sold as nostalgia in coffee-table books from Rolling Stone and in TV movies like Sara Davidson's *Loose Change*. The great criminals of the period—Nixon, Kissinger, and their associates—reaped profits with lucrative book and TV deals. The successful politicians of the 1970s seemed to be those who dealt in symbols, not substance—Jerry Brown, Jimmy Carter, and others; who promised little and offered less; who were calm and self-possessed on TV and downplayed the ability of government to improve society. Howard Jarvis of Proposition 13 fame glared triumphantly from the cover of *Time* in 1978, and *Newsweek* queried on its cover: "Is America Moving Right?"

At one level—the level of visible public consciousness and activity that surfaces in the media—the 1970s were a relatively conservative decade. But there was another level of activity—one less easily discovered by *Time*—which gave at least some promise of progressive political change in the 1980s and 1990s.

Interest in Democratic Management

In the 1960s, business was almost a dirty word. In the 1970s, thousands of activists realized that business need not mean just corporate capitalism—and that *any* society needs business enterprises to produce goods and services for people. These goods and services, however, do not have to be produced under authoritarian work conditions with private profit as the sole criterion. Management can be democratic, and enterprises can be owned by workers and consumers, not just by absentee capitalists.

In 1973, one of the authors went to British Columbia on a story assignment for *Ramparts* magazine. The government in power—the mildly socialist New Democratic Party—had purchased a number of private firms and converted them into public enterprises; but they were still run like private companies. One union official complained, "The government bosses are worse than capitalists. It's harder to strike against them, because they claim they're on our side." The idea of creating a *democratic* business school was born on that trip to Canada.

Economist Richard Parker, publisher of *Mother Jones* magazine (a successor to *Ramparts*), obtained foundation grants and persuaded a sixties activist, David Olsen, to head the New School for Democratic Management in San Francisco. The school has been in existence since 1976. It has run successful summer sessions for over hundreds of students, as well as four-day road sessions in Portland, Oregon; Austin, Texas; and other cities.

The school's staff found that during the 1970s thousands of "alternative" businesses were founded around the country, including food cooperatives, car repair centers, restaurants, arts centers, publishing houses, solar equipment distributors, bookstores, bakeries, housing cooperatives, credit unions, child-care cooperatives, and many more. These enterprises, most of them small-scale, are managed in a relatively humane and democratic fashion.

In some areas of the country, these "alternative" enterprises have banded together organizationally into a kind of alternative chamber of commerce. In the Minneapolis–St. Paul area, for example, more than seventy-five co-ops, worker-owned businesses, and buying clubs formed the All-Cooperating Assembly—an organization that is both a commercial network with certain shared warehouse and transportation facilities, and a political federation. The assembly meets two times a year, maintains a small staff, and publishes a co-op directory for the area as part of its outreach program. In California, Texas, and other states, statewide federations of cooperatives hold annual conferences and publish newsletters on co-op affairs.

In 1978, as a result of the combined lobbying efforts of the Cooperative League of the United States, Ralph Nader's Congress Watch, and presidential consumer advisor Esther Peterson, Congress passed a bill creating the National Consumer Cooperative Bank and provided it with funding and authority to make over $1 billion in loans to consumer co-ops over a ten-year period. The bank revitalized the cooperative movement. In addition to offering financial assistance in the form of loans, the bank, through its technical assistance division, will provide

the co-op movement with expert management training, financial analysis, and market planning; and,
through a special capital development fund, the bank
will make outright grants for start-up equity and
working capital to low-income co-ops. The existence
of the bank and the enthusiasm within the co-op
movement generated by its passage offer the possibility for expansion of cooperative enterprises in the
1980s and 1990s.

Interest in democratic management and worker
ownership was not limited to middle-class veterans of
the 1960s or to old-time cooperative participants
from the 1930s. In 1975, the People's Bicentennial
Commission, a public interest group in Washington,
D.C., asked the Peter Hart Company to take a poll on
public attitudes on the economy. Among other results, Hart found that 66 percent of those surveyed
agreed that people do not work as hard as they could
"because they aren't given enough say in decisions
which affect their jobs." Seventy-four percent would
support a plan whereby consumers in local communities "are represented on the boards of companies that operate in their local region." Fifty-two
percent would support a plan "in which employees
determine broad company policy." Sixty-six percent
would favor working for a company that is employee
owned and controlled.[1]

In 1977, the closure of the Youngstown Tube and
Steel Plant, a division of the Lykes Corporation, generated a grass-roots organization called the Save Our
Valley Campaign. The shutdown of the steel plant
was the biggest nondefense industrial job loss in U.S.
history. The multiplier effect of the plant closing
meant that thousands more than just the 5,000 steelworkers who lost their jobs would be affected by
Lykes's decision. A number of local clergymen decided to fight the plant closing by forming the Save
Our Valley Campaign. They built an ecumenical coalition of local groups, including Steelworkers Union

locals, local small businessmen, and a number of community groups; with a grant from the Department of Housing and Urban Development, the campaign commissioned a study of the feasibility of reopening the plant under worker-community ownership. The study concluded that, "given certain reasonable actions on the part of the community and the federal government, the Works can be reopened and operated as a profitable basic steel manufacturer under community/employee ownership."

The required government actions included loan guarantees of at least $350 million from the federal government. To demonstrate community support for the plan, the ecumenical coalition began a campaign to encourage local residents and businesses to open special accounts at Mahoning Valley banks and savings and loans associations, pledging this money for the purchase of stock in the new steel firm if it received federal assistance. By the end of 1978, more than $1.5 million had been deposited at the nineteen participating banks and savings and loans. Another $1 million had been pledged by national religious organizations.[2]

In April 1979, the Commerce Department turned down the ecumenical coalition's application for $245 million in loan guarantees to reopen the plant under worker-community ownership. The reason given was that the request exceeded the department's $100 million limit on loan guarantees.

Although unsuccessful in reopening the Youngstown steel plant, the campaign of the ecumenical coalition demonstrated that widespread support in a working-class community could be generated around the concept of economic democracy—the concept that workers and community residents should be able to decide their economic futures and run their own economic enterprises.

A number of university researchers and consultants, many headquartered at Cornell, founded the organization, People for Self-Management, which sponsored three national conferences in the 1970s on the democratization of business enterprises. This informal network was responsible for a bill introduced into Congress in 1978 by Congressmen Stan Lundine (D-N.Y.) and Peter Kostmayer (D-Pa.), which would aid workers threatened by plant closures in purchasing the companies where they work.

A few thousand "alternative" businesses or a few worker-owned companies are not sufficient in themselves to reduce substantially the economic power of large corporations. Such democratic enterprises, however, are both working models of more humane ways of producing economic goods—they provide "cultural space" while people engage in political struggle—and training grounds for people with democratic politics to learn the skills that are necessary over the long run, if the rest of the economy is to be democratized.

Political Successes at the State and Local Level

In 1974, the Institute for Policy Studies in Washington realized that many 1960s activists were running for and winning public office at the state and local levels. It seemed that substantial political change could occur only if a base of support could be built in local communities where people actually live and work, not in Washington, a town of bureaucrats and lobbyists. A network was formed called the National Conference on Alternative State and Local Public Policy, which publishes a regular newsletter, produces readers on public policy and model legislation, and sponsors annual gatherings where progressive public officials, community organizers, and labor leaders meet to exchange experience and discuss political program and strategy. The conference provides a vital link for reform efforts in different cities and states.

In Detroit, for example, two 1960s activists have won political office. In 1972, radical lawyer Justin Ravitz was elected to a ten-year term as a judge of the city's municipal court. Ravitz created a stir by requiring courtroom spectators and the judge to stand for the jury; by sentencing store managers who practiced consumer fraud to jail; and by speaking out on the economic causes of crime. In November 1977, Ravitz's former law partner Ken Cockrel, a well-known black activist, was elected to the Detroit city council, after running without the endorsement of the powerful Democratic Party establishments.

As lawyers, Cockrel and Ravitz successfully defended a black auto worker who went on a rampage in the factory and shot supervisory personnel. Cockrel and Ravitz argued in court that working under the unsafe conditions in the plant had driven the man to his desperate action. The case brought public attention to the harsh working conditions inside Detroit's auto plants, and the man was acquitted.

Cockrel, Ravitz, and their supporters built on these two victories by forming a citywide political organization that might run a candidate for mayor in a few years. The organization, known as DARE (Detroit Alliance for a Rational Economy), plans to prepare a comprehensive reform program for Detroit.

In Washington, D.C., city councilman Marion Berry, a former civil rights activist, was elected mayor in 1978. In Minnesota, state senator Alan Spear—the first openly gay public official in the country—state representative Linda Berglin, and others formed the Minnesota Alliance of Populists. In northern California, Congressman Ron Dellums' progressive "machine" elected a county supervisor in Oakland and a state assemblyman from Berkeley. Dellums' Berkeley-Oakland network worked on statewide issues with the Campaign for Economic Democracy, an organization that grew out of Tom Hayden's race for the U.S. Senate.

Progressive officials in some cities and states have set up new public enterprises. In Madison, Wisconsin, left-wing mayor Paul Soglin and his assistant, Jim Rowen, established a city-owned development corporation to provide loans and technical assistance to local cooperatives, worker-owned enterprises, and small businesses. In Massachusetts, progressive state legislators created the Massachusetts Community Development Finance Corporation, which loans funds to community-owned business enterprises and worker-owned firms. Nick Carbone, head of the Hartford city council, successfully passed legislation to create a municipally owned recycling corporation. In New York City, councilwoman Ruth Messinger fought to convert some city-owned housing into tenant-run cooperatives. In Cleveland, populist mayor Dennis Kucinich fought with the city's banks over who would control local economic development.

As attorney general of Arkansas, Bill Clinton, a former McGovern organizer, fought for consumer interests. The consumer protection division of Clinton's office—through lawsuits, investigation of consumer complaints, and mediation—recovered in fines and settlements more than five times its annual budget. Clinton's staff sued nursing homes for double billing of patients; argued successfully against utility company requests for automatic price increases; investigated collusive arrangements between cemeteries and monument companies; and supported price advertising for professional services. Running as an anticorporate, pro-ERA (equal rights amendment) populist, Clinton was elected governor of Arkansas in November 1978.

In Davis, California, seat of the state's major agricultural university, a coalition of environmentalists and antiwar activists won control of the city council and formulated the first comprehensive city energy policy in the country. Davis's new municipal regulations provide strict energy-conservation standards and encourage the utilization of alternative energy sources, such as solar power and wind.[3]

New statewide populist and anticorporate organizations appeared in the 1970s. In Massachusetts, Fair Share—an organization of over 20,000 blue collar families—successfully forced down auto insurance rates and embarrassed major corporations into paying delinquent taxes owed to the city of Boston. The Association of Community Organizations for Reform Now (ACORN), a low- and middle-income populist organization that started in Arkansas and won victories on utility rates, spread to ten other states. In North Carolina, Carolina Action became a statewide force on economic issues. In many states, public interest research groups (PIRGs), funded by student donations, raised economic issues in state legislatures and city council chambers. In some cities, mass membership organizations such as UNO (United Neighborhood Organization) in East Los Angeles and COPS (Communities Organized for Public Service) in San Antonio were started in minority communities.*

The Ohio Public Interest Group (OPIC) was one of the anticorporate organizations that came alive in the decade. Started by antiwar activist Ira Arlook with the support of local churches, OPIC joined with the state's trade unions to challenge corporations' right to move out of communities at will, leaving behind unemployment and depression. Working with state senator Michael Schwartzwalder (D-Columbus), OPIC introduced into the Ohio legislature the Community Readjustment Act, which would require corporations to give two years' advance notice of a plant

---

*Social Policy magazine, in a special September-October 1979 issue on organizing neighborhoods, profiled forty community organizations that appeared in the past decade. All had in common a populist or anticorporate outlook.

closing, pay severance allowances of one week's pay for each year worked to affected employees, and contribute to a community assistance fund that would aid affected towns and cities in redeveloping their local economies.

The issue of plant closings intensified with the shutdown of Youngstown Sheet and Tube. OPIC exposed the way in which the Lykes Corporation, parent company of the steel plant, had run down the Youngstown facility by refusing to modernize it and bleeding it of its profits. OPIC was also influential in the 1977 Cleveland mayoral race (narrowly won by populist Dennis Kucinich), exposing and publicizing the multi-million-dollar tax abatements that City National Bank, Standard Oil of Ohio, and other major corporations were getting from the city council.

The Labor Movement

As many cold-war labor leaders finally began to fade from the scene, union reform groups sprang up in the 1970s in major unions such as the Steelworkers, the Teamsters, and the Mine Workers, and even old hard-liners began to change their minds about working with former antiwar activists and environmentalists.

In California in February 1978, John Henning, head of the state AFL-CIO, gave the opening night speech at a gathering of the state's progressive groups, which included the Campaign for Economic Democracy and Ron Dellums' East Bay machine. Henning spoke about the historical reasons why there is no labor party in the United States and why the labor movement pragmatically has worked within the Democratic Party. He criticized the leadership of the party, however, for being unresponsive to labor's demands and suggested that organized labor look to its left to progressive groups like those at the conference for new political alliances. As part of its more progressive outlook, the state AFL-CIO, in testimony before a state Senate committee, endorsed the concept of a state-owned bank.

At the national level, the heads of many international unions began actively to seek allies on the Left. William Winpisinger, president of the International Machinists Union, was a featured speaker at the 1977 National Conference on Alternative State and Local Public Policy. Jerry Wurf, head of the American Federation of State, County, and Municipal Employees, recruited activists such as Paul Booth, one of the founders of SDS, and Carl Wagner, a McGovern activist, into his union as organizers. A national Labor-Citizen Energy Alliance was formed to lobby Congress on energy issues. Many union leaders, including Wurf and Winpisinger, joined the Democratic Socialist Organizing Committee (DSOC) founded by author Michael Harrington. In November 1979, DSOC sponsored a national conference on "The Democratic Agenda," which attracted hundreds of labor delegates. Even the conservative building trades unions took out ads in DSOC's conference booklet.

The most important labor outreach effort of the decade took place in Detroit in October 1978, when UAW President Doug Fraser called a meeting of left/liberal groups together with representatives of major unions. Groups present at the meeting included women's groups like NOW (National Organization for Women), environmentalists such as the Sierra Club, statewide populist groups like Mass Fair Share, and Democratic Party reform groups such as the DSOC (Democratic Socialist Organizing Committee). Congressman Ron Dellums delivered the keynote address, calling for the creation of a nationwide coalition to create "a more humanistic system" based on the concept of economic democracy.

In the 1970s, unions also began to give more attention to the problem of women workers. The Coalition of Labor Union Women (CLUW) was established, and George Meany announced that he, too, was a feminist. Working women's groups were formed in Boston and Cleveland and joined with unions to organize secretarial and clerical workers.

A number of unions began to show interest in democratizing the work place. UAW vice-president Irving Bluestone initiated a number of work democratization projects in UAW-organized plants around the country. One of the most successful was that at an auto-mirror-manufacturing plant in Bolivar, Tennessee, owned by liberal industrialist Sidney Harman, who was appointed undersecretary of commerce in the Carter administration. The Communications Workers Union received a grant from the German Marshall Fund to send union members to study co-determination in West Germany. In negotiations with Chrysler in 1976, UAW president Doug Fraser raised the question of installing union representatives on the board of that company. In the fall of 1979, Chrysler agreed to nominate Fraser for a position on the company's board of directors to begin serving in May 1980.

Unions also became more aggressive in questioning pension fund investment policies. At the urging of the late Senator Lee Metcalf, the AFL-CIO, at its 1977 convention in Los Angeles, passed a resolution that the "substantial financial power of the AFL-CIO unions be entrusted to financial institutions whose investment policies are not inimical to the welfare of working men and women." Billions of dollars currently controlled by the trust departments of the nation's major banks are at stake.

Led by Bill Winpisinger of the Machinists, unions began to exercise this financial power. As mentioned earlier, a group of ninety unions forced James D. Finley—chairman of J. P. Stevens & Co., the southern nonunion textile giant—to resign from the board of directors of Manufacturers Hanover Trust by threatening to close their accounts or switch to other investment managers. The trustees of the National Union of Hospital and Health Care Employees instructed its money managers to ban any investment that would aid South Africa and to direct "a reasonable ratio" of pension fund monies into socially useful projects. In 1979 negotiations with the UAW, the financially troubled Chrysler corporation agreed to a number of union demands on the investment of worker pension funds. These concessions included the setting aside of funds for investment in home mortgages in targeted cities to be selected jointly by the union and the company; the prohibiting of fund investments in anti-union companies specified by the union; and the removal of investments from corporations doing business in South Africa that refused to accept nonracist hiring practices.

The labor solidarity demonstrated by union support for the striking mineworkers in 1977—much of it arising spontaneously from union locals—recalled the energy and spirit of the old CIO days. Union organizing gains were made below the Mason-Dixon line. In February 1978, the Steelworkers won the right to represent 19,000 workers at Tenneco's Newport News Shipbuilding and Drydock Company in Virginia. The union election was the largest ever held in the South. "It represents a significant advance for the cause of trade unionism in the South," commented Lloyd McBride, Steelworker president. The new union members will provide money and volunteers for political work in that region.

Student Activism

As the *New York Times* reported on March 15, 1978, "After several years of conspicuous quiet, social activists on the nation's college campuses have found an issue to stir the social conscience of their fellow students: South Africa."

Thousands of students at Vanderbilt in Nashville protested the presence of South Africa's tennis team at the Davis Cup matches in March 1977. Students from all over New England met at Yale for a series of workshops and speakers on the apartheid issue. Student protestors at the University of Massachusetts, the University of Wisconsin, and Hampshire College convinced their university's trustees to sell millions of dollars' worth in shares of corporations doing business in South Africa. Demonstrations were held at Cornell, Berkeley, Columbia, and Wesleyan. While many university trustees did not divest, under pressure from students they began to question major U.S. corporations about their involvement in South Africa.

On the University of California board of regents, the issue of investment in South Africa led to the more general question of corporate responsibility and the overall investment policies of the university. Regent Stanley Sheinbaum, an international economist and leader of the left wing of the state Democratic Party, was named to head a special committee on university investment and social policy. Sheinbaum hired a group of progressive economists to advise him on positive investment criteria for the university that would take into account the social consequences of investment in the United States.

Students at the University of California challenged university support for research that aids in the mechanization of agriculture, throwing farmworkers out of jobs. Students in university towns such as Davis and Santa Barbara began to help run progressive candidates for local city councils. Across the country in the 1970s, the student vote helped to elect progressive public officials in such cities as Madison, Ann Arbor, Austin, and Champaign-Urbana.

Students and young adults also formed the core of the anti-nuclear movement that spread rapidly across the country in 1978 and 1979. A national anti-nuclear demonstration organized by Ralph Nader and others brought over 50,000 protestors to Washington, D.C. The accident and shutdown at the Three Mile Island nuclear power plant near Harrisburg, Pennsylvania, created thousands of new activists for the movement.

Innovative Public Policy

In 1973, the Institute for Policy Studies organized the decade's first conference on alternative economic policy from a leftist perspective. One of the participants was professor Bert Gross of the City University of New York, an old New Dealer who had been executive secretary of the first Council of Economic Advisors in the 1950s. Gross presented the conference with an outline for a full-employment bill, which he had drafted for the congressional black caucus. After many rewrites, his outline became the Humphrey-Hawkins Full Employment bill; a weaker version of the bill became law in 1978, committing the country—at least on paper—to a moderate goal of full employment (defined as 4 percent unemployment).

Most of the other conference papers, written by younger policy experts, were amateurish by comparison and did not have as much immediate influence as Gross's contribution—but they were only opening efforts. Boston College economist Barry Bluestone, who attended the conference, later drafted with the help of economist Ben Harrison at MIT, a comprehensive reform program for populist presidential candidate Fred Harris in 1976. The Bluestone-Harrison paper was subsequently published as part of an alternate federal budget study, requested by fifty liberal members of Congress and prepared by the Institute for Policy Studies.

Two other conference participants—Gar Alperovitz and Jeff Faux—formed the Exploratory Project on Economic Alternatives (EPEA). Funded by several foundations, EPEA issued a series of reports on economic policy. In 1977, EPEA received a $300,000 grant from HUD to study the possibility of worker-community ownership for the closed Youngstown steel facilities. In 1978 the project became a permanent operation—the National Center on Economic Alternatives—a kind of left-wing Brookings Institution that continued to provide studies on the national economy for unions and progressive members of Congress.

A number of the papers presented at the 1973 conference later appeared as articles in the premiere issue of a new journal founded in the 1970s—*Working Papers for a New Society*. The publication was created to provide a link between alternative policy thinkers and political activists, and to answer the questions: What is the task of the Left? and What works? *Working Papers* was read by congressional aides, columnists such as Tom Wicker, public officials like the mayor of Cleveland, and thousands of professionals, union officials, and community organizers.

Housing expert Chester Hartman also attended the 1973 conference. In 1977, Hartman, politically active in San Francisco, received a small grant from the Stern Foundation to establish the Planners Network, which links left-wing professionals in urban planning and related areas. Hartman edits a periodic newsletter that describes ongoing policy development, reports on individuals' political work, and keeps network members informed of each others' activities. In 1979, Hartman drafted a rent-freeze measure that appeared on the San Francisco city ballot.

Ed Kirshner, a planner from Oakland, presented a paper at the conference on public ownership of land.

Kirshner became director of Community Economics, an alternative consulting firm which provides technical assistance to progressive public officials, trade unions, and community groups. Kirshner's studies have included plans for new farmworker communities in California's valleys, government sponsored cooperative housing in Santa Barbara, and a comprehensive study of programs for community economic development in Berkeley and Oakland, called *The Cities' Wealth.* He and his associates publish a quarterly newsletter, *The Public Works,* which summarizes their ongoing policy work.

A number of other alternative policy groups focusing on a particular issue or area were established in the 1970s—groups such as the Center for Science in the Public Interest, which specializes in nutrition policy; World Watch, which works on energy matters; the Institute for Local Self-Reliance, which concentrates on neighborhood issues; and Rural America, which is developing new policies for American agriculture.

All of these groups have influenced and initiated legislation. They have educated activists on policy issues and developed alternative experts—people with knowledge and skills, and democratic politics who would be able to staff a national reform government in the 1980s or 1990s.

Public Outreach

Alternative economists and policy researchers were not content to talk only to each other in the 1970s. They produced informational material on economics and related matters from a leftist perspective in popular, easy-to-read form for the mass audience.

The Union for Radical Political Economics (URPE), a professional organization of radical economists, primarily university teachers, grew substantially and matured over the decade. URPE members produced a number of outreach materials on economics. In 1975, a group of URPE economists in Cambridge started *Dollars & Sense,* a monthly publication of popular articles on current economic issues. The magazine became a kind of alternative *Wall Street Journal* or *Business Week* that attempted to unravel economic news and make it comprehensible to a nontechnical audience.

Another group of URPE members, originally graduate students at Harvard, compiled a widely used textbook, *The Capitalist System,* as an alternative to Samuelson's *Economics* and other established texts. During the New York fiscal crisis in 1976, URPE members produced *The Economic Crisis Reader,* offering a radical perspective on the plight of urban areas. As an organization, URPE published materials for teach-ins on such topics as food, energy, inflation, and unemployment. Many URPE members became active in local political efforts—from running progressive candidates to assisting food co-ops and worker-owned firms. URPE members drafted an alternative national urban policy paper at the request of Director Sam Brown at the federal agency ACTION. Other URPE members wrote policy papers for state agencies in California and Massachusetts.

Prospects for the 1980s

Where do all these activities lead, and how do they fit together as parts of an integrated whole?

All of these political activities—as well as many others not described here—are explicitly anticorporate. They also have a common positive side that we have chosen to call economic democracy. During Tom Hayden's campaign for the Senate, the term "economic democracy" was revived to describe not only the campaign program, but a vision of a better society. The term is widely used in Scandinavia to indicate the desire of the labor movement to introduce democracy into the economy.

Henry Wallace and other reformers in the New Deal used the phrase. While vice-president in 1942, Wallace gave a speech at Madison Square Garden in New York, declaring, "The new democracy, the democracy of the common man, includes not only the Bill of Rights but also *economic democracy,* ethnic democracy, education democracy and democracy in the treatment of the sexes."

The people and groups described above have stressed not nationalization of the means of production from the top down, but democratization of the economy from the bottom up, starting with the work place and the community. As we have discussed, public ownership has a role to play, particularly in key industries such as transportation, energy, or steel; but it can be public ownership that includes joint worker-community ownership and substantial work place democracy.

The roots of a movement for economic democracy in the United States, if such a movement develops, will be not in the European socialist tradition, but in the American radical tradition of populism, whose primary value was always democracy.

The great postwar era of American economic expansion is drawing to a close. The expansion—fueled by military spending at home and the primacy of the dollar abroad—placated domestic discontent with a cornucopia of consumer goods. That period of American history is over. The prognosis for the remaining decades of the century is for slower growth, simultaneous inflation and unemployment, and occasional shocks to the system—environmental crises, energy shortages, international monetary disorders, and political and corporate scandals. These are not left-wing predictions of doom, but the consensus of mainstream business journals like *Business Week* and the *Wall Street Journal.*

As *Business Week* commented in an editorial in 1974:

It is inevitable that the U.S. economy will grow more slowly than it has. Some people will obviously have to do with less ... indeed, cities and states, the home mortgage market, small business and the consumer will all get less than they want.

Yet it will be a hard pill for many Americans to swallow— the idea of doing with less so that big business can have more. . . .

The changed situation of the United States in the world economy appears to signal an end to "American exceptionalism"—to the favorable social and economic conditions that worked against the development of a mass-based political movement dedicated to greater democratic control over corporations.

The response of organized big business to slower economic growth has been to "squeeze" labor and to launch an ideological offensive against many existing government programs, such as environmental and worker health and safety laws.

In the 1970s big business deliberately caused at least a temporary breakdown in labor-capital relations. Murray Finley, president of the Amalgamated Clothing and Textile Workers, pointed out that labor and capital had a tacit understanding in the postwar period: "Labor would support free enterprise and business would support a strong, democratic labor movement." But Finley declared to *Business Week* in the summer of 1978 that "there has been a shift on the part of the business community toward confrontation rather than cooperation."[4]

The National Association of Manufacturers, for

example, infuriated union leaders by setting up the Council on a Union-Free Environment. Thomas Donahue, executive assistant to AFL-CIO head George Meany, told union leaders that business lobbying in Washington against labor law reform, tax reform, and consumer bills demonstrated that

it still is, as it always has been, them versus us. Call it class struggle, call it corporate power versus the people, call it the establishment overall. But no one should have any delusions about who we are and who they are. We're the workers who want a bigger share of what they have, and they don't want to give it up.[5]

Corporations began to build a procorporate political movement around the country in the 1970s. Over 600 political action committees (PACs) were established by major corporations to solicit political contributions from employees. The National Association of Manufacturers and the U.S. Chamber of Commerce spent money and energy organizing corporate employees and shareholders into a probusiness political force. The chamber began sending periodic reports on congressional issues to over 350 companies. In the spring of 1978, the chamber sponsored sessions around the country on how to initiate corporate political action programs.

The *Wall Street Journal* profiled one such "model" corporate political program set up by ARCO in 1975. The company assigned a special executive to the task and gave him a budget of $750,000 a year. The ARCO Civic Action Program, as it is called, recruited members by mailing a brochure to each of ARCO's 112,000 shareholders, 22,000 employees, and 13,000 retirees. ARCO organized the 50,000 individuals who responded into forty-five local action committees. The company sponsored educational sessions on public issues for the committee members and mailed to the membership, using a computer breakdown of

members' location and their congressional representatives.[6]

How successful such programs are is not yet clear;
they have been in existence but a short time, and their
impact should not be overrated. It is certain, however,
that American corporations have enormous resources
and the will to mobilize their constituency around
economic issues.

As the decade drew to a close, two clear political
trends were evident: (1) There was a large increase in
citizen action, in participation by "average" people in
community and single-issue action organizations,
particularly those centering around economic issues
that affect their lives. Over a half a million citizens
became members of such groups as Ralph Nader's
Public Citizen, Common Cause, Environmental Action, and a host of local groups like ACORN, Mass
Fair Share, Ohio Public Interest Group, North Carolina Citizens Alliance, and many others. (2) The
business community recovered from the tumult and
self-doubt of the 1960s and began, once again, to
wield its political muscle in Washington and around
the country. Business lobbyists successfully defeated
the consumer protection agency bill and stalled the
Labor Reform Act in committee. Individual corporations such as Mobil began public ad campaigns against
government regulation of business. As Mark Green,
Nader's top aide, wrote in *The Nation,* "business is on
the warpath, and it's incredibly well-financed."

These trends and the political activities we have
mentioned briefly share a common focus: they are
struggles over the allocation of economic resources—
over the control of capital. And these struggles will
grow in number and intensity in the 1980s.

The 1980s, we believe, will be a time of conflict—
what *Business Week,* in a 1976 editorial, called "a
conflict as old as the American republic: The conflict
between political democracy and a capitalist economy."

Because the conflict is an old one, built into the very fabric of American society, we do not claim that it will be decisively resolved in the 1980s; nor do we argue that the progressive trends of the 1970s will necessarily develop into a mass movement for economic democracy. Many factors in American society work against the growth and success of such a movement. Sociologist Seymour Martin Lipset, in considering why the United States did not develop a mass-based labor party as occurred in Western Europe, came to the conclusion that America is, in many respects, unique. Lipset pointed out that the absence of a feudal tradition, the open frontier, the presence of vast natural resources, fluid class lines, a two-party system that absorbed elements of radical programs, a culturally heterogeneous work force composed of ex-slaves and immigrants from Europe, Asia, and Mexico, and affluence (particularly in the period after World War II) all worked against the efforts of organizers to build a popular movement that could challenge corporate capitalism.

Although many of these conditions have diminished in importance, the fact remains that the United States is still the wealthiest nation in the world. Its business and government leaders constitute a powerful ruling elite with great resources at their command to combat change in the direction of economic democracy. But we believe that the major events of the 1970s—the American defeat in Vietnam, the decline of the dollar, the energy crisis, and the appearance of stagflation—all signal an end to American "exceptionalism."

In a period such as this, when the American populace—according to numerous opinion polls—is dissatisfied with the old liberal corporate, cold-war ideology that promoted big government at home and an imperial presence abroad, opportunities exist for the creation of a broad-based, democratic movement that would adopt many of the structural reforms discussed in this book.[7] The *idea* of democratizing the economy is a powerful one, if it can be translated into a tangible politics that touches peoples' lives in the communities where they live.

If it is true that altered economic conditions in the United States have eroded the old business-dominated consensus, what strategy might work to promote a new consensus around the notion of economic democracy? We shall suggest some elements of such a strategy in the chapter that follows.

CHAPTER TEN

Building a Movement in the 1980s

If substantial progress toward economic democracy is to be made in the 1980s and the decade after, several conditions must be met.

State and local multi-issue political organizations and coalitions must appear in a number of cities and states. These must be organizations that consciously build an institutional base by supporting and incorporating cooperatives and other alternative businesses, progressive union locals, and community and neighborhood organizations. These state and local organizations must publicly put forward a transitional economic program by running candidates for office, sponsoring initiatives, lobbying, and issuing investigative reports and exposés as well as educational pamphlets and other materials. Sometime in the 1980s, a candidate should be run for president on a program of economic democracy. The presidential campaign would both rely on the state and local organizations, and help to build their strength.

To do *all* of this, it is neither necessary nor desirable to have a single, centralized national organization directing political activities—at least not one modeled after the Old Left or existing third parties. Networks such as the Alternative Conference on State and Local Public Policy, which links progressives at the state and local levels, and emerging coalitions such as that organized by the United Auto Workers in 1979, in which progressive labor unions play a key role, could be sufficient to the task.

Given the nature of the American federal system, characterized by a strong presidency, a two-party system, and winner-take-all legislative elections, the formation of a left-wing third party would be futile and would only serve to isolate progressives from the majority of Americans. Because party primaries are open in the U.S. political system (there is no ideological test to register for either major party), the challenge for economic democracy can be made within the two-party system.

To carry out this challenge, however, we must go beyond the limited reform strategy of left/liberal groups in the 1970s. These groups did engage in militant public actions centered around various economic issues, and they did build organizations with thousands of members; but their approach was limited to working for marginal, not structural reforms: forcing a corporation pay its back taxes, convincing a governor to allocate funds for a solar energy council, supporting the right of farm workers to unionize. These issues, and many others, were certainly progressive; they were system reinforcing, however, rather than system challenging or system transforming.

In California, for example, there were two statewide left/liberal political organizations in 1979—the California Democratic Council (CDC) and the Campaign for Economic Democracy (CED). The CDC played a major role in the late 1950s and early 1960s in reviving the state's Democratic Party, and many CDC leaders went on to win elected office (California's senior senator, Alan Cranston, was one of the founders of CDC). The CDC, however, while issue-oriented, had no strategy for building progressive political organization in cities and communities, and no mechanism for producing its *own* candidates who would run pledged to a platform generated by the organization. Because of this situation, the CDC found itself simply endorsing or not endorsing self-selected liberal Democrats who chose to run for office. The CDC did take progressive stands on national issues such as the Vietnam war, recognition of China, nuclear testing, and so on; but it failed to develop innovative positions on state and local economic issues and made little use of the initiative mechanism. The CDC has been essentially a *reactive* organization: it responds to the political initiatives of others.

The CDC, like similar liberal organizations around the country affiliated with the New Democratic Coalition, Americans for Democratic Action, or other national organizations, was hindered by the ideological limitations of traditional Democratic Party liberalism. Most CDC members are politically progressive (for example, Tom Hayden received the CDC's endorsement over John Tunney in 1976) and might respond to a movement for economic democracy, but the organization itself seemed incapable of initiating such a movement in the state.

The other statewide left-of-center political organization—the Campaign for Economic Democracy (CED)—grew out of Tom Hayden's unsuccessful 1976 race for the Democratic nomination for the U.S. Senate. At the outset, the CED held the potential to become a model for a statewide, multi-issue organization; perhaps because of its origin, however—one individual's campaign—it has not fulfilled the hopes of many initially associated with it. The organization has centered around one person, Tom Hayden, and its financial support has come mainly from his wife, actress Jane Fonda. While the CED has undertaken some innovative policy initiatives—most notably in its promotion of solar energy—it has not reached out to other activists and included them in the organization in a meaningful way. Some local CED chapters, such as those in Santa Monica and Davis, did form working alliances with other groups and participated in winning electoral campaigns; but they were exceptions, and in the state's major cities—Los Angeles and San Francisco—the CED's presence was minimal.

The CED supported Governor Jerry Brown in his race for re-election in 1978 (the governor had earlier appointed Hayden to a post on his solar energy council), so the CED's political legitimacy appeared to derive as much from Brown's recognition of Hayden, as from its statewide program (which was very uncritical of Brown's administration). The CED's greatest failing has been its reluctance to put forward a comprehensive economic program in the context of a *long-term* political strategy.

The CED shared this fault with other statewide groups of the 1970s such as Mass Fair Share, the Ohio Public Interest Campaign, and ACORN. All of them have had a tendency to seek political legitimacy from alliances with existing public officials and to temper their public programs to what is possible now, rather than redefine what is possible through their own actions. None of the groups has actively educated its members on the issues of economic democracy; in fact, internal education of members, as well as outreach educational efforts, has been minimal. (The groups do teach community organizing skills, but in a very nonideological way.)

All of these groups have had some success in pushing single issues, but their success will remain limited as long as their politics remain timid. Of course, objective circumstances in the 1970s made it difficult for leftist activists to build *any* kind of political organization. The point is that, as conditions change, only organizations that are ready for new opportunities will be able to take advantage of new situations; and only politically bold organizations help to shape their own situations.

Progressive political change will occur in the 1980s if two conditions are met:

1) People—not hard-core activists, but regular working people with families and jobs—must become politically active by taking steps, however small, in the direction of democratic participation, aimed at bringing about better lives for themselves as well as a more decent society. Such steps could include the following: renters attend a meeting in their building to set up a tenants' union; workers in a plant strike or organize around demands for a greater voice in running the company; community residents appear at a hearing or at a meeting in support of needed community facilities; families donate a small sum of money to a grass-roots campaign or initiative or attend a demonstration or rally as part of that campaign.

2) The vision of economic democracy must begin to emerge as a *majority* viewpoint. This is what Italian social thinker Antonio Gramsci called "ideological hegemony." People frequently act against their own objective interests: tenants vote against rent control; propertyowners vote for corporate tax relief and cuts in services they really want; many tenants and lower-middle-class families do not vote at all. Socioeconomic problems and their solutions are shaped by the media and by reigning politicians and commentators—and, without a clear alternative vision and explanation, most people will accept the dominant view, which is inherently undemocratic and anti-egalitarian. In the 1960s, many single-issue movements did win a measure of ideological hegemony for their positions: majority views on women shifted because of the women's movement, which began with a very small group of feminists; majority views on race shifted because of the civil rights movement, which began with a small group of white and black activists in the South and in northern universities; majority views on America's role in the

world shifted because of the antiwar movement, which began with a small group of antiwar activists based on college campuses.

It is possible for a movement to lose many times in the conventional sense—in elections or initiatives or bills in the legislature—and yet to win in the long run, in the construction of a more democratic society.

A movement must define political progress more broadly than do conventional politicians—and it must fit a notion of political progress into the overall framework of a transitional program and a long-term strategy.

Such a transitional program would have the following characteristics: it should, as enacted, increase the power people have over their own lives and reduce the power of corporations and those with money; it should be easily explainable to people and embodied in clear measures such as bills, initiatives, or organizing demands; it should have a simple identifier (such as EPIC—End Poverty in California—in the 1930s); elements of it should, in theory, be realizable at the level of political struggle in which people are engaged—state government, county government, and city government; as much as possible, it should *relate to the needs of people in their daily lives;* and, finally, the program should reflect the constituency that can make up a *majority* movement for change.

One possible unifying theme for such a program would be: fighting inflation together. An anti-inflation program would focus on the expenditures that constitute 80 percent of a typical family's budget—food, health, housing, energy, and transportation. It would also include taxes, which have been rising with inflation and are viewed by most families as a payment to government for services that, under current governmental arrangements, are not worth the price they pay. The program would offer *structural* economic reforms that would save people money and improve the quality of life; at the same time, these reforms would reduce corporate power and increase democratic control over capital.

Such a statewide reform program would include the following elements:

Tax reform: progressive taxation based on the ability to pay, including a tax on intangible wealth (i.e., stocks and bonds). A "split roll" property tax under which homeowners would be taxed at a lower rate than owners of income-producing and business property.

Housing: a concrete program of tenants' rights, including the right of renters to form tenants' unions and receive legal recognition as bargaining units vis à vis landlords. This has been done in Madison, Wisconsin, and in Saskatchewan, Canada. In New Jersey, a Truth-in-Renting Bill requires that all landlords provide tenants with a booklet (at landlord expense) spelling out tenants' rights. This renters' rights bill could be an initiative or an omnibus bill in the legislature, or could consist of local initiatives. It also lends itself to tenant organizing and direct actions related to tenants.

A state bank or housing finance agency might be advocated to lend mortgage money to tenants for co-ops and to lower- and middle-income families for homes.

A stiff antispeculation tax to slow down inflation of urban housing should be included.

In some areas, rent control would also be part of the program.

Energy and transportation: strict energy-conservation codes for new housing; "lifeline" rates for utilities; state promotion of solar energy, including low-interest loans for solar home installations; state support for mass transit, including the new electric light-rail car and trolley; creation of Nader-inspired RUCAGs (residential utility consumer action groups) funded by a voluntary check-off on utility bills.

Insurance: a system of state-run, nonprofit, no-fault auto insurance as operated in three provinces in Canada. Public insurance in Canada is cheaper than private insurance—so consumers would save, service would be better, and, most important, the public would take control of millions of dollars in premiums, which public authorities would be required to invest only in the state through a public investment board whose members included labor and consumer representatives. People would purchase their insurance through the Department of Motor Vehicles or possibly their local agent—but the state would have a monopoly on auto insurance. In addition, the state insurance authority might offer home, life, and other insurance in competition with private firms. Auto insurance must be a monopoly to insure the no-fault provisions and prevent the state from being saddled with the worst drivers, while private companies skim off the better risks.

Such a public insurance authority could be created by means of an initiative procedure. It offers lower prices for consumers, jobs for labor and the unemployed, public control of capital, and greater control over auto repairs through the leverage of the public authority.

Health: a state program of health insurance coupled with tight cost controls and an emphasis on community-based health care, with health providers and consumers represented on policy boards. Health education systems at the state's public universities should require doctors to participate in public health centers for a certain minimum number of years after graduation. Again, this could be done through an initiative or a legislative bill. Features of Ron Dellums' national health bill could be adapted to the state level.

Food: promotion and financial/technical support for food cooperatives, urban gardens, and community canneries; state support for direct-marketing efforts such as weekend farmers' markets.

Consumer rights: an aggressive program to inform consumers of their rights through pamphlets, public interest radio and TV spots, and the creation of neighborhood "consumer action" centers where information and advice would be provided.

Employee bill of rights or economic bill of rights: measures to increase the rights of workers and consumers in economic decision making. Embodied in one bill or initiative or a series of measures, such a bill of rights would include: employee and consumer representation on the boards of all enterprises incorporating in the state, beginning with the publicly regulated utilities and banks; employee control over health and safety by means of in-plant health committees modeled after Sweden's new, far-reaching plant safety laws; additions and amendments to state industrial relations laws to include an employee bill of rights guaranteeing the rights of workers on the job in all Bill of Rights areas—free speech, free assembly, due process, and so on—and establishing special labor courts to enforce the law.

These are the major areas and general measures that should form the core of a statewide program. Obviously there are other issues that concern people—immigration, the arts, telecommunications, and so on. What is advocated is *unity* around these basic issues because they go directly toward dealing with the economics of inflation, taxation, and work alienation, and offer the broadest possible appeal to a potential constituency without dividing the potential coalition. Every measure is prolabor and proconsumer. Minorities and middle- and low-income families all benefit in tangible ways. It is a majority program that is relatively simple to understand and that can be embodied in measures at the state level.

Elements of this program can be translated into a metropolitan program. Housing is a key area for city political action, which could be organized around the issues of tenants' rights, the transformation of apartments into co-ops with city-loaned money, and the use of city employee pension funds for housing loans. The idea of city-owned banks should be part of a city program; such banks would focus on housing and economic development. The other powerful idea at the city level is neighborhood government: the creation of neighborhood controlled services, planning boards, and governmental units. Progressives should be fighting for people's rights to maintain a decent neighborhood. The inhabitants of a city relate not so much to city government as to their neighborhoods. As long as neighborhoods fight for *equal* funding for services and education and equal portions of federal and state aid, building neighborhood political units is the best strategy; then neighborhoods can unite in citywide coalitions with labor to put forward citywide measures.*

City and State Politics

A state or city transitional program would be put forward by a statewide or citywide political organization or a coalition. At the state level, where there are partisan elections, the effort should focus on the Democratic Party primaries—in effect, as a "party within a party." In many cities, on the other hand, elections are nonpartisan; here progressive groups could work either within the Democratic primaries or through an independent citizens' organization.

In a number of states and cities, such organizations could put on the ballot at least one, if not more, of the program issues as initiatives, and introduce the rest as bills in the legislature or city council.

*A comprehensive urban program is spelled out in more detail in the booklet *The Cities' Wealth,* produced by the Cooperative Ownership Organizing Project in Oakland.

A statewide or citywide slate of candidates for office, pledged to the program, should be fielded. Not only should candidates be run for all state offices, but candidates should be put up for *selected* Assembly and Senate seats where there is a *reasonable* chance of defeating a right-wing Democratic incumbent or a standing Republican, or where there is an open seat. Candidates should not be fielded against strong liberal Democrats; instead, the latter should be urged to support the program.

The candidates would have to agree to run for office under a centrally controlled, integrated campaign arrangement whereby *all* fund raising, campaign decisions, and media buys would be carried out by a *single* campaign operation. No money would be spent by independent campaign committees for individual candidates. Separate committees *might* be operated for Assembly or Senate candidates, depending on the desires and needs of the local candidates—for instance, the need for locally targeted direct mail or media. Every attempt would be made to distribute slate cards in *every Democratic* district for the state and local slate.

The slate might include one or two initiatives from the program, in an effort to "ride the initiative" as Jerry Brown did in California with campaign disclosure in 1974 and the Republicans did with Proposition 13 in 1978.

The slate and local add-ons would serve as a foundation for mobilizing a potential electoral base—students, women, minorities, labor—as well as a potential fund-raising base—entertainers, unions, sympathetic businessmen, and so on.

Citywide political organizations should become the real building blocks of statewide organization *over the long run.* Dynamic statewide slates can be run using mass mobilization techniques, canvassing, and imaginative television advertising; progressives can win some offices and also score ideological victories by defining the issues. The existence of citywide political organizations would enable progressives to build on statewide victories by providing vehicles for mobilizing support for the statewide issues after the state-level campaign, and by developing leaders who speak for the movement in cities around the state and who with time can become visible leaders of the statewide effort.

Such citywide political organizations exist in other countries, particularly in Canada. In Montreal, for example, the Montreal Citizens' Movement (MCM)—a left-wing coalition organization—won 45 percent of the popular vote in 1974. The MCM ran a slate of candidates on a common program under the general slogan, "A City for People." The Movement won a number of seats and continued as an *action* organization, not simply as an electoral coalition. MCM members, including elected officials, took part in direct action, lawsuits, demonstrations, educational events, lobbying, and so forth, on basic economic issues such as housing and economic development. The MCM redefined political issues and political debate in Montreal, shifting the focus away from development benefiting upper-income segments and toward community-controlled, neighborhood oriented development benefiting middle- and low-income groups.

Building a city or statewide organization or coalition is not easy. In 1977, for example, the Montreal Citizens' Movement split into two groups; both fielded a slate of candidates in the fall 1978 elections, which helped the party of incumbent Jean Drapeau, a conservative, to sweep the city.

In Berkeley, California, a left-wing slate has been fielded in city elections since 1971. The sponsoring electoral organization, Berkeley Citizen Action (BCA), has suffered a number of internal conflicts. In the initial electoral effort, some candidates on BCA's slate, after winning office, repudiated or ignored the common left program. In 1977, the BCA almost split over the issue of including a member of the Communist Party on its slate of candidates for city council. Despite these ups and downs, the BCA has provided a continuous left presence in the city.

The BCA enjoyed its largest electoral victory in the spring 1979 elections, winning the mayor's office, the city auditor's position, and three out of four open council seats. These election successes brought the BCA within one vote of a full majority on the council and increased its ability to begin to implement its program (based, in part, on Kirshner's *The Cities' Wealth*).

All across California, the spring elections of 1979 indicated a counterreaction to the conservative, anti-government sentiment of Proposition 13, which had passed the previous year. In Santa Monica, a middle- and lower-income city of 100,000 primarily renter families, the combined effects of Proposition 13 cutbacks and inflation in rents led to a "tenants' revolt." A coalition of community activists formed Santa Monicans for Renters' Rights and fielded a slate of council candidates and a strong rent-control initiative. The prorenter candidates swept the elections and rent control was enacted. The new law called for an elected rent board, and when elections for the board were held in June, the renters' rights slate of five candidates won all the seats. The renters' slate included a member of the United Auto Workers and a member of the Retail Clerks union. The local organizers had put together an alliance of activists, union locals, senior citizens, families with children in search of affordable housing, and minorities to win electoral victories and shift some power away from the local establishment of bankers, real estate developers and "old" families that had dominated the city's politics for decades. Left/progressive coalitions also won city elections in Santa Cruz, Santa Barbara, and Davis, California.

The difficulties in running slates of candidates on a common program should not be ignored—but the potential benefits far outweigh those to be gained by simply supporting "good" individuals as they appear. It takes a person with a strong ego and a personality open to public exposure to run for public office in the United States. Organizers of state and city electoral efforts should keep this fact in mind: some people make better candidates than others; but it should be possible, by careful preparation, to find individuals who are both good candidates and committed to building a movement for economic democracy.

Current public officials around the country who style themselves as progressives or populists should be evaluated according to how strongly they support the creation of slates and common programs for future races, and how well they attempt to build a community base of alternative enterprises, progressive unions, and strong neighborhood organizations. Individuals who are elected to office and fail to construct a base that will not only support them, but *survive* them, are not very useful, in the long run, in building a movement for economic democracy.

An important principle in this strategy is that *one does not compromise in advance.* Neither the program nor the slate should be tailored to just what is possible in the present, given existing political forces. The goal is to redefine what is politically possible. With few exceptions, existing politicians tend to be weak and vacillatory, however well-meaning, because they have already compromised so much on the issues, and because they are not interested in building an organization and stirring people into motion to take control over their own lives. They are building careers, not a movement.

It is also imperative to take a longer view than is common for most well-meaning, single-issue activists. A movement must think five, ten, even twenty years ahead, and be willing to suffer defeats in the short run to assure victory over the long term. The strategy of running slates may seem foolhardy to some—even suicidal. What if every candidate loses badly? What if the people ignore the movement? Progressives need to create a *dynamic,* to draw on the energy and resources of the potential constituency; this can be done only by *being bold,* by taking chances and venturing much.

Only a slate with a common program will break through people's complacency or cynicism—through the psychic surface of the "Me Decade"—and tap people's deeper yearnings for a more democratic and decent society.

Not only is it necessary to be bold and to take a long-term view. The notion of politics should include the construction of a number of ongoing institutions, linked together as part of the overall political movement in states and cities. This means working closely with cooperatives and supporting the expansion of the co-op movement. It means encouraging union allies to fight for and support the establishment of cooperative ventures, particularly in health care, food, retail establishments such as travel agencies, bookstores, and movie theaters, and in enterprises such as newspapers.

The establishment of a significant number of alternative enterprises is important in meeting some of the basic needs of a movement: the need for movement members to communicate with one another; the need to reach out to potential supporters with information and analysis; the need to gain experience in running business enterprises so that, as political victories are won, there are trained people ready to move into positions of responsibility; and the need to create some "human space" within the dominant business culture for activists, so that people do not become spent in a few years, so that people can maintain a lifelong commitment and still have fun, enjoy children and each other, vacation, play, go to movies and theater, have picnics, participate in sports—in short, make a life while making history.[1]

National Politics

Most of the attention and energy in the decade of the 1980s should go toward building city and state political efforts. Only when such a base has been constructed in a number of cities and states is a movement prepared to contend seriously for national office. A movement for economic democracy can claim legitimacy only by demonstrating the ability to win elections, to govern cities or states, and to spread a new, democratic viewpoint among a majority of citizens.

This is not to say that national politics should be ignored—that would be both absurd and impossible. It does mean, however, that the movement need not concentrate on building a national political organization. National politics hardly exists in the United States, except on television. The two national political parties are weak, both organizationally and ideologically, and the decline of the seniority system and of the "solid South" has reduced the importance of party discipline in Congress. Congressmen have increasingly become ombudsmen and service-centered operators for their constituents. Few members of Congress act on any consistent or readily discernible set of political principles. The cabinets and policies of presidents of both parties in the postwar period show greater similarities than differences.

Single-issue groups of all political persuasions do lobby in Washington—and, on some issues, such as the establishment of a consumer cooperative bank, progressive groups have been successful; but this is rare. A national movement such as the women's movement is not centered on Washington; its strength is derived from its activities in cities and states across the country. There is no one single women's organization that issues topdown commands to party cells.

Once all this has been said, we can still see that there is one integrating factor in national politics—the presidency—an office that a movement for economic democracy should attempt to win. Under the American federal system, some elections for the presidency have in the past been key issue-defining events—watersheds in U.S. history. MIT political scientist William Dean Burnham studied what he calls critical election periods—an election or closely related series of elections that resulted in a dramatic realignment of political forces in the country. Such election periods are characterized by abnormally high intensity of feeling. They are issue-oriented affairs "involved with redefinition of the universe of voters, political parties, and the broad boundaries of the politically possible." Such critical elections occurred in the 1850s over slavery, in the 1890s over industrialization and the populist response, and in the 1930s over the Depression and the New Deal.[2]

Such a critical election period focused around the issue of economic democracy could occur in the late 1980s or the 1990s. The shape of the realignment could resemble that in Western Europe, with more clearly defined parties of the Left and Right emerging from the election.

To reach such a point—and to be ready for it when it comes, as a national crisis of confidence in the old, dominant ideology develops—a movement for economic democracy must begin to run a candidate for the presidency in the Democratic primaries in the 1980s.

The potential for such efforts can be seen by imagining for a moment that George McGovern's campaign had been a part of such a movement, rather than the individual effort of a liberal Democrat. McGovern's campaign raised over $30 million, primarily in small donations through a well-run direct-mail campaign. Millions of people voted for McGovern, and a number of unions bolted from the AFL-CIO's political fold to support him. Thousands of volunteers in cities around the country worked for him. Had the base created by the McGovern campaign been consciously developed over four years, an organized left wing of the Democratic Party could have fielded its own candidate in 1976 around a strong platform of economic reform—and that effort, if unsuccessful, would have been built upon for 1980.

Similarly, imagine that the Progressive forces in 1948 had adopted the strategy of running Henry Wallace in the Democratic primaries rather than as a third-party candidate. Wallace probably would not have won the nomination from Truman, but he would have carried a number of large states—particularly California, where veterans of Upton Sinclair's 1934 campaign dominated the Democratic Party, and possibly Michigan and Ohio, where Wallace had strong support among union rank and file. The existence of a national progressive network *within* the ranks of the Democratic Party might have substantially diminished Truman's cold-war policies and might have provided a stronger defense against cold-war repression of the Left.[3]

A presidential candidate running on a program of economic democracy in the Democratic primaries, even if unsuccessful the first few times out, could accomplish a number of things: development of a national mailing list of progressive supporters and activists; public education and definition of the economic issues facing the country through TV and radio spots, newspaper coverage, and appearances on TV news shows required by equal-time provisions; creation of a national "shadow" or alternative cabinet of knowledgeable alternative policy experts who would continue, after the campaign, to serve as critics of existing policies and proponents of alternative policies; identification and inspiration of new activists in cities and states where primaries are held, stimulating them to join the movement and to build up a base in their own cities and states.

Progressives have the technical capacity to run a presidential campaign—the media specialists, time buyers, direct-mail experts, advance men and women, speech writers, and policy researchers are all there. Many know each other through such networks as the Conference on Alternative State and Local Public Policy, the Institute for Policy Studies, the Exploratory Project on Economic Alternatives, and Ralph Nader's Center for the Study of Responsive Law. The Progressive Alliance organized by the United Auto Workers might be able to serve as a national forum for planning such an effort and selecting possible candidates.

The campaign might bring together many of the progressive anti-inflation efforts that appeared across the country in the decade of the seventies (see the chart on pp. 400-1), so that its program would combine the idea of economic democracy with the notion of fighting inflation in a progressive rather than a regressive way. The message would be that the structural reforms described in earlier chapters are the way to combat and eventually eliminate inflation over the long run.

In the spring of 1979, the Progressive Alliance lobbied against President Carter's proposed cuts in federal social programs. If, however, the alliance or any similar group of unions and community groups remains simply a lobbying operation in Washington, and does not build an organizational base in cities and states, it will contribute little to a movement for economic democracy.

On August 22, 1979, the United Auto Workers— the key union in the Progressive Alliance—called what the *Los Angeles Times* labeled "America's first union-led European-style political strike." The nearly

Some Specifics of a Progressive Anti-Inflation Program

| | Government Actions Advocated or Initiated | | | Citizens' Actions (in addition to Inquiry, Advocacy and Electoral Politics) |
	FEDERAL	STATE	LOCAL	
Price Controls	Permanent, selective controls, starting with *Fortune* 500 Opposing Carter on decontrol and anti-control	Tough utility regulation Public interest advertising	City price commissions Extensive consumer education, dealing with product quality as well as prices and helping in comparison shopping	Monitor sellers Monitor public officials at all levels Widespread initiatives in consumer self-education and protest
Spending	Cut war budget and corporate subsidies Regulate capital flight and foreign investment	Reduce business subsidies More efficient public administration	Reduce tax abatements More efficient public administration	Protest welfare handouts to corporate rich and local speculators Support public officials who resist private pressures
Taxing	Close major loopholes General fund financing of Social Security	Antispeculation taxes Progressive income taxes Lower taxes for homeowners	Anti-speculation taxes Less reliance on sales taxes Lower taxes for homeowners	Tax-reform initiatives Tax withholding under certain circumstances
Credit	Reduction of interest rates Credit allocation Activation of new national co-op bank Promote credit unions	State banks Productive use of pension funds	Municipal banks Productive use of pension funds	Protest redlining Withdraw deposits from certain banks Withhold mortgage payments under certain circumstances
Energy	Public corporations for oil imports and energy development	Antitrust actions against oil companies State power generation and distribution	Municipal public power, with elected consumer representation on boards	Antinuclear demonstrations Install solar devices

	Major shift to solar, biomass and neglected hydro energy, as well as hard and soft coal			Voluntary conservation and recycling
Transport	Massive mass transport expansion and improvement Require more efficient, safer cars	Improved land-use planning to minimize trips to work	Bicycle lanes Free downtown buses Minibuses	More bicycling and walking More car pools
Housing	Revive public housing for both rehabilitation and new construction	Low-interest loans for rehabilitation and new housing Public land purchase and maintenance	Rent control More public rehabilitation, construction and co-op promotion Public land purchase Zoning to prevent, not promote, speculation	Oppose condominium movements, gentrification, planned shrinkage and shortage creating demolitions Tenant unions and rent strikes
Food	Less price support for agribusiness and factory farms Family farm aid Promote direct marketing More antitrust action	Promotion of co-ops Consumers on marketing boards Consumer protection laws and enforcement	Promotion of co-ops Sponsor farmers markets Consumer protection laws and enforcement	Consumer co-ops, food gardens Boycotts Protest automatic check-out scanners
Medical Care	National health service Regulation of medical-drug-hospital costs	Support health co-ops Cost regulation	City-owned health maintenance organizations, health promotion education in schools	Self-care in home; improved diet; more physical exercise and activity; client-controlled health clinics
Insurance	Public insurance companies Clear-wording laws	State insurance companies Better consumer information	City insurance Better consumer information	Buy term life insurance only Protest discriminatory auto rates

SOURCE: Prepared by D. Shearer and B. Gross; from B. Gross, "Anti-Inflation for Progressives," *The Nation*, June 23, 1979.

million-member union stopped work for five minutes to protest the "rip-off of America by the oil industry." Among other demands, the UAW called for the creation of a public energy corporation. On October 17, 1979, the Progressive Alliance sponsored a one-day national protest against big oil interests. Both events displayed a new willingness on the part of some major unions to mobilize their memberships around political issues.

In the 1980s, the unions themselves will have to move beyond conventional liberalism and adopt as their political program many of the structural reforms discussed in previous chapters, particularly Sweden's industrial democracy legislation and the alternative corporate plan approach pioneered by the unions at Lucas Aerospace in England. At the collective bargaining table, as well as in the political arena, unions will have to redefine economic issues and raise such matters as worker representation on corporate boards and worker control over in-plant decision making.

Public interest figures such as Ralph Nader and local equivalents in cities and states will have to go beyond lobbying and exposés of corporate wrongdoing and try to win government power by standing for election. As has been stressed throughout this book, the government—at all levels—is the key arena in the struggle for economic democracy.

The cooperative movement, as it grows in the 1980s, will have to reach out to the unions and to progressive politicians both to obtain support and to educate them on the day-to-day realities of democratic enterprises.

Together, these political forces, along with some women's groups and minority organizations, can make great strides in the 1980s toward building a national movement for economic democracy. It is possible. It can be done—but only if the task is seen clearly and is viewed within the context of *structural* economic reforms.

A Closing Word

The American progressive movement was destroyed in the 1950s; its rebirth in the 1960s was centered around young people, mainly students. Of necessity, young activists focused on single issues such as civil rights, the Vietnam war, women's rights, gay rights, and the environment. There was no time, amidst crises and Nixonian repression, to devise a long-term strategy nor develop a long-term program; many of the institutions that were built—communes, magazines, liberation schools—did not survive the turmoil of the sixties.

We are now at the stage of constructing a movement which will be rooted permanently in American communities and American experience, and not based on the needs or perceptions of foreign "revolutionary" parties or ideologies. We should not underestimate how difficult this task will be. America is still the most powerful and, in many ways, the most flexible advanced capitalist country in the world. The nation's capacity for simultaneously coopting change and repressing it, remains immense. The ideology of the dominant business-oriented culture is still almost all-pervasive, though inroads have been made in the past ten or fifteen years through single-issue movements.[4]

While we should not underestimate what we are up against, neither should we sell ourselves or our prospects short. Above all, we should not let ourselves be satisfied with minor alterations, with a few small changes, with a bit more access to public officials, with a few "interesting" job offers or "pilot" programs.

Ideas have a power that can free untapped hope and energy in a people. The democratic idea of America has been and can again be a powerful weapon. It is a living heritage which we can apply to the economic system in which we live, and with it we can build a new reality.

Notes

CHAPTER 1

1. Charles E. Lindblom, *Politics and Markets* (New York: Basic Books, 1977), p. 356.
   For an extensive analysis of power in American society from a radical perspective, see G. William Domhoff, *The Powers That Be* (New York: Random House, 1978).
2. Robert Heilbroner, *Boom and Crash* (New York: W. W. Norton, 1979).
3. See Stanley Aronowitz, *False Promises* (New York: Basic Books, 1974).

CHAPTER 2

1. E. F. Schumacher, *Small Is Beautiful* (New York: Harper and Row, 1975), p. 259.
2. C. A. R. Crosland, *The Future of Socialism* (London: Macmillan, 1957), p. 496.
3. Ibid., p. 464.
4. Ibid., p. 483.
5. Stuart Holland, *The State as Entrepreneur* (London: Weidenfeld and Nicolson, 1972), p. 7.
6. Andrew Shonfield, *Modern Capitalism* (London: Oxford University Press, 1965), p. 84.
7. National Economic Development Office, *Relationships of Government and Public Enterprises in France, West*

Germany, and Sweden, Background Paper 2 (London, 1976).

8. Quoted in John B. Sheahan, "Experience with Public Enterprise in France and Italy," in *Public Enterprise,* ed. by William Shepherd (Lexington, Mass.: D. C. Heath, 1976), p. 161.

9. Ibid., p. 147.

10. Richard Pryke, *Public Enterprise in Practice* (London: MacGibbon and Kee, 1971).

11. W. A. Robson, *Nationalized Industry and Public Ownership,* 2nd ed. (London: George Allen and Unwin, 1962), pp. 432-34.

12. William G. Shepherd, "British and United States Experience," in *Public Enterprise,* p. 110.

13. Gordon Adams, "Nationalizing Rolls Royce," *Working Papers for a New Society,* Spring 1974, p. 46.

14. Stuart Holland, *The Socialist Challenge* (London: Quartet Books, 1975), pp. 275-77.

15. Stuart Holland, *The State as Entrepreneur,* p. 10.

16. Sheahan, op cit., p. 20.

17. "West Germany: Long-Range Entrepreneur," *The Economist,* December 30, 1978, p. 41.

18. See "Public Enterprises in Germany," in *The Evolution of the Public Enterprises in the Community of Nine* (Brussels: European Centre for Public Enterprises, 1973).

19. See Jesse Jones, *Fifty Billion Dollars* (New York: Macmillan, 1951).

20. Lloyd Musolf, *Mixed Enterprise* (Lexington, Mass.: D. C. Heath, 1972), p. 56.

21. Ibid., p. 68.

22. See Philip Selznick, *TVA and the Grass Roots* (New York: Harper and Row, 1966); and Peter Barnes, "The Lessons of TVA," *Working Papers for a New Society,* Fall 1974.

23. Annmarie Hauk Walsh, *The Public's Business* (Cambridge, Mass.: MIT Press, 1978).

24. William Shepherd, "Public Enterprise and Accountability," paper commissioned by the

Exploratory Project on Economic Alternatives (Washington, D.C., 1974).

25. Geoffrey Cowan, "TV Without Commercials," *Working Papers for a New Society,* Winter 1976.

26. Sheahan, op. cit., p. 176.

CHAPTER 3

1. See Maurice Zeitlin, "Who Owns America," *The Progressive,* June 1978.

2. See Achim von Loesch, *North American Workers' Banks in the Twenties,* Commonweal Economy pamphlet no. 7 (Frankfurt: Bank für Gemeinwirtschaft, 1974).

3. See Mario A. Milleti, "Amalgamated: Cautious Bank with Union Label, *New York Times,* July 3, 1978.

4. Paul P. Harbrecht, *Pension Funds and Economic Power* (New York: The Twentieth Century Fund, 1959), pp. 4-5.

5. Ibid., pp. 95-96.

6. Ibid., pp. 269.

7. Peter Drucker, *The Unseen Revolution: How Pension Fund Socialism Came to America* (New York: Harper and Row, 1976), pp. 1-2.

8. Harbrecht, op. cit., p. 236.

9. U.S., Congress, Joint Economic Committee, *Broadening the Ownership of New Capital,* report, June 17, 1976, p. 15.

10. See Edward S. Herman, *Conflicts of Interest: Commercial Bank Trust Departments* (New York: Twentieth Century Fund, 1975).

11. E. F. Ehbar, "Those Pension Funds Are Even Weaker Than You Think," *Fortune,* November 1977.

12. In testimony before the U.S. Congress, Joint Economic Committee, Subcommittee on Fiscal Policy, hearings, April 27-30, 1970, p. 216.

13. Nathaniel Keith, *Politics and the Housing Crisis Since 1930* (New York: Universe Books, 1973), p. 130.

14. U.S., Congress, House, Committee on Banking, Finance, and Urban Affairs, Subcommittee on

Economic Stabilization, *Catalog of Federal Loan Guarantee Programs,* September 1977.

15. Martin T. Katzman and Belden H. Daniels, *Development Incentives to Induce Efficiencies in Capital Markets,* report to the New England Regional Commission, June 15, 1976, p. 50.

16. Ehbar, op. cit., p. 146.

CHAPTER 4

1. Arie Shirom, "The Industrial Relations System in Industrial Cooperatives in the United States, 1880-1935," *Labor History,* Fall 1972.

2. Derek Jones, "The Economics and Industrial Relations of Producer Cooperatives in the U.S., 1890-1940" (1976; mimeographed).

3. Ibid., p. 16.

4. Paul Bernstein, "Run Your Own Business: Worker-Owned Plywood Factories," *Working Papers for a New Society,* Summer 1974; and Edward Greenberg, "Producer Cooperatives and Democratic Theory: The Case of the Plywood Firms" (Palo Alto: Center for Economic Studies, 1978).

5. Bernstein, op. cit., p. 31.

6. Greenberg, op. cit., p. 32.

7. Ibid., pp. 64-65.

8. See Alastair Campbell, et al., *Worker-Owners: The Mondragon Achievement* (London: Anglo-German Foundation, 1977).

9. *The Economist,* December 11, 1976.

10. William F. Whyte, "The Emergence of Employee-Owned Firms in the U.S., *Executive,* Spring 1977, p. 23.

11. Ben Achtenberg, "Working Capital," *Working Papers for a New Society,* Winter 1975.

12. See reports in the *Wall Street Journal,* March 31, 1978, and April 10, 1978; also, *Dollars and Sense,* May-June, 1978.

13. See Martin Carnoy and Hank Levin, "Workers' Triumph: The Meriden Experience," *Working Papers*

for a New Society, Winter 1976. Carnoy revisited Meriden in July 1978 to update the case study.

14. Alan Baumgartner et al., "Conflict Resolution and Conflict Development: A Theory of Games Transformation with an Application to the Lip Factory Conflict" (1977; mimeographed).

15. Ibid., p. 35.

16. See Peter Herman, "Workers, Watches, and Self-Management," *Working Papers for a New Society,* Winter 1974.

17. "Offspring of Lip," *Worker Control Bulletin,* November 1975.

18. Jean-Pierre Dumont, "Le Dificile Retour sur Realités," *Le Monde,* June 15, 1978.

19. See, for example, Seymour Melman, "Industrial Efficiency Under Management vs. Cooperative Decision-Making," *Review of Radical Political Economics,* Spring 1970; and the extensive survey, "Productivity and Worker Participation" (Ann Arbor: Institute for Social Research, University of Michigan, 1977); Paul Blumberg in his study *Industrial Democracy: The Sociology of Participation* (London: Constable, 1968), gives an extensive survey of the literature on alienation and participation in work.

20. Juan Espinoza and Andrew Zimbalist, *Economic Democracy: Workers' Participation in Chilean Industry, 1970-73* (New York: Academic Press, 1978), p. 156.

21. Ibid., p. 131.

22. Greenberg, op. cit., p. 24.

23. Ibid., pp. 24-25.

24. Martin Leighton, *London Sunday Times* magazine, June 11, 1978.

25. *Wall Street Journal,* March 31, 1978, p. 33.

26. Espinoza and Zimbalist, op. cit., p. 130.

27. Quoted in Greenberg, op. cit., p. 45.

28. Ibid., pp. 19-20.

29. Richard Hyman, "Workers' Control and Revolutionary Theory," in *The Socialist Register, 1974,* ed. by Ralph Miliband and John Saville (London: Merlin Press, 1974).

CHAPTER 5

1. John K. Galbraith, *The New Industrial State* (New York: New American Library, 1967), p. 44.

2. David Noble, *American by Design: Science, Technology and the Rise of Corporate Capitalism* (New York: Alfred A. Knopf, 1977).

3. Barry Stein, *Size, Efficiency and Community Enterprise* (Cambridge, Mass.: Center for Community Economic Development, 1974).

4. Stanley Boyle, "A Reorganization of the U.S. Automobile Industry," U.S., Senate, Committee on the Judiciary, Subcommittee on Antitrust and Monopoly, February 28, 1974.

5. John Blair, *Economic Concentration* (New York: Harcourt Brace Jovanovich, 1972), p. 151.

6. Lewis Mumford, *Technics and Society* (New York: Harcourt, Brace, 1934).

7. Alfred Chandler, Jr., *The Visible Hand: The Managerial Revolution in American Business* (Cambridge, Mass.: Harvard University Press, 1977), Introduction.

8. William Shepherd, *Market Power and Economic Welfare* (New York: Random House, 1970), p. 246.

9. Harry Braverman, *Labor and Monopoly Power* (New York: Monthly Review Press, 1977).

10. Quoted in Stanley Boyle et al., *Radical Technology* (New York: Pantheon, 1976), p. 131.

11. David Dickson, *The Politics of Alternative Technology* (New York: Universe Books, 1975), p. 204.

12. President's Council on Environmental Quality, *Solar Energy: Progress and Promise,* April 1978.

13. Tom Bender, "Why Big Business Loves A.T.," *RAIN,* January 1978, p. 5.

14. J. P. Smith, "Giants Harnessing Solar Development," *Washington Post,* October 15, 1978.

15. "The Coming Boom in Solar Energy," *Business Week,* October 9, 1978, p. 102.

16. Doris Nieh, "Arco Is Making an Attempt to Harness the Sun's Power in Hopes of Becoming the General Motors of Solar Energy," *Executive,* August 1978.

17. "Sun Wars," *New Times,* September 30, 1977.
18. U.S. Office of Technology Assessment, *Application of Solar Technologies to Today's Energy Needs,* June 1978.
19. Richard Merrill, *Radical Agriculture* (New York: Harper and Row, 1976), p. xv.
20. Earl Heady, *Scientific American,* September 1976.
21. *The Family Farm in California,* (Sacramento: State of California, Small Farm Viability Project, 1977), p. 44.
22. Sidney Baldwin, "Lessons of the New Deal," in *The People's Land,* ed. by Peter Barnes (Emmaus, Pa.: Rodale Press, 1975), p. 17.
23. Baldwin, op. cit., p. 20; see also Sidney Baldwin, *Poverty and Politics: The Rise and Decline of the Farm Security Administration* (Chapel Hill: University of North Carolina Press, 1968).
24. Jim Hightower, *Eat Your Heart Out* (New York: Crown, 1975), p. 42.
25. See Joe Belden, "Toward a National Food Policy," (Washington, D.C.: Exploratory Project for Economic Alternatives, 1976).
26. See *New Directions in Farm, Land and Food Policies,* (Washington, D.C.: National Conference on Alternative State and Local Public Policies, 1979).
27. David Elliot, *The Lucas Aerospace Workers' Campaign* (London: Young Fabian pamphlets, 1977), p. 5; see also "The Lucas Plan," in *The Right to Useful Work,* ed. by Ken Coates (Nottingham: Spokesman Books, 1978).
28. Quoted in Elliot, op. cit.
29. Quoted in ibid., p. 7; see also Mike Cooley, "Design, Technology, and Production for Social Needs," in *The Right to Useful Work.*
30. Quoted in Elliot, op. cit.
31. Ibid.
32. Quoted in Derek Shearer, "Swords into Plowshares," *Working Papers for a New Society,* Summer 1973.

CHAPTER 6

1. Quoted in Larry Kramer, "Exxon Suit Drags on as

Lawyers Celebrate," *Washington Post,* July 20, 1978.

2. All quoted in John Holosha, "Trust-Busters Unable to Calm Merger Wave," *Washington Star,* August 13, 1978.

3. Quoted in Peter Barnes and Derek Shearer, "Beyond Antitrust," *The New Republic,* July 6, 1974.

4. Judy Kinkaid, *Extending Divestiture,* Exploratory Project on Economic Alternatives (Washington, D.C., 1977), p. iv.

5. Quoted in John Winslow, *Conglomerates Unlimited: The Failure of Regulation* (Bloomington: Indiana University Press, 1973), p. 270.

6. William Domhoff, *The Powers That Be* (New York: Random House, 1978), p. 32.

7. U.S., Congress, Joint Economic Committee, *The Economics of Federal Subsidy Programs,* report, January 11, 1972.

8. See Milton Derber, *The American Idea of Industrial Democracy* (Urbana: University of Illinois Press, 1970).

9. Quoted in Milton Derber, "Collective Bargaining," *The Annals,* May 1977, p. 92.

10. William Winpisinger, "An American Unionist Looks at Co-Determination," *Employee Relations Law Journal,* Autumn 1976, p. 129.

11. Quoted in *Report of the Committee of Inquiry on Industrial Democracy,* chairman, Lord Bullock (London: Her Majesty's Stationery Office, January, 1977), p. 24 (hereafter cited as Bullock Report).

12. See Ralph Nader, Mark Green, and Joel Seligman, *Taming the Giant Corporation* (New York: W. W. Norton, 1976); and Christopher Stone, *Beyond the Law: The Social Control of Corporations* (New York: Harper and Row, 1976).

13. Quoted in the Bullock Report, p. 22.

14. Eric Batsone, "Industrial Democracy and Workers Representation at Board Level," in *Industrial Democracy-European Experience* (London: Her Majesty's Stationery Office, 1977), p. 35.

15. Bullock Report, p. 93.

16. P. L. Davies, "European Experience with Worker Representation," in *Industrial Democracy,* p. 59.

17. Quoted in the Bullock Report, p. 67; see also Myles L. Mace, *Directors: Myths and Realities* (Cambridge, Mass.: Harvard Business School, 1971).

18. Batsone, op. cit., p. 25.

19. *The Biendenkopf Commission on Co-Determination in the Company,* translated by Duncan O'Neill (Belfast: Faculty of Law, Queen's University, 1976).

20. Peter Brannen et al., *The Worker Directors* (Nashville: David Hutchinson, 1976).

21. Alfred Diamant, "Democratizing the Workplace: The Myth and Reality of Mitbestimmung in the Federal Republic of Germany," in *Worker Self-Management in Industry: The West European Experience,* ed. by David Garson (New York: Praeger, 1977), p. 45.

22. Quoted in the Bullock Report, p. 109.

23. Martin Slater, "Worker Councils in Italy: Past Development and Future Prospects," in Garson, op. cit., p. 197.

24. Ibid., p. 207.

25. *Jenkins' Work Report* (Paris, December 1977); see also Andrew Martin, "Sweden: Industrial Democracy and Social Democracy," in Garson, op. cit.

26. Michael Watson, "Planning in the Liberal Democratic State," in *Planning, Politics and Public Policy—The British, French and Italian Experience* (Cambridge University Press, 1975); see also Stuart Holland, *Beyond Capitalist Planning* (Oxford: Basil Blackwell, 1979).

27. Quoted in Derek Shearer and Lee Webb, "How to Plan in a Mixed Economy," *The Nation,* October 11, 1975.

28. John Sheahan, "Planning in France," *Challenge,* March-April 1975, p. 18.

29. Quoted in Shearer and Webb, op. cit., p. 337.

CHAPTER 7

1. Arthur Okun, *The Political Economy of Prosperity* (Washington, D.C.: The Brookings Institution, 1970), p. 37.

2. Herbert Stein, "Fiscal Policy: Reflections on the Past Decade," in *Contemporary Economic Problems,* ed. by William Fellner (Washington, D.C.: American Enterprise Institute, 1976), p. 55.

3. Arthur Okun, *Further Thoughts on Equality and Efficiency* (Washington, D.C.: The Brookings Institution, September, 1977), p. 3.

4. Stein, op. cit., p. 57.

5. Daniel Q. Mills, *Government, Labor and Inflation: Wage Stabilization in the United States* (Chicago: University of Chicago Press, 1975), p. 10.

6. See *Fact Sheets on Sweden* (Stockholm: Swedish Institute); "The Aims and Means of Swedish Economic Policy (October 1965); "Active Manpower in Sweden" (October 1974); "Labor Relations in Sweden" (January 1975); "Taxes in Sweden" (June 1975); "The Swedish Economy, 1971-75" (January 1977).

7. Assar Lindbeck, *Swedish Economic Policy* (Berkeley: University of California Press, 1974).

8. Swedish Institute, "Labor Relations in Sweden," 1976.

9. Andrew Martin, "Is Democratic Control of Capitalist Economies Possible?" in *Stress and Contradications in Modern Capitalism,* ed. by Leon Lindberg (Lexington, Mass.: D.C. Heath, 1975), p. 53.

10. Howard Wachtel and Peter Adelsheim, "The Inflationary Impact of Unemployment: Price Mark-ups During Postwar Recessions, 1947-70," U.S., Congress, Joint Economic Committee, November 3, 1976, p. 3.

11. Ibid., p. 5.

12. Leslie Nulty, *Understanding the New Inflation* (Washington, D.C.: Exploratory Project on Economic Alternatives, 1977).

13. Serge Kolm, *La transition socialiste* (Paris: Edition du Cerf, 1977).

CHAPTER 8

1. Testimony in U.S., Congress, House of Representatives, Committee on the Budget, Task

Force on Distributive Impacts of Budget and Economic Policy, *Hearings on President Carter's Welfare Proposals,* October 1977, p. 31.

2. Reischauer, testimony in ibid., p. 31.

3. Bennett Harrison, *Urban Economic Development* (Washington, D.C.: The Urban Institute, 1974).

4. Statement of Frankie Mae Jeter, *Hearings,* 1977.

5. Frances Fox Piven, and Richard Cloward, *Regulating the Poor* (New York: Pantheon, 1972), pp. 76-77.

6. Ibid., p. 190.

7. Ibid., p. 177.

8. Louise Lander, *National Health Insurance* (New York: Health Policy Advisory Center, 1975).

9. Leif Holgersson and Stig Lundstrom, *The Evolution of Swedish Social Welfare* (Stockholm: Nyokpking, 1975); see also Walter Kopki, "Poverty, Social Assistance and Social Policy in Sweden," in *Readings in the Swedish Class Structure,* ed. by Richard Scase (Oxford: Pergamon, 1976).

10. R. D. Cramond, "Housing Without Profit," *Public Administration,* Summer 1965.

11. Ralph Husby and Eva Wetzel, "Public Assistance in Sweden and the United States," *Social Policy,* March-April, 1977.

12. Jerald Hage, and Robert Manneman, "The Growth of the Welfare State in Four Western European Societies" (Madison: University of Wisconsin, Institute for Research on Poverty, November 1977), p. 1.

13. Piven and Cloward, op. cit., p. 348.

14. James O'Connor, *The Fiscal Crisis of the State* (New York: St. Martin's Press, 1973).

15. Leonard Goodwin, *Do the Poor Want to Work?* (Washington, D.C.: The Brookings Institution, 1972), p. 115.

CHAPTER 9

1. See Jeremy Rifkin, *Own Your Own Job* (New York: Bantam Books, 1977), which contains an extensive description of the Hart poll.

2. Charles Lally, "Does Youngstown Have a Prayer?", *Beacon* (Sunday magazine of the *Akron Beacon Journal*), May 21, 1978.

3. See Neil Peirce and Jerry Hagstrom, "Watch Out, New Right, Here Comes the Young Progressives," *The National Journal,* December 30, 1978.

4. Quoted in Peter Gall and John Hoerr, "The Growing Schism Between Business and Labor," *Business Week,* August 14, 1978, p. 80.

5. Quoted in Philip Shabecoff, "Class Struggle Has Become Washington's Latest Rage," *New York Times,* July 30, 1978.

6. Neil Ulman, "Business Lobby: Companies Organize Employees and Holders into a Political Force," *Wall Street Journal,* August 15, 1978.

7. See, for example, Barry Sussman, "New Right in U.S. Politics May Only Be an Expression of Discontent Not Ideology," *The Washington Post,* March 5, 1978. John Magney's "Mountains, Molehills, and Media Hypes: The Curious Case of the New Conservatism" (*Working Papers for a New Society,* May-June 1979) is an in-depth analysis of polling data in the seventies. Magney concludes, "Over the last decade, popular dissatisfaction not just with high taxes but with the whole structure of class and corporate privilege has risen enormously. And there would seem to be a greater potential for progressive change now than at any time in recent history."

CHAPTER 10

1. On the role of cooperative enterprise in past mass political movements on the Left, see Lawrence Goodwyn, *Democratic Promise—The Populist Movement in America* (New York: Oxford University Press, 1976); and Walter Lippmann, "On Municipal Socialism, 1913," in *Socialism and the Cities,* ed. by Bruce M. Stave (Port Washington, N.Y.: Kennikat Press, 1975).

2. William Dean Burnham, *Critical Elections and the Mainsprings of American Politics* (New York: W. W. Norton, 1970).

3. For a brilliant description of the Progressive Party's activities, see Curtis McDougall, *Gideon's Army,* 3 vols. (New York: Marzani and Munsell, 1965).

4. For a consideration of the less progressive roads facing America, see Bert Gross, *Friendly Fascism* (New York: Avon, 1980). A positive vision is offered by Gross in "Anti-Inflation for Progressives," *The Nation,* June 23, 1979.
Many of the proposals also appear in *There Are Alternatives* published by COIN (Consumers Opposed to Inflation in the Necessities) (Washington, D.C., 1979).

Resources on Economic Democracy

ORGANIZATIONAL RESOURCES

COMMUNITY ECONOMICS, INC.

6529 Telegraph, Avenue, Oakland, California 94609

This is an economic consulting group which works with public officials, community groups, and unions on economic analysis of community development projects, including cooperatively owned and run housing developments and business enterprises. It publishes a regular newsletter, *The Public Works* ($5.00 a year), and a number of excellent technical studies. It is one of the best groups of its kind in the country and the first place any progressive official or community group should look for technical assistance in developing proposals for economic development projects.

CONFERENCE ON ALTERNATIVE STATE AND LOCAL POLICIES

2000 Florida Ave., N.W., Washington, D.C. 20009 (202) 387-6030

Contact: Lee Webb. This national organization of progressive state and local public officials and community leaders works to develop innovative and forward looking proposals for state and local government. They have a wide selection of publications and also publish a bimonthly magazine *Ways and Means.*

DOLLARS & SENSE

A monthly bulletin of economic affairs written by a group of progressive economists. Best source of up-to-date information on the economy. A good summary of business publications for those who don't have time to read the *Wall Street Journal* and

Business Week themselves. Subscriptions: $7.50 a year. Write: Dollars & Sense, 324 Somerville Avenue, Somerville, Massachusetts 02143.

EXPLORATORY PROJECT ON ECONOMIC ALTERNATIVES

This foundation-sponsored project has produced a series of economic policy reports on such subjects as inflation, food policy, cooperatives, citizen access, and capital and community. For a publications list, write: EPEA, 2000 P Street, N.W., Suite 515, Washington, D.C. 20036.

IN THESE TIMES

1509 North Milwaukee Avenue, Chicago, Illinois 60622

Nonsectarian, weekly left newspaper. Regularly reports on progressive political officials, union struggles, and left activities abroad. A readable, nonrhetorical style distinguishes the paper from many past left publications. Essential reading for keeping up with progressive, grass-roots and national left politics in the U.S. $17.50 a year.

NATIONAL ASSOCIATION OF HOUSING COOPERATIVES

1522 K Street, N.W., Suite 1036, Washington, D.C. 20005

Best source of information on housing co-ops, how to form them and run them, sources of finance, etc.

CO-OP MAGAZINE

North American Student Co-op Organization, Box 1301, Ann Arbor, Michigan 48106

The best single source of information on the North American co-op movement. A subscription to the journal includes a monthly newsletter on co-op affairs with updates on legislation such as the National Consumer Bank Bill. Special back issues deal with a variety of issues from co-op finance to worker democracy in co-ops. $10.50 a year.

THE NEW SCHOOL FOR DEMOCRATIC MANAGEMENT

589 Howard St., San Francisco, California 94105

The country's first alternative business school offers courses and workshops—in San Francisco and other cities—for people in worker-controlled or collective and cooperative enterprises. The school also has a program for union members and for women and minorities in starting successful businesses. The school maintains a series of case studies of democratically run firms and will soon be publishing a reader on democratic management.

SELF-RELIANCE

Institute for Local Self-Reliance, 1717 18th Street, N.W., Washington, D.C. 20009

A very useful publication that reports on the efforts of communities in the United States to become more self-sufficient and politically independent. The Institute publishes a variety of studies on waste management, urban farming, solar energy, city-owned financial institutions, and neighborhood government. The newsletter regularly publishes short news items on what's happening in communities around the U.S. $6.00 a year.

UNDERCURRENTS

12 South Street, Uley, Dursley, Gloucestershire, England

The best publication that reports on technology from a Left political perspective. $7.50 a year.

WAYS & MEANS

Conference on Alternative State and Local Policies, 2000 Florida Ave., N.W., Washington, D.C. 20009

The newsletter of the national conference. Published six times a year. Regular information on progressive legislation and programs at the state and local level. Best source of information on alternative policies for state and local government. $10.00 a year.

WORKERS' CONTROL

Institute for Workers' Control, Bertrand Russell House, Gamble Street, Nottingham NG7, 4ET, England

The bulletin of the Institute for Workers' Control. The institute is the best source of information on worker control efforts in Europe. The bulletin, published six times a year, includes news updates on worker-owned plants, new industrial democracy legislation, and union bargaining efforts over workplace democracy. The institute also publishes a series of books and pamphlets (e.g., *Can Workers Run Industry?*, *Full Employment, State Ownership and Workers Control*, etc.).

WORKING PAPERS FOR A NEW SOCIETY

Write: Subscriptions, 4 Nutting Rd., Cambridge, Massachusetts 02138

Published every other month, *Working Papers* is the best progressive policy journal in the country. Newly designed, it is a kind of *Fortune* magazine of the Left, which runs substantial articles on politics and policy. It's a must for anyone seriously concerned with social change in the U.S. Back issues available.

PUBLISHED RESOURCES

Popular Economics Press, *Why Do We Spend So Much Money?* and *What's Happening to Our Jobs?* Popular Economics Press, Box 221, Somerville, Massachusetts 02143. Two illustrated pamphlets, written in easy-to-read, question-and-answer style, illustrated with original drawings. One book deals with the sources of inflation, the other with unemployment and working conditions. Ideal for community education programs. Over 75,000 copies sold to date. Single copies $1.45 each. Bulk rates on request.

Edwards, Richard, *The Capitalist System: A Radical Analysis of American Society,* URPE, 41 Union Square West, Room 901, New York, New York 10003. The authors belong to the Union for Radical Political Economics (URPE), which publishes a journal, a newsletter and a bibliography called "Readings List in Radical Economics." URPE also publishes readers for teach-ins on a variety of economic issues. For information on publications write to URPE at the address given.

Kapp, K. William, *The Social Costs of Private Enterprise.* Schocken Books, 1971. Best single book on the failings of an economy dominated by large, private corporations.

Seligman, Ben, *Economics of Dissent.* Quadrangle, 1972. Collection of essays ranging from the economics of labor to converting the military economy by an economist who combined practical work in the labor movement with academic research.

Blair, John, *Economic Concentration.* Harcourt, Brace, 1972. This is the classic work on economic power in the American economy by the economist who directed the investigations of the congressional Subcommittee on Antitrust and Monopoly for two decades. Blair's other books, *The Roots of Inflation* and *Control of Oil* are also outstanding.

Nader, Ralph and Mark Green, *Corporate Power in America.* Grossman, 1973. Of the many Nader studies on the economy, this gives the best overview. It contains some of the best thinking on what to do about corporate power, see particularly Robert Dahl's essay, "Governing the Corporation." Other Nader studies are listed in the front of the book.

PROGRAMS OF ECONOMIC REFORM

Working Papers for a New Society. "Left with the Democrats?" Fall 1975, Number 3. Write: Working Papers, 4 Nutting Rd., Cambridge, Massachusetts 02138. A collection of articles spelling out alternative national policies that a left-wing Democratic administration might enact.

Institute for Policy Studies, *The Federal Budget and National Reconstruction.* Institute for Policy Studies, 1901 Q Street, N.W.,

Washington, D.C. 20009, 1978. $5.95. At the request of 54
members of Congress, this left-wing think tank produced a
collection of papers critiquing the federal budget and offering
alternative programs.

Campaign for Economic Democracy, "Working Papers on
Economic Democracy." CED, 304 South Broadway, Room 501,
Los Angeles, California 90013, 1977. $10.00. A detailed
program of reform at the state level, prepared for a conference
of California activists.

Conference on Alternative State and Local Policies, *Public Policy
Reader.* Conference on Alternative State and Local Policies, 2000
Florida Ave., N.W., Washington, D.C. 20009, 1976. $5.00. A
650-page reader of alternative economic programs for cities and
states, prepared for a national gathering of state and local public
officials.

Lindblom, Charles, *Politics and Markets.* Basic Books, 1977. A
new and provocative study of the relationship between economic
institutions, markets, and political freedom. Lindblom concludes
that markets are useful for insuring economic efficiency, but that
some form of market socialism under worker self-management
is more democratic than a corporate-dominated economy.

Piven, Frances Fox and Richard A. Cloward, *Poor People's
Movements.* Pantheon, 1977. A study of four political movements:
the Unemployed Councils of the 1930s; the CIO; the civil rights
movement; and the national welfare rights movement. The
author's conclusions don't follow from the case studies; however,
the discussions of the four movements are excellent, and readers
can draw their own conclusions on the relationship between
militancy around economic issues and the role of political
organization.

Goodwyn, Lawrence, *Democratic Promise.* Oxford University
Press, 1976. A superb book about the Populist movement of the
1880s, which began with farmers' efforts to escape poverty
through cooperatives and ended in a great third-party challenge
to corporate America. One of the best books on American
politics ever written.

Jaggi, Max, Roger Muller and Sil Schmid, *Red Bologna.* Writers
and Readers Publishing Cooperative, 233A Kentish Town Road,
London NW5 2JT England. $5.00. 1978. Distributed in U.S. by
Pathfinder Press. A report, in depth, by a Swiss collective of
journalists, on the urban policies enacted in the Italian city of
Bologna under Communist Party rule over the past two decades.
This is one of the few works in English which deals with the
public policies actually carried out by a left city government in a
Western European country. It covers urban planning, consumer
policy, education, health, senior citizens, and economic de-

velopment. The book includes a detailed interview with Bologna's "red" mayor Renatoa Zangheri.

WORKPLACE DEMOCRACY

Jenkins, David, *Job Power*. Penguin, 1974. Journalist Jenkins surveys worker-control efforts in Western Europe, Israel, Yugoslavia, and the United States. The book is the best, single introduction to the worldwide movement for democracy in the work place.

Strongforce, *Democracy in the Workplace*. Strongforce, 2121 Decatur Place, N.W., Washington, D.C. 20008. 1977. Produced under a grant from the federal government, this is the best how-to-do-it manual on work-place democracy in the U.S.

Rifkin, Jeremy, *Own Your Own Job*. Bantam Books, 1976. This is a popular introduction to worker control and includes the results of a national poll on citizens attitudes on the issue. The book also describes a few U.S. companies under worker management. The book was produced by the Peoples Business Commission, 1346 Connecticut Avenue, N.W., Washington, D.C. 20036.

Vocations for Social Change, *No Bosses Here*. Vocations for Social Change, 353 Broadway, Cambridge, Massachusetts 02139. $3.00. A useful manual for working collectively with case studies.

Strongforce, *Non-Profit Food Stores*. Strongforce, 2121 Decatur Place, N.W., Washington, D.C. 20008. $3.00. An excellent resource manual, complete with detailed case studies of food co-ops in four cities including one started by a United Auto Workers local.

National Association of Housing Cooperatives, 1522 K Street, N.W., Suite 1036, Washington, D.C. 20005. Best source of information on housing co-ops, how to form them and run them, sources of finance, etc.

Case, John, Leonard Goldberg, Derek Shearer, "State Business," *Working Papers*. 4 Nutting Rd., Cambridge, Massachusetts 02138. $3.00. Spring 1976. The single best article on state-government owned enterprises. The article covers the state-owned Bank of North Dakota, state-run insurance programs in Wisconsin and Canada, and state ownership of utilities. The article includes an extensive and useful bibliography on public enterprise.

PUBLIC ENTERPRISE AND PUBLIC CONTROL OF CAPITAL

Shearer, Derek, *Public Control of Public Money*. Conference on Alternative State and Local Policies, 2000 Florida Ave., Washington, D.C. 20009. $5.00. A report on the pros and cons of state ownership of financial institutions. An updated, revised version is now available. The study includes an extensive bibliography of books and articles on banking, redlining, and the state bank of North Dakota, and the appendix contains copies of model legislation on state banks.

Shepherd, William G., *Public Enterprise*. Lexington Books, D.C. Heath and Company, Lexington, Massachusetts, 1976. The best available survey on public enterprise economics in the U.S. A bit academic, but contains a highly useful section on the experience with public enterprise in Western Europe. Extensive notes on further sources.

Walsh, Annmarie Hauck, *The Public's Business*. MIT University Press, Cambridge, Massachusetts, 1978. A study of government-owned corporations focusing on the limited experience of the U.S. A detailed discussion of the problem of controlling public corporations such as the Port of New York Authority, public power systems, and highway authorities.

Holland, Stuart, *The Socialist Challenge*. Quartet Books, 27 Goodge Street, London WIP 1FD England. $6.00, paperback. A provocative book by a young British economist on the imperative for public ownership in the dynamic, profit-making sectors of the economy, coupled with workers' representation in national economic decision making. Holland is noted for his conceptualization of "planning agreements" under which government, business, and labor jointly plan for long-term economic strategy. The best introduction to the thinking of the labor left in Western Europe. Indications of directions for U.S. economic policy under a new New Deal.

ALTERNATIVE TECHNOLOGY

Dickson, David, *The Politics of Alternative Technology*. Penguin, 1978. An excellent essay that puts in political context the hopes of those who believe that "small is beautiful" and that small-scale technology will some day transform America.

Noble, David, *America by Design*. Knopf, 1977. A brilliant description of how financial institutions, patent law, university education, scientific research and the federal government combined to generate multinational high-technology firms such as General Electric, Du Pont, and AT&T.

Braverman, Harry, *Labor and Monopoly Capital*. Monthly Review Press, 1974. A classic work which analyzes the relationship between technology, scientific management and the working conditions under which most Americans toil.

Boyle, Godfrey, and Peter Harper, *Radical Technology*. Pantheon Books, 1976. *Rainbook—Resources for Appropriate Technology*. Schocken Books, 1977. The two best guide books to resources produced by the movement for a more humane technology.

Elliot, David, *The Lucas Aerospace Workers' Campaign.* Young Fabian Group, 11 Dartmouth Street, London SW1H 9BN England. $1.00. A detailed report on one of the most exciting happenings in the union movement in Western Europe. A group of unions representing workers in the Lucas Aerospace plant produced a detailed Alternative Corporate Plan, listing new products that the company could produce. The plan has become part of the union's bargaining strategy to avoid layoffs. One of the first times a union group has taken the initiative in economic planning.

Index